Preparing For End of Life

by Virginia Chang, Ph.D.

Table of Contents

INTRODUCTION 1

    About This Book. 1

    Foolish Assumptions. 3

    Icons Used in This Book 3

    Beyond the Book. 4

    Where to Go from Here 4

PART 1: PLANNING FOR THE END OF LIFE 5

CHAPTER 1: Understanding End-of-Life Basics. 7

    Birth, Life, and Death 8

    I Will Die 9

    Moving Closer to Death Every Second 11

    Death Happens Once 12

CHAPTER 2: Planning for End of Life Begins Now 15

    Remembering Death Can Happen Anytime 16

    Starting to Plan When You're Healthy 17

    Thinking of It Like Wedding Planning — No, Really 17

    Preparing for Death Is a Gift to Those You Love. 20

CHAPTER 3: Making Death Personal. 23

    Personalizing Death 24

    Identifying the Important Things in Life. 25

        Who matters most. 26

        What matters most 27

    Incorporating Personal Elements 28

        Keeping true to *you* 28

        Multicultural blending. 30

PART 2: PHYSICAL PREPARATION. 33

CHAPTER 4: Completing the Legal Paperwork. 35

    Organizing Your Files 36

        Using a good ol' file cabinet. 36

        Gathering your important docs. 36

        Using the new and improved digital file cabinet. 38

    Estate Planning 41

        Basic components of estate planning 42

        Estate plan: Will, trust, and DPOA together. 45

        Getting help with estate planning. 46

        Keeping your estate planning docs up to date 47

Advance Care Planning. 47
Having the conversation. 48
Advance directives. 49
ADs: HCP and living will together 58
Sharing your ADs. 59
Keeping your ADs up to date. 60

CHAPTER 5: **Managing Medical Logistics**. 61
Making Medical Decisions 62
Asking the essential question 62
Thinking about goals of care 64
Deciding where you want to die 64
Discussing your goals with others. 65
Establishing Your Medical Orders. 66
Knowing your medical orders 67
Completing medical orders 69
Changing your mind 70
Understanding End-of-Life Care 70
Touring the origins of hospice. 70
Knowing what hospice is (and isn't) 71
Knowing what palliative care is (and isn't) 72
Hospice versus palliative care 73
Meeting Your Healthcare Team. 74
The doctor 74
The nurse 76
The social worker. 77
The end-of-life doula. 78
The spiritual care counselor. 79
The home health aide. 80
The bereavement counselor 80
The volunteers. 81
Other support staff 82

CHAPTER 6: **Expecting Death: Pre-Death Planning**. 83
Finally, It's All About Me 84
Celebrating Your Life. 84
Sensing Death Is Near. 85
The exception: Sudden death 86
Natural death. 86
Planned death 87
Creating a Vigil Plan. 90
Realizing the benefits to a vigil plan 90
Understanding the elements of a vigil plan. 91
Getting help for a vigil plan 93

CHAPTER 7: **Making Post-Death Arrangements** 95

Why Should I Bother? I'll Be Dead! 96

Deciding What Happens to My Body 96

Plowing through paperwork 97

Understanding body disposition options. 98

Remembering Me After Death 103

Gathering together after death. 103

Writing your own obituary 109

Personalizing Post-Death Arrangements. .110

Religious 110

Cultural 111

PART 3: EMOTIONAL PREPARATION 113

CHAPTER 8: **Facing Aging, Illness, and Death** 115

I'm Afraid of Dying. 116

Becoming Friends with Death 118

Acknowledging death 119

If you can't beat them, join them 119

Embracing Death. 121

Taking a daily mortality vitamin 122

Living healthier. 123

Prioritizing what's important 124

Appreciating the now 125

CHAPTER 9: **Losing Who You Once Were**. .127

I'm Scared of What's Happening to Me 128

Who Am I?. 130

Navigating Dimensions of Loss 132

Physical loss 132

Mental loss 138

Social loss 141

Spiritual loss. 143

Seeing Yourself Anew 146

Who are you now?. 146

Sitting with loss 148

CHAPTER 10: **Being in Grief** 149

I'm So Sad 149

Grief and Mourning. 151

Anticipating grief 152

Experiencing grief 152

Letting grief transform 158

CHAPTER 11: **Takin' Care of (Unfinished) Business** 161

   I Want to Be at Peace 162

   Investing in a Peaceful Death 163

   Shedding Emotional Baggage 164

      Regrets 165

      Guilt...166

      Shame 168

CHAPTER 12: **Reviewing Your Life** 171

   I Am Pretty Darn Amazing 172

   Looking Back at Your Life.....................................173

      The tapestry of you 173

      The roller coaster of life 175

   Conducting a Life Review 176

      Benefits of a life review 177

      Methods of a life review..........................178

CHAPTER 13: **Deserving of Self-Care** 187

   I Love Myself..188

   Caring for Yourself 189

      Physical self-care 190

      Mental self-care......................................191

      Emotional self-care 192

      Social self-care 192

      Spiritual self-care....................................193

   Caring for Yourself Better 194

      Taking a self-care assessment.................194

      Evaluating your self-care assessment 198

      Creating a self-care plan.........................201

PART 4: SOCIAL PREPARATION 203

CHAPTER 14: **Connecting to My Community** 205

   Humans Are Social Creatures 206

   Creating a Community of Care 208

      Needing each other.................................208

      Allowing others to care............................209

      Feeling good about your care 210

   I Don't Need Help! I Can Do It Myself!...................211

      Asking for help.......................................212

      Gifting a good feeling 212

      Choosing to be alone 213

CHAPTER 15: **Creating a Support Network**................................215

Caring Takes a Village...216

Implementing the Ring Theory...............................217

Identifying your circles of care...........................218

Dumping out..219

Support in..220

Being the center of attention...........................222

Gathering Tools and Apps for Your Village.............223

Communication and organization 224

Medication management..............................225

Resources and community..............................225

CHAPTER 16: **Valuing and Healing Relationships**.................227

Understanding that Relationships Change...............228

Appreciating friends.....................................228

Making new friends......................................229

Losing friends..230

Healing Relationships...231

The Ho'oponopono Prayer.............................233

Putting it all together....................................236

CHAPTER 17: **Leaving a Legacy**.......................................237

Defining Legacy..238

Meaning-Making in Legacy....................................238

Honoring yourself...238

What's my legacy?..239

Creating a Legacy Project.......................................240

Painting your last portrait...............................241

Reconnecting to me 241

Considering Common Legacy Ideas.........................242

Letters and notes...242

Legacy and memory books.............................243

Photo books..245

Audio and video...245

Legacy and memory boxes.............................246

Recipe collections and more..........................247

Crafts, quilts, and more.................................248

PART 5: SPIRITUAL PREPARATION..........................249

CHAPTER 18: **Embracing Spirituality at End of Life**.............251

What Is Spirituality 252

Spirituality is universal..................................252

Spirituality is diverse.....................................252

Distinguishing Spirituality and Religion 253
    Spirituality versus religion 254
    Global religious landscape 255
Recognizing Spiritual Distress 256
    Feeling scared, needing comfort 256
    Experiencing existential distress 257
    Losing faith 258
    Making sense of death 259

CHAPTER 19: **Leaning into Spiritual Care** 261
Finding Support in Spirituality 262
Leaning into Others for Spiritual Support .262
    Your spiritual leaders 263
    Your spiritual community 263
    Spiritual care counselors 264
    Caregivers 264
Leaning into Personal Spiritual Practices .264
    Deep inner work 265
    Contemplation 265
Leaning into Spiritual Traditions 265
    Rituals and ceremonies 266
    Ancestor worship 267

CHAPTER 20: **Letting Go and Compassion** 269
The Value of Compassion 270
    Defining compassion 270
    Compassion, empathy, and sympathy 270
    Compassionate care at end of life 272
    Self-compassion 274
Easing into Death 275
    Attachment versus non-attachment 275
    Holding on versus letting go 275
    Giving permission 276

PART 6: THE PART OF TENS 279
CHAPTER 21: **Ten Myths About Death and Dying** 281
Nobody Thinks About Death 281
Thinking About Death Will Make It Happen 282
Thinking About Death Just Makes Me Sad .282
Preparing for End of Life Is Only for Old or Sick People 283
Hospice Means Giving Up 283
Pain Is a Part of Dying 284

Morphine Kills You 285
I Need a Lawyer to Complete My Advance Directives 285
My Family Knows What I Want 286
Living Longer Gives Me More Time. 286

CHAPTER 22: **Ten Tips for Thinking More Positively**
and Getting Started 287
Stopping to Smell the Roses 288
Living in the Now. 288
Saying I'm Not Fine 288
Writing Down Your Thoughts 289
Talking to The Elderly 290
Volunteering in Hospice 290
Relishing Simple Joys. 291
Writing a Letter to Your Future Self 291
Writing Letters of Gratitude. 292
Spending the Inheritance. 292

INDEX. 293

Introduction

Welcome to *Preparing For End of Life For Dummies*! I'm so glad you're here.

Death is not easy. Most people avoid doing any kind of preparation because it can be heavy and complicated stuff. *Preparing For End of Life For Dummies* presents a particularly positive and comprehensive approach to aging, illness, and dying. The book offers a whole-person approach to end of life, looking at the physical, emotional, social, and spiritual aspects that impact the end-of-life experience. The book aims to provide you with information, tools, resources, and tangible steps to adopt a healthy, secure, and celebratory state of mind toward facing your own mortality.

By taking time today to prepare for the end of life, you will make a difficult time in the future a little less uncertain. You will approach end of life with peace of mind knowing that you have done everything you could to ensure the kind of end of life you want.

About This Book

If you are reading this book, you want to know what it takes to do death better and get the death that you want. The last few decades, culminating with the COVID-19 pandemic, have shown us that we are not dying well. Too many people are caught unaware, unprepared, and afraid. As a society, we have moved away from the community-based care model that once was the basis for everyone at the end of life. As a result, many people now approach end of life with fear, loneliness, and avoidance. However, there's a rising public demand for doing death better, resulting in an increase in public awareness, education, and conversation around preparing for end of life. This book addresses this need with a unique upbeat, accessible approach.

Some of the content in this book you may already know about, and maybe you've done some initial work. Some of the content in this book may be new to you, and hopefully, you will do additional work. I appreciate your curiosity and desire to find out more and discover what end of life can be like for you.

I've organized the content into six parts:

>> **Part 1: Planning for the End of Life.** This part is a reframing of what a healthy and positive relationship with death can look like. I introduce you to the concepts, attitudes, and perspectives toward aging, illness, and dying that are the foundation of this book.

>> **Part 2: Physical Preparation.** This part introduces you to the myriad of logistical and practical matters that arise before, during, and after death. The aim is to help you understand, determine, and retain control over your end-of-life process, including legal, financial, medical, and pre- and post-death arrangements.

>> **Part 3: Emotional Preparation.** This part addresses the complex and complicated emotions experienced at end of life and how to anticipate, acknowledge, and adapt with a more positive mindset.

>> **Part 4: Social Preparation.** This part explores the importance of social connection and community at end of life. Social support affects everything from the quality of care received to knowing that you will be remembered by others after death.

>> **Part 5: Spiritual Preparation.** This part emphasizes the value of spirituality as support at end of life. Spirituality can offer hope, comfort, strength, and connection and has the ability to transcend the end-of-life experience.

>> **Part 6: The Part of Tens.** This part addresses some of the common misconceptions surrounding death and dying and then offers some positive tips for getting started with preparing for end of life.

Throughout this book, I have included personal stories as well as stories from dying people from my work as an end-of-life doula. I am honored to have accompanied and supported many individuals in their transition from this world. The lessons I have learned about life and death — and how to prepare for end of life — are shared with you, the reader; their stories are highlighted in sidebars in the book. While their names have been changed and personal details omitted, *these are real people.* When you read their stories, think, *This could be me, or my dad, best friend, or grandmother.* Because we will all die.

You'll find *Preparing For End of Life For Dummies* an easy-to-read and conversational guide on the topics of aging, illness, death, and dying. Contrary to popular thinking about what death is, this book is positive and not at all depressing. In fact, you might find it uplifting, inspiring, and motivating. You'll also like the easy-access organization, modularity, and hands-on information, exercises, and resources.

Note: No artificial intelligence was used in this book.

Foolish Assumptions

This book makes some assumptions about you, the reader:

>> You aren't dead yet.

>> You haven't experienced dying or had a near-death experience.

>> You haven't had a close experience with someone else dying.

>> You may be scared, afraid, worried, or anxious about dying yourself.

However, here are some positive assumptions about you, the reader:

>> You are curious.

>> You want to learn more about the end of life and prepare for it.

>> You want something more, different, or better than what you currently know about end of life.

>> You are brave.

This book doesn't make any particular assumptions about your age, current health, or life experiences. All you need is a desire to do death better for yourself whenever it is your time.

Icons Used in This Book

Throughout this book, icons in the margins highlight certain types of valuable information that call out for your attention. Here are the icons you'll encounter and a brief description of each.

TIP

This icon alerts you to important insights, clarifications, or ways to do things better.

REMEMBER

This icon highlights information that's especially important for you to know.

NEW

This icon marks information that provides a new way of looking at things or a new way of thinking about things.

This icon tells you to watch out! It marks important information for you to be aware of or which may present problems later on. (Beware!)

WARNING

Beyond the Book

In addition to the abundance of information and guidance related to aging, illness, death, and dying that I provide in this book, you can find even more help and information online at Dummies.com. Check out this book's online Cheat Sheet: Just go to www.dummies.com and search for **Preparing For End of Life For Dummies Cheat Sheet.**

Where to Go from Here

You, the reader, can decide how to use this book. You don't need to read the chapters in sequential order, although I would recommend that you begin with Part 1. These first three short chapters provide the foundation and basic concepts to start you off with the positive mindset and proper framework for understanding the rest of the book. After Part 1, you can then choose whichever chapter interests you and dive in; each chapter is organized to provide a rich experience.

When you're done reading this book, you'll want to keep it, not just as a reference, but to monitor your own progress in preparing for end of life. Not everything can be done all at once or right away. The thoughts and ideas presented in this book are like seeds. Keep coming back to this book for constant watering.

Ultimately, you are living until the moment you die. So, if you want to prepare for end of life . . . in order to die well, you have to know how to live well. Thank you for reading this book.

1

Planning for the End of Life

IN THIS PART . . .

Get an introduction to basic end-of-life concepts to reframe your relationship with death to a positive one.

Understand that end-of-life planning should begin when you are healthy and well.

Make death meaningful by personalizing the end-of-life process to you.

Chapter **1**

Understanding End-of-Life Basics

Thank you for your curiosity and desire to prepare for end of life. It takes a lot of courage to do this — to want something different, more, or better for yourself.

Each of us who prepares for end of life is doing something to make this world a more humane place to live and die. For many of us, the process of dying is not one to look forward to in our society. We face death and dying with a lot of ignorance, uncertainty, and anxiety. What I want to say to you is it doesn't have to be that way. What you can do is empower yourself in the process so you can approach the last phase of life with knowledge, preparedness, and awareness. And to do that, you have to start now while you are still well enough, alert, cognitive, and capable.

Since it is your life and death, you need to do the work to bring about a positive end-of-life experience. To be prepared for the end of life involves developing a relationship with death and addressing each of the aspects that impact the end-of-life experience. These aspects are the physical, emotional, social, and spiritual components of what makes up you as a unique individual. I discuss the questions, issues, and preparation for each of these aspects in the rest of the book: physical (Part 2), emotional (Part 3), social (Part 4), and spiritual (Part 5). When you address all these aspects, you develop a thorough and comprehensive approach to end of life. You are doing the best that you can for yourself.

Throughout this book, I ask you to check in with yourself about what you think, understand, and feel about what is being discussed. From there, you'll know what you need to work on. The aim of this book is to help you reframe your relationship with death to one that is positive, meaningful, and affirming. Consequently, you will be more prepared for end of life. I will be your guide and am grateful you're here.

In this chapter, we discover the basic end-of-life concepts that are the foundation of this book. The concepts may seem simple and obvious but are profoundly deep and transformative. They help you to rethink what death means and are the basis for developing a new relationship with death and dying.

Birth, Life, and Death

Birth and death are the bookends of life. We are born and we die. Everything else in between is life (see Figure 1-1).

FIGURE 1-1:
The story of your life occurs between birth and death.

Your story begins at birth. You won't clearly remember the beginning, but it is usually a time of joy and celebration. You have probably been told the story of your birth many times by your parents. You may have faint memories of the early years of life as a wee child, but your story really begins a few years later when memories become more set in your mind. And the more you live, the more pages you add to the story of your life. Only you know your whole story since no one else has lived your life under the exact same circumstances. Your life story is unique. Isn't that cool!

But every story has an ending, and your life too shall come to an end. If you are reading this book, you haven't yet come to the end of your story. And because you are reading this book, you still have time to shape that ending. Some story endings are happy, while others are sad. Some endings are full of pain and sorrow, while others are full of joy and reverence. Many stories leave the readers wanting more. And that's a good thing in life, because the people whose lives you touched — your readers — wish your story could go on and on.

REMEMBER

Regardless of how your story ends, it will end. While this fact may make you sad, what's truly wonderful is that you still have a chance to write those last chapters yourself, to shape the narrative of the end of your life. There is every possibility that you can have a joyous, celebratory end to life, similar to your birth. But in the case of end of life, you have to make it happen. Unlike at birth when your parents prepared for your arrival, it's up to you to prepare for your departure.

So, it's good that you're here. I am certain that you would like to have a happy and peaceful ending to your life story. This book can help you get there. It's not easy; it's hard work. But your desire to write the ending to your story is the first step to getting there.

I Will Die

I will die. Yup, that statement sums it up.

How do you feel when you say this? *I will die.* This statement is a basic truth, yet understanding how you feel about it can key you in as to how you feel about death. It's a good idea to understand your relationship with death and dying. And if you're saying to yourself, "What relationship?" Well then . . . now you know something too.

I will die. Do you accept this? Do you truly accept that it will happen to you? If so, that's good. Acceptance is the first step to understanding death and dying. Where does the understanding of the truth of this statement lie for you? Does it reside in your head? If so, you accept death as intellectual knowledge. It exists like a fact. It's like knowing about atomic fusion or traveling to the moon. You know of these things, that they are possible, but they don't affect you. Similarly, you know that you will die, but you probably never think about it.

I will die. Does this truth reside in your heart? Instead of residing in your mind, you feel the truth of this statement in your body or in your emotions. Do you worry about dying? Do you fear what it will be like when it is your time? Or do you think about death a lot but not know what to do with all the feelings it generates? Just tuning in to how you feel when you realize *I will die* helps you identify the nature of your relationship with death. By understanding your feelings about death, you will know what to work on to prepare for end of life.

Say you have some relationship with the concepts of death and dying and accept the statement, *I will die.* The next question is this: Do you live by this truth? As human beings, we all hold on to some principles, ideals, or basic truths that we use to guide our life and live by. Do you live with the realization of *I will die* and allow it to guide your life?

For example, honesty may be a truth that you try to live by. You try to always tell the truth and never lie. You use honesty in your relationships with others and hope that they respect you back with honesty too. For you, it is one way to stay true to yourself. Or maybe you live with equity as a guiding principle. You make decisions and view life through a lens of being fair and just. You create allies and fight against injustice. You work hard to live in an equitable world. Honesty and equity are just two examples of qualities that can be used as guiding principles for living.

NEW

You can use the truth *I will die* to also guide your life (see Figure 1-2). Understanding this truth in your heart and mind will do much for how you view the world and live life. You see how precious life is. How fleeting it is! You appreciate more and more what you have and what is around you. To realize and live by this truth changes how you make decisions, how you spend your money, and who you love.

FIGURE 1-2:
Facing your mortality affects how you live life.

Historically, people were more aware of this truth. They lived by it because the threats of death lurked everywhere. But now, we actually live in a safer society, and medicine is able to treat and cure so many ailments that once would have been fatal. While the causes of death are still numerous and threatening, we are not aware of them as much as we once were and have removed them from our daily consciousness.

Well, now, you have an opportunity to make a conscious choice to live by the truth of *I will die*. To choose to face your own mortality and let it affect how you live. To choose to embrace death.

Moving Closer to Death Every Second

If it feels like you have endless time in front of you, you don't. Thinking you will live forever is an illusion. In fact, you don't actually know when you will die. You could die suddenly. You could die tomorrow. You could die years from now. You could die when you are very old. You just don't know when you will die, but you are moving ever closer to death as time passes.

Remember the first end-of-life concept of this chapter: birth, life, and death. From the moment of birth, you begin to live, but you also begin to die. Every breath you take affirms life, but takes you further from birth and brings you closer to your inevitable death. Every day you live is one day further from your birth and one day closer to your death. You just don't know how many breaths you will take or days you will have before you die.

Here's another way to think about this: Your life is like the sand in an hourglass (see Figure 1-3). The first grain of sand that falls represents your birth. All the grains that come after make up your life. You can't control the pace or stop it. Sand just keeps falling. Unfortunately, you also don't know how many grains of sand there are. The last grain of sand to fall represents your death.

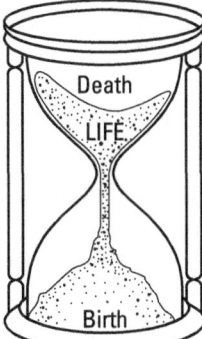

FIGURE 1-3:
Life is like an hourglass of sand.

Now you understand that life-lived is continually increasing (the bottom half of the hourglass), while life-yet-to-live is continually decreasing (the top half of the hourglass). The fewer grains of sand that remain in the top portion of the hourglass, the closer you are to death. When the last grain falls, life is over.

Death Happens Once

Think of death as a milestone event that only happens once. It is the end of this reality or existence as we know it and the beginning of whatever is next. Maybe there is an afterlife. Maybe there is a different plane or dimension of being. Maybe it is energy or consciousness. Or maybe there is nothing.

What we are certain of is that each of us will die once and that it is a departure from this reality. So it's a once-in-a-lifetime event. It's like hitting the jackpot! (See Figure 1-4.)

FIGURE 1-4:
Death can be a happy, celebratory event, like hitting the jackpot.

Many other once-in-a-lifetime events happen in life. Certainly, every birthday is a once-in-a-lifetime event; you only experience your 8th, 37th, or 63rd birthday once. But what about the more significant birthdays, such as the first? Sweet Sixteen? Your 50th or 100th? You mark those days as having reached a major milestone in life. More than likely, you celebrate those birthdays. You may have a big party and invite all your family and friends. You eat, drink, and be merry. You probably reminisce about your life up to that point and share memories with others. You laugh, love, and possibly cry. You probably think about the future and what is to come — how many more years you might live and what you still want to accomplish in the time remaining. This milestone event becomes an occasion to notice the passage of time and to reflect on what is past and what is yet to come.

Why can't death be exactly the same?

TIP

I propose to you that it can. It is possible for death to be just like that. Death is a once-in-a-lifetime event. Death can be a celebration of you — of who you are and the life you have lived. It can be a time to bring people together to celebrate, honor, and remember you. It can be joyous and celebratory. It can be full of love, laughter, and tears. It can be one giant good time for everyone.

If a big party at end of life sounds irreverent to you, that's okay. You needn't think of your death in this fashion. But what I do want to tell you is that there are other ways to think about it than those you're used to, have been told, or have been conditioned to believe by society. Death doesn't have to be scary, morose, morbid, heavy, sad, and tragic. There are other ways to think about death that embody honor, celebration, reverence, joy, and remembrance.

The basic premise here is death only happens once. So how do you want to experience it?

Chapter **2**

Planning for End of Life Begins Now

Just about any event is better experienced when you're prepared. That goes for death too. The more that you are prepared, the more likely your experience will be better and positive.

Preparing for end of life is a lengthy process. Unfortunately, too many people wait and don't begin preparing until either they receive a terminal diagnosis or are old and aged. In these situations, you are not in the best of health. You are likely grappling with a lot of difficult emotions, including those of grief, anger, sadness, doubt, and more. Your mind may not be as sharp or perceptive as it once was. And you may be filled with worry and anxiety for yourself and those you love, and for the future. These are not the circumstances in which you should be making important decisions about the rest of your life.

In this chapter, I share with you why it is so important to begin planning now, what the planning process may look like, and the benefits of planning ahead.

Remembering Death Can Happen Anytime

You don't know when you will die. While you would like to think that you will live to old age, you just don't know. Accidents happen; illness occurs. That's why it's so important to be prepared at all times.

TIP

Think of it this way: People who live in natural disaster–prone regions are prepared. They don't know if a tornado will ever strike them or their home, but they are prepared. Maybe they have prepared physically by building an underground shelter and stocking it with food, water, battery-powered lights, medicines, and other supplies. And of equal importance, they have prepared mentally for the possibility and the likelihood of a tornado striking. They have chosen to face it with resilience, fortitude, calm, and determination. By physically and mentally preparing, they have increased their chances for a positive outcome. And they have done all this preparation knowing that a tornado may never strike them, their family, or their home for their entire life.

If you can prepare for something that may never happen, then you can prepare for something that will definitely happen, as illustrated in Figure 2-1. The tornado may never strike you, yet you are prepared. Death is certain, yet you are unprepared.

IF YOU CAN...　　　　**THEN YOU CAN...**

FIGURE 2-1:
Being prepared for all eventualities leads to better outcomes.

The only uncertainty about death is when it will happen. Just because you don't know, do not ignore the reality of death! You don't ignore the possibility that a tornado could occur suddenly. The uncertainty becomes all the more reason to be prepared. So be ready to face death whenever it should present itself, regardless of your age, health, family, living circumstances, and wealth.

Just like being prepared for a tornado, being prepared for end of life increases your chances for a more positive outcome. You, and your loved ones, will be better able to face end of life, move through it, and cope — whenever it happens — if you are prepared.

Starting to Plan When You're Healthy

Perhaps you accept that you will die and that death can happen anytime, but if you're still feeling some anxiety about it, maybe one reason is that you're not prepared.

We can better face tragedy when we are prepared. And there are many components to being prepared: physical, emotional, social, and spiritual. You — like each of us — are a whole person, so we have to consider all the aspects that make up a person. It's important to address all four of the components because each of them will be affected and impacted at end of life. This book goes into detail and thoroughly discusses what it means to be prepared in each of the components so that you understand what is involved.

REMEMBER

Begin preparing for end of life now! Begin while you are still healthy, alert, cognitive, and fully able. You will want to make important life decisions while you still have full capacity to understand what you are deciding on and its implications. These kinds of decisions — pertaining to end-of-life, medical, financial, and legal issues — should not be made when your mind and judgment are clouded by worry, anxiety, or fear. Instead, think and begin planning for end of life now when you have the strength and clarity to address the difficult questions of end of life.

NEW

The good news is that preparing for end of life will change how you live starting the moment you begin preparing. It will change how you view yourself, your life, and your relationships with others. Preparing for end of life crystallizes what is most important and who is most important to you. Because at end of life, that is all that matters.

So why wait to be at Death's door to know what and who are most important to you? If you prepare for end of life now, it will not only affect your end of life but also your current life. That's pretty amazing! What a wonderful byproduct of preparing for death!

Thinking of It Like Wedding Planning — No, Really

NEW

What does planning for end of life look like? It's similar to planning a wedding. It's a big event that's all about you and celebrates a major transition in life. In the case of a wedding, you are transitioning from being a single person to being in a committed relationship with someone else. At end of life, you are transitioning from this life to whatever may be next.

Think of it this way: Your wedding day is a special event that most people antici-pate and plan for extensively. It is a special day, and you want it to be memorable.

Imagine your upcoming wedding. You are intimately involved in all the planning and all the decisions, down to the tiniest detail. First, you decide where the wed-ding will be held — the location and the venue. Then, you might decide upon the theme and color scheme of the wedding. Next, you decide who will attend, the food, the décor, the dress code, and the flowers. You consider the atmosphere, the pro-gram, and what kind of music to have. You decide upon each and every element of your wedding based upon what you wish and prefer.

Planning a wedding is hard work and a lengthy process. There are many things to consider and a lot of decisions to be made. You might even hire a wedding planner, as shown in Figure 2-2, to help you think through everything, present options, handle some of the logistics and coordination, and just make the whole process a little more manageable and smooth. Having a wedding planner takes some of the burden off you and allows you to enjoy more of the time leading up to the wedding.

FIGURE 2-2:
A wedding planner helps you in the planning process and eases some of the burden.

And if everything goes as planned, the day is grand. You are the center of atten-tion. You can relax and enjoy yourself. You can bask in all your glory! Everyone is having a wonderful time. There are smiles all around, laughter, and tears. Much love is present, in the air and in everyone's hearts. Congratulations! What a won-derful wedding!

Of course, even all the planning that you do doesn't guarantee that the wedding day will be picture-perfect. Most times, the wedding will be beautiful and go without a hitch. Yet, you cannot anticipate or plan for every eventuality. There may be snafus or little hiccups. And possibly, if something major goes wrong or a drunk guest makes a scene, you'll have established a system of response so that somebody else will take care of it for you. There will be others who can handle complications that arise and provide support so that you can continue to enjoy your wedding day.

All right, now that I have set the scene for your wedding, imagine that your death can be exactly the same. Yes, it can!

NEW

Approaching end-of-life planning may be easier for you if you conceptualize it like a wedding. It's a similar process with similar issues and questions to address, but with a longer timeline and an uncertain date. So just as you plan a wedding, plan for the end of your life.

You wouldn't go to your wedding with no planning at all, would you? Nor would you have someone else plan your whole wedding for you without your input. That sounds crazy! It's the same at end of life. Move through the process in accordance with your wishes and preferences. Retain control and make the decisions, big and small. In this fashion, you move toward the "big day" knowing more about what it's going to be like and what's likely to happen. There is a greater sense of security and calm about everything because you have planned.

TIP

Get help if you need with the planning. Just like wedding planners, there are end-of-life doulas who can help you prepare for end of life, as shown in Figure 2-3.

FIGURE 2-3: An end-of-life doula helps you in the planning process and eases some of the burden.

Doulas can work and support you through the lengthy planning process. They can talk through your options, act as sounding boards, be your cheerleader when the subject of death gets you down, and help keep you focused on the big picture. Bring in an end-of-life doula early on in the planning process. It helps smooth the way, eases your conscience, relieves some of the burden, and allows you time and space to savor living.

Lastly, when the big day arrives, it will be all about you. You will be the center of attention. You may not be awake or conscious or even aware of what is going on around you, but there is a sense of security, calm, and even relief going into the end having planned it out. All the while, your family and friends are present, remembering, honoring, and celebrating you. You are surrounded by love, laughter, and tears. How lovely!

Preparing for Death Is a Gift to Those You Love

While death is about you, the impact of your death is about those you love — your family and friends. The pain of your absence will be acutely felt. They will be in intense grief and very, very sad. It may even pain you to think of your loved ones in such pain from grief.

It may surprise you to realize that upon your death, the world does not stop. And if you are a bereaved person, you may be surprised to discover that the world does not stop because someone you loved died either. Someone so important, kind, loving, and essential to you is gone; why aren't more people taking notice? Bills still need to be paid, laundry needs to be done, the lawn needs to be mowed. Groceries need to be bought and food prepared. Friends and family return home and go back to work. Meanwhile, you want to just retreat from the world and daily life. You try, but you can't. The world does not stop. You are still dealing with the affairs of the death and its aftermath.

Many people are incapacitated by the depth of grief they feel after a death. Grief can be complicated for many personal reasons, but is also compounded by the *secondary losses* of grief. These are the other effects that can arise as a result of a primary loss. Think of secondary losses as the ripple effect of a death.

There are many potential and possible secondary losses which can arise from a death. The following are two examples:

>> **Loss of financial security:** Financial instability may arise because of the loss of income from the death of the person who may have been the breadwinner. It can even come from the loss of your own income as you take time off from work. Perhaps you are only given a short time off for bereavement and feel you are unable to go back to work so soon. This may result in job instability too.

>> **Loss of dreams for the future:** Perhaps you and your spouse had always talked about taking that special trip together. Now it will never happen. The loss of that dream causes grief and is deeply felt. This is also considered a secondary loss.

Secondary losses may be immediate after a death, or they may unfold over time. Whenever they occur, secondary losses are just as impactful to the experience of grief.

If you have felt intense grief from the death of someone, you know how challenging and painful grief can be. But now, you are the one thinking about your own death and what you can do. (Thank you for reading this book!) Preparing for end of life is not only good for you, but also good for the people that you love.

REMEMBER

Let me say it again: *Preparing for end of life is not only good for you, but also good for the people that you love.*

If you prepare for end of life physically, emotionally, socially, and spiritually, then you will be better prepared to face death whenever it happens. And if you are prepared, your loved ones will be better prepared to face your death and cope physically, emotionally, socially, and spiritually.

Before death, you are giving yourself and your loved ones the gift of time to be with you in a positive and meaningful way. Together, you will talk, share, laugh, love, and cry. Nothing is more beautiful than giving them memories to hold and cherish forever.

After death, you are giving your loved ones the gift of time and space to grieve. The more that you take care of before your death, the less that they will have to deal with after death, including those secondary losses. And for them, this would be a luxury. Because they will be in so much grief from your absence, each thing that they don't have to worry about, handle, or deal with is a gift (see Figure 2-4). Instead, your loved ones can focus more on their grief — feeling it and moving through it to find a new reality of life without you.

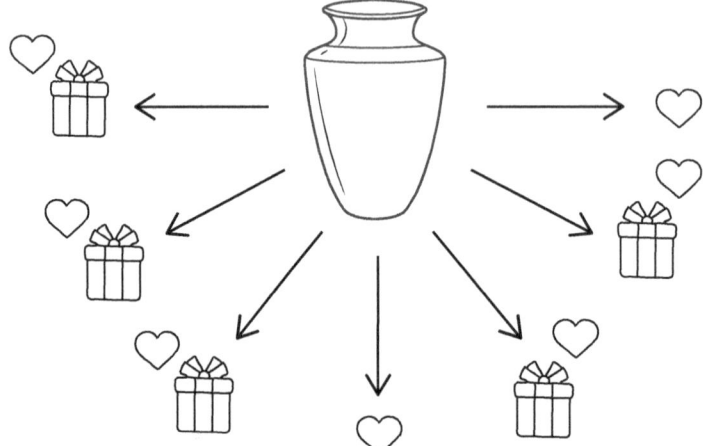

FIGURE 2-4:
After death, you can still positively impact the lives of your loved ones by having prepared ahead.

Therefore, your thoughtfulness, generosity, and love will continue to touch those you love. Even in death, you have the potential to give many little gifts to your loved ones.

Chapter **3**

Making Death Personal

I n order for death to be meaningful, it must be all about you and feel personal to you. If there's ever a time in your life when the world revolves around you, let it be at the end of your life.

No event in your life is more significant than your death. Not your birth, marriage, 50th birthday, or 100th birthday. All those events happen and then life continues on. The memories of those events became part of the giant repository of memories about you. However, your death will be the last event, creating the very last memory of you. There will be no more memory deposits after your death, so you want to make this last memory wonderful. Not just meaningful and memorable for others, but personal, significant, and beautiful for you too.

Think of this chapter as a call to action. Grant yourself the permission to think about yourself for once — to prepare for end of life and plan for this event of death and make it all about you. If this idea of making it all about you makes you feel uncomfortable, that's okay. You might need time to get used to the idea of death and reframing it this way. Give yourself time. In the end, it will be better for you in facing death, and it will be better for your loved ones in coping and living on afterwards. In fact, death can be truly amazing!

In this chapter, you discover how to personalize the end-of-life process, determine who and what are most important to you, and incorporate your unique cultural heritage and style into the process.

Personalizing Death

Death can be so impersonal.

In our current highly medicalized society, most people are dying like this: You are hooked up to life-sustaining machines in a sterile hospital room devoid of comfort, familiarity, and meaning, either alone or with strangers. You are cared for by kind-hearted healthcare professionals, who dictate and control everything that you do and that is done. You eat at set hours, not when you want, and are given bland, soft food that won't do any harm. You are visited occasionally, or often, by family and loved ones, but there is no way to interact or be together in a loving way. You do nothing most of the time and sleep a lot. When you are awake, your eyes see nothing that gives hope, comfort, or happiness.

Do you want to die this way?

On the other hand, you are living until the moment of death. So really, the question is,

Do you want to live this way?

It is a choice that each of as a human being have, but too often, we don't stop ourselves to ask: Is this what I really want? Does this feel right? Is this consistent with who I am as I have lived my life?

I would like to suggest that it is possible to get off the assembly line of dying anonymously. Or at least, move away from the *feeling* of being anonymous, unseen and unheard, and just a cog in the machine of today's institutions.

NEW

Make. Death. Personal.

Death can be meaningful by personalizing it to you. It means living by what's most important to you and with the people you love close to you. It means incorporating your values, beliefs, traditions, and culture into your end of life, reminding you each and every day of the meaning of your life.

In my experience, making death personal is like a *big* sigh. It is like taking a huge breath, exhaling it all out, and relaxing into a huge space of rest. Imagine your end of life being like that.

Where does your big sigh exist?

Identifying the Important Things in Life

Have you heard the saying, "How we live is how we die?" It's true. The way you are living life now — your attitudes and propensities — will be reflected in how you die. That is because the way that you have approached life will become the way that you will approach death. And what you currently think and feel about death will be carried into the dying process with you.

Imagine an ideal death for yourself, what would it look like? How do you want to die? Write down your answer here.

_____

_____

_____

_____

_____

_____

_____

_____

NEW

When most people talk about this, they talk about it as if it is a dream, an unattainable goal. I would like to say to you that whatever you have written down as your answer above can be a reality. But you have to know what you want for end of life and start living your current life toward that goal.

You will be glad to know that there still is time to achieve this or at least move in that direction. If you are reading this book, you are thinking about the end of your life and how you will die and what you can do about it. This book will help you get there. Thank you for reading it.

Who matters most

Did your answer include the names of anyone? I bet you thought of at least one, or maybe a few people, that you would like to be with you when you die, such as, *I would like my spouse or partner, my children, or these close friends to be with me.* And if you didn't approach the question of "How would I like to die?" in that way, think about it now. Who would you like to be present with you? Write down their names here:

_____

The people you thought of are the ones who are the most important to you. They matter. These are the people you love. And when you are at the end of life at Death's door, you want to be surrounded and held in their love. Because then, you know that you were loved and will be remembered by the people that you loved the most. It feels good when it is reciprocal.

So, are the people you love in your life now? Are they close or distant? Will they show up for you out of love or obligation or not at all?

If the people you love are in your life now, good. Keep them close. Tell them how much you love and appreciate them. Give them love and receive their love. When you are at end of life, they will be there for you with their love.

If the people you love are not in your life, how can you restore the relationship? How can you bring them close again? It may not be easy; in fact, right now, it may seem impossible. To bring them into your life again may require some difficult work on your part. But if this is what you want at end of life, then preparing begins now and there is still time. In Chapter 16, I talk about valuing and healing relationships.

What matters most

Once you've identified *who* matters most to you, think about *what* matters most to you.

Go back and read your answer to "How do I want to die?" This may give you clues as to what matters most to you. Look for descriptive keywords, such as peaceful, pain-free, love, laughter, music, simple, or sunshine. Write down your words here.

_____

Some of the keywords may be things that matter the most to you, such as love and laughter. Other keywords may not be things that matter as much, but they can give you clues to what matters the most. For example, if you wrote "sunshine," then nature might be something very important to you and may be tied into your spirituality (see Chapter 18). Or if you wrote "peaceful," you need to identify what would give you peace first. This takes a bit more introspection and work by you to figure out what would give you a peaceful state of mind (see Chapter 11).

Or maybe what matters most to you is not reflected in your dying scenario. It could be that you value honesty or justice. These qualities are more abstract yet very real. If you think of more ideas or values that you feel are very important to you, write them down here.

_____

_____

_____

REMEMBER

If you want to manifest an end of life that embodies who and what matter the most to you, then you have to be living a life embodying who and what matter the most to you.

WARNING

If you are living a life mostly angry at the world, you will die angry. And let me tell you that it is not a pleasant way to leave this world. Anger results in tension, both physical and mental, in yourself and with others. This tension can manifest in ugly symptoms that produce more pain and suffering. Dying angry is not pretty.

Therefore, it is essential to realize that the life you are living now will shape and determine how you die. If you aren't living the life that will result in the kind of death you want, then determining how you want to die *is* just a dream.

Incorporating Personal Elements

So much of what makes up you is your personality, your likes and dislikes of anything and everything. Your personality with your age, race, sex, health, location, socioeconomic status, and family environment, combined with your beliefs, values, traditions, and culture, makes you unique. Realizing that you are special — and dying knowing that you are special — is a very powerful way to leave this world.

If this appeals to you, it becomes important to incorporate personal elements into your end of life. That is what makes dying meaningful and personal.

Keeping true to *you*

There is no one "right" way to die. Don't worry about what is typically done or what other people do or think. If you plan ahead and prepare, then you have the time to dream big. Isn't this the way with anything in life? So you see, end of life is not so different than life itself.

A key part of end of life is staying true to who you are and your style. If you stay true to you, then you will feel good about your situation and circumstances. If you stay true to your style, you will feel happy.

As you come to find out, end of life is very much about loss, so it can become tricky to balance loss with staying true to yourself. In Chapter 9, I discuss the many kinds of losses you may encounter and experience at end of life. The more you can be aware and prepare ahead of time for what's to come, the better you'll be mentally and physically. And by anticipating loss, you can respond in a way that stays true to you and your style.

Do you know who you are and what your style is?

First, let's take a look at who you are. This simple 5-word exercise is a great way to get a quick description of yourself. Think of five words to describe your current self. Describe who you are now, not who you wish you were or want to be. The words can be qualities (e.g., curious) or skills (e.g., organized). It is important to be honest. Write down your five words here:

_____

If you were really honest with yourself, you may have written down one or two words that currently describe you but that you don't like. That's okay. Thank you for your honesty; it takes a hard look at yourself to admit this. This is between you and the book; no one else needs to know. Besides, these types of exercises only work if you are honest.

Now, think about the end of life. Imagine that you are dead and no longer on this earth. How would you like to be remembered by the people left behind? What words do you hope your friends and family use to describe you? Write down five words here:

_____

Now look at your two lists of who you are now and who you'd like to be at death. Are some words the same? Are some words different? If some words are the same, that's good. It means that you're living the life that you want and the way you'll be remembered at death. If some of the words are different, how can you shed the words that currently describe you to become the words that you would like to be? Consider what steps you would need to take.

There's probably no more important self-evaluation you can take than determining what kind of person you'd like to be at death. You may think, "Why should I care about who I'll be at death when I'll soon be dead?!" Yes, it's okay to question why it should matter when you won't be alive. The answer is this: It matters because that is how you will be remembered by your loved ones left behind. And knowing that gives your life meaning now.

Lastly, die with style — with your style. That is also staying true to yourself. Whatever your form or way of expression is, stay with it.

Do you have an idea of what your style is? If you don't have any particular style or it isn't important to you, that's okay too. But if you do have a particular style that's important to you, write it down here. Examples of styles could be "I live simply" or "I love the color orange" or "I like to be well put together" or "I'm a big football fan."

_____

_____

_____

WARNING

Don't let the process strip you of what makes you special as a person. The anonymization of people within the care system combined with the many losses experienced at end of life can make death demoralizing. This contributes to the feeling of despair many people feel when thinking about death. Therefore, it is essential that you counter this possibility with staying true to yourself in the process of dying. By anticipating and acknowledging what may happen, you can prepare.

Staying true to yourself doesn't mean being stubborn (unless *stubborn* is one of the words you wrote down)!

Stay true to yourself and your style, but clearly communicate with others as to how or why you like or dislike something, why you want or don't want certain things, and what's important to you. If you want to be seen, you have to communicate clearly, calmly, and openly.

The end of your life should be all about you, but you can be kind at the same time.

Multicultural blending

Each person has a unique cultural heritage consisting of all the different cultural elements in their life. Some of the predominant cultural factors include race, gender, country of birth, current location of residence, ethnicity, language, religion, and socioeconomic status.

Culture influences our values, our meaning in life, our beliefs, and our traditions. It establishes our sense of self, our interconnectedness with others, and our lifestyle. Culture plays a significant role in shaping who we are and what our style is. Culture even defines who and what are most important to us.

Some cultural factors play a more significant role in your life than others. Some may play a larger role in defining self and your identity. Or certain cultural factors may play a greater role in how you live and make decisions. It's important to acknowledge and recognize the significance and contribution of culture in shaping who you are.

For example, many immigrants strive all their lives to assimilate and integrate into the societies of their new country. Yet, they may hold very close to their hearts a special connection to their homeland, language, and traditions. I have seen immigrants at the end of life revert to this sense of identity. For some, they reminisce of their childhood, their country, and stories of the past. Even more pronounced, some individuals revert to speaking only in their language of birth, refusing to speak English anymore. For these immigrants, the connection to their identity at birth is so strong and important that this is what gives them the most comfort at end of life.

Another example is the LGBTQ+ community. They have struggled all their lives to be accepted for who they are and in their gender representation. Sadly, the LGBTQ+ community carry past trauma from the AIDS epidemic of the 1980s, when so many young, gay men died horribly, having faced discrimination and/or abandonment by their families, employers, landlords, and the medical establishment. As a result, the LGBTQ+ community have created their own culture of care, support, and protection at end of life. For them, it ensures that they are seen, safe, and secure and offers a death that is respected and honored. No one should have to explain themselves or be harmed for who they are, and certainly, not at the end of life.

REMEMBER

Instead, everyone deserves to have as many positive qualities, attributes, and factors as possible working in their favor when facing death. No one need face unnecessary suffering or pain, unless it is of their own choice. Death can be hard enough for some to realize and accept; let everyone enter into end of life with grace, love, and support.

REMEMBER

It is clear that the impacts of culture on an individual are vast and wide. Cultural influences also take many different forms of expression, some overt and obvious, and others strong and hidden. It is important to consider, identify, and recognize which cultural factors play significant roles in your end of life. If you're not sure, that's okay. Perhaps the first step is identifying and being aware of them. Discussions of personal cultural elements, such as religion or identity or ethnicity, occur throughout this book as they relate to certain end-of-life topics. As they come up, consider them as they pertain to you and make note. Later on, you will want to incorporate as many cultural elements as possible into your end-of-life process. That is what makes death personal.

2

Physical Preparation

Get your legal, financial, and medical affairs in order to ensure the end of life you want.

Understand the medical logistics and decision-making process that affect end-of-life care.

Discover options for controlling and celebrating approaching death.

Explore options for after-death arrangements and remembrances.

Chapter **4**

Completing the Legal Paperwork

You may know what you want at the end of life, or maybe you're just beginning to prepare. Figuring out what you want — how it will go, who will be there, how you will be cared for, and how your affairs will be taken care of — is the initial part of the process. Even when you get to the point of knowing what you want, ensuring that what you want happens sometime in the future is a whole different matter.

Many things are within your control, and you can determine the process and outcomes for many situations, unexpected and at end of life, by expressing your wishes and preferences in legal documents. By planning in advance, you anticipate and prepare for the logistics and decisions of how things will be handled and taken care of by everyone involved.

Physical preparation is about getting your affairs in order, figuring out what you want, making decisions, and completing the paperwork. The process can be lengthy and time-consuming, but in the end, you will have a set of legal documents that ensure you have communicated how your life and your death are to be handled. The process of completing this paperwork helps identify the issues that you need to know more about and the questions to ask.

In this chapter, I discuss organizing your personal information, planning for how your legal and financial affairs will be handled at death, and determining how you will be treated medically at end of life.

Organizing Your Files

It is amazing how many important papers and legal documents you can accumulate over a lifetime. It is key to prepare and organize all your important records and files — to know what you have and where everything is. Because planning and accessing your important information can make all the difference in an emergency and at the end of life.

Using a good ol' file cabinet

Being prepared and having important documents in a single place allows you and your loved ones to know and access what's needed, when it's needed. It reduces confusion and uncertainty, instead giving you peace of mind and security. You know important information is available and accessible in an emergency and at the end of life.

TIP

Start by setting up a file. You can put your important papers in a desk drawer or file cabinet. Alternatively, you can make an index of all your paperwork and the location of each document in a notebook. AARP provides a simple template called "Valuable Documents at Your Fingertips." It lists important contacts for you to fill in, along with their information, and important documents for you to fill in, including their location.

REMEMBER

For added security, you can store your documents in a fireproof and waterproof safe. If you use a bank safe deposit box, you can keep the original documents there, but be sure to keep copies in your file at home.

Gathering your important docs

What documents about you are important? A lot more than you expect. After all, you have lived a lifetime. I have organized the essential information and documents into three main categories: personal, financial, and health.

TIP

This is a good place to start in gathering your paperwork together. If you have or find additional information specific to you, add it to your file. Be comprehensive and include any information that might be useful to know about you.

Personal information

Here is a checklist of important personal information:

>> Passport

>> Social Security information

>> Birth certificate

>> Citizenship and naturalization papers

>> Certificates of marriage

>> Divorce/separation papers

>> Military discharge papers

>> Adoption papers

>> Names and phone numbers of spouse and children

>> Names and phone numbers of close friends and relatives

>> Names and phone numbers of faith leaders

>> Names of associations and organizations of which you are a member

>> Safe combination

>> Location and keys to safe deposit boxes

Financial information

Here is a checklist of important financial information:

>> Wills/trusts/estate planning documents

>> Names of banks and account numbers (checking, savings, CDs)

>> Income and assets (pensions, IRAs, 401(k)s, interest)

>> Investments (stocks, bonds, property)

>> Insurance policies (life, auto, homeowners, property, accident, liability, long-term care, health)

>> Retirement and death benefit information

>> Income tax information — copies of tax returns for the last two years

>> Property tax information — copies of tax bills, deeds, and liens

>> Other liability information

- » House deeds

- » Mortgages and debts/loan information

- » Car titles and registrations

- » Other documents of ownership

- » Credit/debit cards and account numbers

- » Names and phone numbers of your attorney, accountant, stockbroker, financial planner, insurance agent, and the executor of your will

Health information

Here is a checklist of important health information:

- » Advance directives, or
    - Healthcare proxy
    - Living will
- » Medical orders forms (DNR, DNI, POLST)
- » Health and hospitalization insurance policies
- » Health insurance cards
- » Current prescription list
- » Organ donation information
- » Funeral home information
- » Burial/cremation information
- » Names and phone numbers of doctors and funeral director

Using the new and improved digital file cabinet

More and more, the business of our lives occurs in a digital world. We communicate and transact online. We research information and invest our money. We purchase items, take photos, and play games. Even if a meeting or event is in-person, the arrangements are set up online. As a result, a lot of our business — and personal information — exists digitally.

Organizing your digital information

For the same reasons explained earlier about your physical paperwork, it's a good idea to organize your digital information into one location. That way, you and your loved ones know and can access what's needed, when it's needed.

You can create a physical list of all your important digital information in an index and add that to your documents file.

Alternatively, you can select software to centrally organize your digital information. Managing and storing your digital information just on your main device is a risk; if your device crashes, you lose access to everything. Therefore, it's best to back up your digital information in the cloud. There are many personal cloud storage solutions, such as Google Drive, OneDrive, Dropbox, and Apple iCloud. Or, you can subscribe to a secure online organizer with digital vaults and data encryption, including password and document management, like Trustworthy or Evernote. Look for applications with high security measures and safeguards in place to protect your information.

While some people are hesitant to shift from storing paper documents in a filing cabinet to digital alternatives, there are some advantages. First, digital storage solutions safeguard against physical threats like fire, theft, or natural deterioration. Second, you can access your documents from anywhere with an internet connection. This reduces complications from not having something important on hand when you didn't know you needed it.

If you go with a digital solution, be sure to write down your login information and keep it in a safe place, perhaps with your paperwork file, or inform a trusted person on how to access your digital file cabinet.

Taking stock of your devices

Consider all the devices that may hold important personal information. In particular, check out your old and unused devices and transfer any important information or documents to your central storage location.

Electronic devices include the following:

>> Desktop computers

>> Laptops

>> Mobile phones

>> Tablets

>> eReaders

>> External hard drives

>> Flash drives

Consolidating your digital information

Creating a digital file cabinet can be as simple or extensive as you want it to be. Be aware that the information world is moving toward everything being digital and paperless. You can keep up with the current trend or figure out a balance of paper versus digital that works for you.

TIP

All the information listed in the earlier section "Gathering your important docs" can be included in your digital file cabinet, especially if you already have that info in a digital format. Or if you want to convert to digital storage, you can scan the documents and destroy the paper versions.

Here is a checklist of important digital assets with some listed examples:

>> Email accounts (Gmail, Outlook, Yahoo)

>> Social media accounts (Instagram, YouTube, X)

>> Website domains and blog sites

>> Financial accounts (banking, brokerage, credit cards)

>> Medical accounts (patient portals, pharmacy)

>> Utility accounts (cellphone, internet, gas, and electric)

>> Shopping accounts (Amazon, Temu, Etsy, Poshmark)

>> Subscription service accounts (Netflix, Spotify, news)

>> File storage accounts for documents, photos, music, and so on

>> Other online accounts, such as gaming, dating, travel, and so forth

REMEMBER

Most of your personal information is accessed through your online accounts. Therefore, keeping track of your login information for these accounts — username and password — is critical. You can use a password manager to secure your sensitive data. Later on, the personal information in these accounts can be removed or deleted, and the accounts closed and deleted.

Estate Planning

Estate planning is the process of determining how your estate is to be handled in the event of death or incapacitation. Your estate consists of everything you own: your car, home, other real estate, bank accounts, investments, life insurance, furniture, art, jewelry, and personal possessions. Everyone has an estate — no matter how large or small it is. Everyone owns some *stuff*. You get to determine what happens to your stuff after you die, because you can't take it with you.

If you have already done your estate planning and have a will completed, congratulations! I applaud you for taking that step forward, because in order to have done any type of estate planning, you had to be thinking about your death. And really . . . that's the subject of this book.

I can't tell you how many people tell me, "I'm prepared for death. I have my will done." Most people think that being prepared for end of life is about having a will. I appreciate that the act of completing a will forced you to think about death. You had to consider a time when you are no longer alive, envision the world going on without you, imagine how your loved ones would be, and then decide what to do with your belongings. The process probably brought you an acute sense of death and that it will happen to you one day.

However comforting or difficult you found that process to be, it was necessary. A will is the one instrument you have to make sure of how your *stuff* — your estate — will be taken care of after your death, and that your property and assets will be divided and distributed according to your wishes.

NEW

But there is so much more to being prepared for death than taking care of your stuff. As you come to understand by reading this book, being prepared for end of life is about having peace of mind when faced with the idea of or actual death. Being prepared for end of life is about you, the life you are living now, and the kind of death that you want in the future, and then taking the steps to get there emotionally, socially, spiritually, and physically. You are so much more than your things.

So, if you have done your estate planning and have a will completed, you can skip the next few pages if you'd like. (Yes! All of estate planning is only a few pages in the whole book of end-of-life planning!)

If you haven't done your estate planning or completed a will, I offer a summary viewpoint of it here. This is because estate planning can be quite complicated and is markedly different for every person. It depends upon you, your personal priorities and goals, your financial situation, the assets you own or control, your family circumstances, and many other factors.

TIP

Estate planning also has significant legal, financial, and tax implications for you now and your beneficiaries in the future. While doing all your estate planning by yourself is possible, consulting with an attorney or other estate planning specialist is advisable. All estate planning documents use legal language. If you're not a lawyer, it is very challenging to state what you want, and do so using legal terminology. To that end, estate planning professionals will dot the i's and cross the t's — making sure the documents say what you want. Mistakes are avoided, and your plan accurately reflects your wishes.

If you want to find out more about estate planning, there are many resources, books, and experts on the subject. In fact, I recommend *Estate Planning For Dummies* (by Jordan S. Simon and Joseph Mashinski; Wiley) or *Wills and Trusts Kit For Dummies* (by Aaron Larson; Wiley), especially if you have done very little or no estate planning and/or are feeling overwhelmed even thinking about it. Both of these books are great guides for getting started and dive into the details and complications you may encounter.

Since most of end-of-life planning is associated with estate planning, and consequently gets a lot of attention (although that doesn't mean a lot of people have a will!), I am going to focus on the areas of end-of-life planning that get less attention but are equally important — which comprise the rest of this book! So, I thank you for being here, wanting to know more, and reading on.

But first, you need to take care of your stuff! The next few pages contain a summary review of the important components of estate planning.

Basic components of estate planning

Estate planning involves making a plan in advance that establishes the people or organizations who will receive your things after you die. It sounds simple, but ensuring that it happens later on can be the complicated part of estate planning.

WARNING

If you don't properly prepare for the future, you'll have no say in how your estate is divided and distributed, and what your loved ones receive. The government will decide, according to your state's intestacy laws, who receives your property. Wouldn't you prefer to keep control of who gets what and when?

The process of estate planning usually involves the following tasks:

>> Reviewing your property, assets, and debts

>> Writing a will

>> Setting up trusts

- >> Naming beneficiaries
- >> Making charitable donations to limit estate taxes
- >> Choosing guardians for children or pets
- >> Naming an executor of the estate
- >> Establishing a guardian for living dependents
- >> Setting up a power of attorney

Completing these tasks results in several legal documents, which make up your estate plan. Together, these documents form a powerful representation of your final wishes on what to do with your stuff after you die.

Last will and testament

A *will*, formally known as a Last Will and Testament, is a legal document that describes how you would like your property and assets to be distributed after your death. A will also provides instructions about the guardianship of any minor children. You state your wishes in a will and name an *executor,* someone you trust, who is your personal representative in charge of your estate after you die.

There are several types of wills, and it can be hard to know which one is the right type for you. Working with an attorney who understands all the legalese and technicalities of wills is advisable. Then you can be sure that your will accurately reflects your situation and preferences. See more about this in the "Getting help with estate planning" section, later in this chapter.

After death, the authenticity of a will is determined through a legal process known as probate. *Probate* is the method by which your estate is administered and processed by the legal system.

The probate process varies greatly from state to state and is often a lengthy process, taking anywhere from a few months to two years or longer. Because of this, probate can become expensive with attorney's fees, executor commissions, and court costs. Unfortunately, these drawbacks of the probate process have resulted in probate getting a bad rap. An attorney can advise you of what alternatives are available in your state and what may make sense for you.

After probate is granted, your executor can legally access your assets, pay any debts and taxes, collect and distribute the remaining assets of your estate, and fulfill your wishes according to the instructions in the will.

Revocable living trust

A *living trust* is a trust fund and a legal document that is created and in effect while you are still alive. *Revocable* means you can change your mind, thereby retaining the power to amend or terminate the trust at any time. A trust also has a beneficiary who will receive the assets at a preplanned time or upon your death.

A revocable living trust is one of the most common trusts established and preferred by many families and estate planning professionals. Some of the benefits are as follows:

>> Brings all of your assets into one plan

>> Avoids probate at death

>> Prevents court control of assets if you become incapacitated

>> Provides increased privacy

When you create a revocable living trust, you transfer your assets into a trust and appoint a person as trustee to manage and use the trust. You may even appoint yourself as the trustee of the trust! In this way, you are controlling the assets as trustee, even though technically, your assets are owned by the trust. For all intents and purposes, there is no significant change from the way you may be currently living your life.

While this all sounds great, take the time to understand trusts, in detail and in-depth, to see if you really benefit from having one. There are many different types of trusts, and choosing a trust depends upon you, your needs and those of your family, and your goals and what you want to accomplish by having one.

REMEMBER

A revocable living trust or any other trust does not replace a will. A will is still necessary to address assets outside of a trust and the issue of guardianship for minor children.

Trusts are only one element of estate planning, and determining what works best for you and your overall situation can be complicated. Consult with qualified legal and estate planning experts to ensure proper planning.

General durable power of attorney

A *general durable power of attorney* is a legal document that authorizes someone to make legal and financial decisions for you and remains in effect even if you become incapacitated. This document is also known as a financial durable power of attorney or a durable power of attorney for finances.

The person you appoint in your general durable power of attorney (DPOA) is called your *agent* or attorney-in-fact. Your agent can access all your assets and act on a wide range of business matters (non medical) for you. This includes managing your bank and investment accounts, paying bills, buying and selling property, filing tax returns, applying for benefits, and more. You have the flexibility to grant broad powers to your agent and also to limit them. You can leave very specific instructions to your agent as to your wishes and goals regarding your financial matters.

A DPOA can be effective immediately or only when you are incapacitated and no longer able to make decisions for yourself. In most cases, a durable power of attorney remains in effect until you cancel it or die.

The agent is your personal representative and carries an enormous responsibility to you. Your agent will have a great deal of control over your assets to manage your legal and financial affairs. Therefore, it should be someone:

1. you trust

-AND-

2. who is capable of performing the tasks to manage your affairs.

WARNING

The agent does not need to have any special knowledge of legal matters or finances, but they should not have financial interests that compete or conflict with yours, a history of financial instability, or money problems of their own. You don't want your agent to "loot" your estate for their personal gain.

REMEMBER

Ultimately, your agent should be someone you trust to protect your assets and your interests. When thinking of who to appoint as your agent, think of someone with integrity.

The POA agent can be a spouse, other family member, or close friend. If you do not have a close family member or friend you feel comfortable appointing, you can also name a professional, such as an attorney or accountant. This will cost more, but it means that you'll be protected and avoid family conflicts.

TIP

You may want to appoint an alternate agent in case your first choice is unavailable or unable to manage your affairs when the time comes.

Estate plan: Will, trust, and DPOA together

An estate plan manages your assets and ensures your wishes are carried out while you are alive and after your death. It also takes care of and provides financial security to your family and loved ones after death. Having an estate plan in place reduces the burden to everyone involved and offers peace of mind and security knowing that your affairs are in order.

The will, trust, and DPOA, as discussed in the previous section, are three important elements in estate planning:

>> A will outlines how your assets should be distributed after death.

>> A trust manages those assets during your lifetime or after.

>> A general DPOA fills the gap of allowing someone to manage your affairs during your lifetime if you're unable to do so yourself.

When the three combine together — will, trust, and DPOA — you create a comprehensive and proactive estate plan.

There may be additional estate planning tools that apply to your situation and circumstances. Consult with estate planning professionals to explore options and what makes sense for your situation.

Getting help with estate planning

It is wise to get help with estate planning. What you want to do — your decisions — will have legal, financial, and tax implications. What you want to say has to be done in legal terminology. Therefore, to make sure you understand everything and your paperwork is done correctly, work with professionals in estate planning.

Your estate planning team will likely consist of one or more of the following professionals:

>> Attorney

>> Accountant

>> Financial planner

>> Insurance agent

Which professionals are involved will depend upon whether your estate is complicated or simple and straightforward. Most estate plans can be set up by an attorney experienced in estate law, but there are also estate planning companies with a variety of expertise in-house.

TIP

Explore your options for who can help you create an estate plan. Even if your estate isn't overly complicated, working with estate planning professionals is helpful to make sure you are on the right path.

Keeping your estate planning docs up to date

Once you have created your estate plan, it's crucial to keep the documents up to date so that they reflect your current personal, family, health, and financial situation. It would be horrible if you had a fatal accident and your estate plan hadn't been amended to include your youngest child.

TIP

Therefore, it's good to review and update your estate plan whenever you have any major life change. This includes a change in marital status; a move to a different state; a change in health; if there are new family members in your life, such as the birth of a grandchild; or if a close friend dies. You'll need to update your estate plan to include, remove, or replace people. And your estate plan has to be in compliance with the state regulations where you live.

REMEMBER

Estate planning is an ongoing process, not a one-time event. Periodic reviews will ensure that your estate plan reflects your current values, wishes, and circumstances. Over time, your thoughts and feelings about end-of-life care may change.

Advance Care Planning

Advance care planning is about doing what you can to ensure that your wishes and preferences are consistent with the healthcare treatment you might receive if you are unable to speak for yourself or make your own decisions. Advance care planning covers the medical side of you and your affairs in advance, for the future.

While many of us do not like to think that we will ever need such a plan, advance care planning ensures an end of life that you want, consistent with your values, beliefs, traditions, culture, and spirituality. Too often the lack of advance care planning results in questioning, confusion, or disagreement among family members trying to envision what you would want when you're unable to speak for yourself. Doing advance care planning relieves the burden, and instead, becomes a gift you give yourself and your family for the future.

Please see Chapter 5 for a more in-depth discussion about what to consider in making decisions affecting your medical care and how to manage the medical side of your affairs.

Having the conversation

An important part of advance care planning involves having conversations with family members and other loved ones about what you would want in the event of a life-threatening illness or injury.

Planning ahead of time relieves family members from wondering if they "did the right thing" on your behalf. It allows them to make healthcare decisions that are consistent with you as a person and your wishes and preferences. It gives everyone involved, family members and loved ones, a sense of security and comfort during an intense, emotional time.

REMEMBER

It takes many conversations and time for everyone involved to come to an understanding. This can be a hard subject for some people to not only think about, but to talk about as well. Therefore, be patient with yourself and your loved ones. It can take time to wrap your heads around what all this means.

TIP

Having conversations with your loved ones about life-threatening illness or injury, including dying and death (see Figure 4-1), can be difficult to initiate and hold for you and your loved ones. The Conversation Project, an initiative of the Institute for Healthcare Improvement, offers great guides to help everyone talk about their wishes for care through the end of life. And if you need someone to guide and facilitate the conversations, an end-of-life doula can be a helpful presence.

FIGURE 4-1:
Talking with your loved ones about your end of life wishes can be difficult but helpful.

In the end, the most important thing is to have open and honest conversations with the people who matter the most to you in life. They will be the ones involved in caregiving and supporting you at end of life. It makes their job easier — emotionally and physically — to know what it is that you want. By having these conversations, you are sharing the way you want to live through the end of your life.

After having these important discussions on end-of-life care, document your medical wishes and preferences in writing in an advance directive.

Advance directives

Advance directives (ADs) are the legal documents that express your wishes and preferences regarding healthcare treatment and appoint someone to communicate for you in the event that you can't speak for yourself.

All fifty states permit and recognize ADs, although the particulars can vary. Advance directives are generally accepted even if prepared in another state. Without such directives, families may find it necessary to obtain court orders to deal with their medical situations.

Advance directives are also known as:

>> Living wills

>> Medical directives

>> Healthcare proxies

>> Advance healthcare directives

Regardless of the name your state gives to these documents, their purpose is to allow you to express your preferences concerning medical treatment in an emergency medical situation when you can't communicate.

Most commonly, this type of situation occurs either because you are unconscious or because your mental state is such that you no longer have the capacity to make your own decisions. These situations can occur at any time, unexpectedly, because of accidents or a sudden change in your health. And these situations arise more frequently at end of life. For all these reasons, it is important to complete your ADs regardless of your age or current health condition.

Advance directives are comprised two components:

1. A healthcare proxy
2. A living will

I discuss each of the components of ADs in detail so you understand how important these documents are to ensure an end of life that you want.

The healthcare proxy

The *healthcare proxy* (HCP) is someone you appoint to make healthcare decisions for you if you lose the ability to make decisions yourself. The HCP is your medical advocate.

The person you appoint as your HCP has the authority to make medical decisions for you in the event you are unable to express your preferences about medical treatment.

TIP

Appointing an HCP is a good idea regardless of your age or health. You never know when a medical emergency may happen. An HCP acts on your behalf when you are unable to make your own healthcare decisions, even if only temporarily. For example, a situation might arise when you are under general anesthesia for a surgery or in a coma because of an accident. Then you need an HCP to make medical decisions for you.

But don't worry! When you are again able to make your own healthcare decisions, your HCP is no longer authorized to act.

SELECTING MY HCP

The HCP carries a great responsibility to speak for you in the event you are unable to speak for yourself in a medical situation. Therefore, it should be someone:

1. you trust

-**AND**-

2. who is assertive.

It is very important to consider *both* criteria in your selection of someone as your HCP.

TRUSTING SOMEONE AS HCP

The HCP should be someone you trust to honor *your* wishes and preferences, *not* apply their own wishes and preferences in a situation.

When making medical decisions for you, the HCP must set aside their own feelings and desires about what they want done for you or what they would do for themselves in a similar situation. The HCP must speak *as if they are you* — what they know you would want done based on their knowledge of you and the many conversations with you.

REMEMBER

Therefore, consider people who respect you enough to do what you want, not what they want. When in a medical emergency, doubt and uncertainty are removed because your HCP is doing what they know you want. It relieves the HCP of the burden of wondering, "Did I make the right decision?"

FIGHTING FOR YOU AS HCP

The second criteria for selecting an HCP is very important. By appointing an HCP, you can expect the HCP to ensure that the healthcare providers follow your wishes and other family members respect your wishes. You can also expect the HCP to decide how your wishes apply as your medical condition changes, especially if complications arise unexpectedly. Ideally, the HCP is someone who can be assertive enough to enforce your wishes and preferences in the face of adversity or contrary opinion.

The HCP may be confronted with pressure and coercion. Doctors may recommend a different course of medical action that's contrary to what your HCP knows you want. In the end, the medical professionals will respect your wishes — especially if legally documented and backed by your HCP — but family members may disagree. The HCP may be exposed to anger, hostility, and guilt for doing what you want. In a medical emergency, emotions run high, and people do not always act rationally or reasonably.

REMEMBER

So choose an HCP who can stand up for what you want and remind everyone that they are acting on your behalf. Ultimately, everyone should know that the HCP is just doing what you want.

CHOOSING MY HCP: FAMILY OR FRIEND

The HCP can be a spouse, other family member, or close friend. The HCP doesn't have to be the person closest to you or the person naturally expected to be the HCP.

Keep in mind that when the HCP's role becomes effective and is speaking for you, you are no longer able to speak for yourself. You're likely to be in a medical emergency, unable to communicate.

REMEMBER

During any crisis situation, the threat of you dying is real, for you and your loved ones. Emotions are grave and intense, filled with worry, anxiety, and stress. It can be crazy and chaotic. So you need to think about how your HCP will react in an emergency concerning you. In this type of situation, the HCP must be calm and reasonable and able to make decisions for you. *Can they do that for you in an emergency situation?*

Sometimes a spouse may not be the best choice as HCP because they're too emotionally involved. Sometimes they are the best choice because they know you best. Only you know who may be the best person to serve your interests.

Some of the people to consider as your HCP are shown in Figure 4-2.

FIGURE 4-2:
When choosing your HCP, think about who can best make decisions for you in an emergency situation.

TIP

The best thing that you can do is talk to the people you are considering as HCP. Be honest. Tell them what you want and why you want it. Explain your wishes and preferences for end of life, and your motivations behind them. Give them the opportunity and time to think about it, ask questions of you, and understand exactly what it is that you want. Have many conversations with your potential HCPs.

TIP

When you have decided upon an HCP and that person has agreed, share your decision with the important people in your life. Explain your thinking and why you are choosing so-and-so to be your HCP. Communication ahead of time can go a long way in preventing misunderstandings or hurt feelings later on.

REMEMBER

Whether you choose a spouse, another family member, or a close friend as your HCP, it is more important to talk to everyone — often and in detail. Have many conversations. Prepare.

DON'T WAIT!

Begin the conversations with your loved ones as soon as possible. Don't expect someone to agree to be your HCP right away. Give everyone enough time to come to an understanding of what you are asking.

The HCP carries a major responsibility for you, so have open and frank discussions with them about your wishes, preferences, and beliefs. This is a process, and it takes time. In the end, your HCP will be in a position to act on your behalf with confidence and knowledge of what you want.

TIP

I recommend that you designate an HCP as soon as possible — at whatever point in life you're at — because you never know when a medical emergency may occur. Better to have someone that you know and trust — someone who loves and cares about you — to make decisions for you.

APPOINTING YOUR HCP

So you have had multiple conversations with your potential HCP, and they've finally agreed to be your HCP. What do you do next? You need to officially appoint this person as your HCP in a legal document, generally a healthcare proxy form.

Every state has their own HCP form, which can be obtained from the state's government site. Forms are also available for every state from organizations such as CaringInfo, a program of the National Alliance for Care at Home. Other organizations, such as the two in the following list, have created forms that are user-friendly and still meet the legal requirements for the different states:

>> Five Wishes

>> PREPARE for YOUR Care

Here are a few helpful points to keep in mind for the HCP form:

>> **Check out the forms accepted for your state.**

>> **Most states will recognize an HCP from another state, but one state's form does not always work in another state.** Be sure to fill out forms in all the states that you spend significant time in.

>> **You don't need a lawyer to complete an HCP form.** The states vary in their requirements for witnesses and notarization, so please check out your state's requirements.

>> **Be sure to give your HCP a signed copy of the form.** Also give copies to your doctors, family, and anyone else who may be involved.

Even though you have signed this form, you have the right to make healthcare decisions for yourself as long as you are able to do so. Your HCP will only start making decisions for you when your doctor determines that you are unable to make healthcare decisions for yourself.

Congratulations! You have now completed the first component of your advance directives and are one step closer to ensuring the kind of end of life that you want.

RECOGNIZING SYNONYMS FOR HCP

Be aware that there are many other names for an HCP. Since each state has their own state requirements and forms, many terms have been developed to mean essentially the same thing.

Other terms for an HCP that you may see include the following:

>> Healthcare agent

>> Healthcare surrogate

>> Healthcare representative

>> Durable medical power of attorney

>> Healthcare power of attorney

>> Healthcare attorney-in-fact

>> Medical decision-maker

APPOINTING AN ALTERNATE HCP

Normally, one person is appointed as your HCP. However, it is common to appoint one or more alternate persons, in the event your first choice proxy is unavailable.

Be sure to have in-depth discussions with any alternates that you consider appointing as your HCP, not just the primary person, to see whether they are willing and able to make decisions for you and carry out your wishes.

CHANGING YOUR HCP

It is easy to cancel or change the person you have designated as your HCP. Simply fill out a new form.

Appointing an HCP is voluntary. No one can require you to appoint one, but designating someone to be your HCP is a good idea.

The living will

A *living will* is a legal document that provides specific instructions about certain medical treatments in the event that you are unable to communicate. It is recognized as evidence of your wishes and decisions regarding future medical care.

The living will is based on the common law right that a competent adult can determine what will be done to their own person or body. This is known as the right of self-determination, which includes the right to accept or decline medical treatment.

A living will doesn't determine your medical treatment in situations that don't affect your continued life, such as routine medical treatment and non-life-threatening medical conditions.

REFLECTING ON WHAT'S MOST IMPORTANT

Reflecting on what matters most to you can help you decide on the types of care and medical treatment options you want to include or not include in your living will.

NEW

Many people begin the process by thinking about their values and wishes. For example, if your heart were to stop or you were to have trouble breathing, would you want to undergo lifesaving measures? What if it meant that you couldn't speak and were kept alive on machines? Or what if it meant that, sometime in the future, you could be well enough to spend time with your family? For some people, staying alive as long as medically possible, or long enough to experience an important life event, is the most important goal. Others have a clear idea about when they would no longer want to prolong their lives. (For a more in-depth discussion about the goals of care in making medical decisions, see Chapter 5.)

You should consider the following questions in order to complete a living will:

>> How important is it to be independent and self-sufficient?

>> If your health worsens, where do you prefer to be — at home or in a hospital or nursing facility?

>> Do you want treatment at all costs to prolong life or is quality of life more important?

>> What are your biggest fears or worries about a severe illness?

>> What circumstances make life worth/not worth living?

>> What abilities are so critical to life that you cannot imagine living without them?

Take stock of your thoughts and feelings about these important questions. Your answers may change based upon your age, health, and circumstances. Or you may already know the answers to many of these questions and feel strongly about how you want to be cared for at end of life.

A living will is personalized, just about you. It takes into consideration what's most important to you and your values, beliefs, traditions, spirituality, and culture.

DECIDING ON FUTURE MEDICAL TREATMENTS

The living will specifies what type of medical treatments you would or would not want. It is most often used by people who want to express their feelings about the use or the withholding of life-sustaining treatment that prolongs the process of dying. For example, you are able to decide in advance whether to be given food and water intravenously or other medical procedures that impact your care, including at end of life.

Most standardized living will forms address the following medical treatments, but you should list as many possible end-of-life care decisions in your living will as you feel confident about.

» CPR (cardiopulmonary resuscitation)

» Mechanical ventilation

» Pacemakers and ICDs (implantable cardioverter-defibrillator)

» Artificial nutrition and hydration

» Dialysis

» Antibiotics and other medications

» Comfort (palliative) care

» Organ and tissue donations

» Donating your body to science

The preceding list can be overwhelming to think about. Unless you are a medical professional yourself, you may not understand what all these medical treatments are and their implications to you in a life-threatening situation. It is vital to understand these medical treatments — even if you think they don't apply to you — before completing your living will.

GETTING HELP TO COMPLETE YOUR LIVING WILL

Begin by talking to your doctor or another healthcare provider. Tell them that you are completing your living will and want to understand and think through your choices before you put them in writing. Find out about your current health status and the kinds of decisions that are likely to come up. Ask questions about the medical treatments in a living will and what these medical decisions mean for you.

Next, talk to the important people in your life, your family, and close friends. Remember a living will is about what you want and don't want. It reflects your values, beliefs, religion, spirituality, and culture. But anything you decide will affect the care and support of those closest to you.

Also consider talking to any other persons who know you well and can help you work through these issues in the context of your family and medical history. These may include members of your faith community or any other trusted family or friend.

CREATING YOUR LIVING WILL

So you have had multiple conversations with your doctors, family, and friends. You understand and are ready to make decisions about future medical care. Now what do you do? You need to officially state your medical decisions in a legal document, the living will form.

A range of living will forms is available. Some living wills are incorporated under the broader umbrella term of advance directives. If so, the part of the advance directives that refers to medical care and treatment is essentially the living will component.

Living will forms are not standardized. The language in some forms is quite legalese with lists and check boxes, while other forms allow you to convey a range of feelings and preferences with regard to future medical care. Some medical scenarios may be more black-and-white to you, while others are more nuanced.

Some states have forms that can be obtained from the state government sites, while some allow you to create your own. Forms are also available for every state from organizations such as CaringInfo, a program of the National Alliance for Care at Home. Other organizations, such as the two in the following list, have created forms that are user-friendly and still meet the legal requirements for the different states:

» Five Wishes

» PREPARE for YOUR Care

Here are a few helpful points to keep in mind for the living will form:

>> **Check out the form accepted for your state.**

>> **Each state has its own rules and regulations.** Most states recognize living wills and ADs legally notarized from another state, but it is not guaranteed.

>> **You don't need a lawyer to create a living will.** The states vary in their requirements for witnesses and notarization, so please check out your state's requirements.

>> **Be aware that two states currently do not officially recognize a living will: Massachusetts and Michigan.** Despite this, a living will is still potentially useful because it can guide an HCP and healthcare professionals about the types of choices you would make.

>> **Be sure to give a signed copy of the living will to your HCP.** Also give copies to your doctors, family, and anyone else who may be involved.

Congratulations! You have now completed the second component of your advance directives and are one step closer to ensuring the kind of end of life that you want.

ADs: HCP and living will together

The HCP and the living will, together called advance directives (ADs), express your attitudes and wishes about future medical care. These documents allow you to remain in control, with the authority to dictate how you want to live and die. Considering that the majority of dying people are unconscious, in distress, or otherwise unable to speak, your ADs serve as your voice when you may not have one.

An HCP and a living will both have the same purpose: to see that your medical wishes are expressed and honored, even when you can't do so yourself. They work best *in tandem.*

The language in standard living wills is usually too narrow to apply to many common medical situations. The living will is intended to anticipate an end-of-life situation with no reasonable expectation of recovery. These include if you are in any of the following states:

>> A terminal condition

>> Permanent unconsciousness (persistent vegetative state)

>> Conscious but with irreversible brain damage

Because living wills focus on terminal illnesses, permanent unconsciousness, and cognitive decline — and these situations are rarer — it is best to have an HCP to make medical decisions on the most current situation and information. Since you can't anticipate all situations ahead of time, designating an HCP helps you be prepared for the unexpected.

This is why it is so important to have both components of advance directives.

A living will with no HCP

If you do not have an HCP, or if the person you have appointed is not available, then it is essential that you have a living will.

The limitation of a living will is that it applies to only specific medical situations and does not account for every possible medical scenario. Without an HCP, healthcare providers will be left to interpret your intention for medical care in an unanticipated situation based on the living will and also consult with family, if available. The healthcare providers may have to make difficult judgments about how to proceed in your care.

If you lack an HCP, the state may designate someone else, according to state laws, to make decisions on your behalf, and it may be someone you didn't intend.

An HCP with no living will

Your HCP can make medical decisions for you in all unforeseen circumstances that a living will may not cover. In addition, all fifty states recognize an HCP. So you may be thinking that you don't need to have a living will.

Creating a living will is a good idea even if you have appointed an HCP. Your HCP is making medical decisions for you based on in-depth past conversations with you about your wishes and preferences for medical care and end of life. The more that you can support and prepare your HCP — through conversations and a living will — the better position your HCP will be in to act with confidence on your behalf when necessary.

Even though a living will covers only specific medical situations, it can be used as a guide to your intentions about future medical care. Removing ambiguity about your intentions will help your HCP to be your medical advocate.

Sharing your ADs

Once you've completed your advance directives, ensure that copies are provided to your HCP, your healthcare providers, and others whom you think should have the information, such as your family, friends, or clergy.

REMEMBER

If you go to the hospital for any reason, bring a copy of your ADs with you. Check to see if your local hospital will maintain your ADs on file in case you are admitted in the future.

Keeping your ADs up to date

You can change your ADs, or just one component of your ADs, at any time. If you want to make changes, you must create a new form, distribute the new copies, and destroy the old copies.

TIP

It is a good idea to review your ADs when you have a major life change that affects your health or family circumstances. This includes getting a new diagnosis or having a change in marital status. When you marry, divorce, become separated, or become a widow or widower, you may need to reconsider your HCP.

REMEMBER

Advance care planning is an ongoing process, not a one-time event. Periodic reviews will ensure that your ADs reflect your current values, wishes, and circum- stances. Over time, your thoughts and feelings about end-of-life care may change.

Chapter **5**

Managing Medical Logistics

G etting good medical care is a complex matter at any time in life, and even more so at end of life. The more you know about how the process works — who is involved, what is happening, what to expect, and what you need to know — the better prepared you will be for end of life.

The sheer nature of the timing being at end of life or life-threatening can make everything seem more fraught and final. It can be an emotional, difficult time for you and your loved ones. There may be anxiety, uncertainty, and worry. The time to make important medical decisions is not when you are feeling scared or too ill to think clearly, stressed, or in an emergency situation. Therefore, it's important to consider your thoughts and emotions around the topics of end of life — illness, dying, and death — when you are healthy, calm, and of a clear mind.

In this chapter, you discover the important medical decisions that arise at end of life, goals of care and the essential question to ask yourself, care options at end of life including hospice, and who the members of your healthcare team are.

Making Medical Decisions

At end of life, the things that drive your decision-making may be very different from how you made decisions previously in life. And in regard to making medical decisions, your decision-making process may be greatly influenced by your age, health, whether or not you are ill, the symptoms of disease, the level of pain and suffering you experience, where you live, who is able to support you, and many other factors.

It is helpful to first establish the goals of your end-of-life care. Keeping these goals in mind:

>> Drives your decision-making toward achieving those goals of care

>> Helps you feel more in control of your life and the decisions that affect it

>> Eases the sense of doubt and uncertainty in decision-making

>> Reminds you of the "big picture" and to live fully in the time remaining

REMEMBER

Try to be realistic and hopeful in thinking about your end-of-life goals of care. Wishing for something unrealistic, such as a miracle cure, can result in disappointment, frustration, and other negative emotions.

Asking the essential question

Determining your end-of-life goals of care begins with asking yourself this essential question:

Do you want to do everything possible to prolong your life, or do you prefer to minimize treatments and procedures that might cause pain and suffering?

A decision of this nature will impact the course of your end of life and affect the medical plan of care. It is a complex and complicated question.

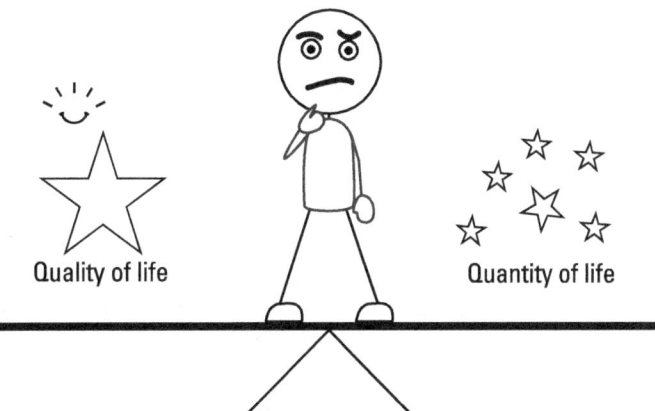

Quality of life   Quantity of life

Quality versus quantity of life will always be one of the hardest decisions you make for yourself. Only you know what value you place on time left to live and at what cost.

Having information as well as different perspectives on this question helps you to be well-informed and comprehensive in your thinking about what is important to you. Please consider the following:

>> **Your health:** Talk to your doctors about your current medical condition, the severity of illness, and prognosis. Doctors are required to communicate fully about available treatment options and the related risks and benefits of specific treatment interventions.

>> **Your family and loved ones:** Talk to them about this. Any decision you make will affect them as well. You want their support, so give them time to understand your thinking.

>> **Personal values:** End of life is associated with loss of dignity, autonomy, and control, in terms of what is happening to you and how you are treated and cared for. Consider the importance and retention of these values to you.

>> **Your spirituality or faith:** Your spiritual or religious beliefs may influence or be a factor in your decision-making process. Consult with your spiritual faith leaders for guidance.

You may know immediately what your goal for end of life is. Or, it may take a long time to come to a decision that feels right to you. That's okay. Take the time you need to think seriously and come to a decision that feels best for you.

What feels right for you now may change as you age or your illness progresses. It's okay if your inclination toward one or the other changes, even frequently. As circumstances change, it is vital to reassess the situation: you, your current condition, how you feel, and the quality of the life you are living. And you can adjust your goals of care to reflect your current state.

There is no "wrong" decision. No matter what you decide, you will not make the wrong decision if you keep your needs, wishes, and preferences foremost in your decision-making process. Whatever decision you make, you know that the choice reflects who you are as a person and what's important to you, given the information you have at the time.

The question of quality versus quantity at end of life is not an easy one. In the end, it is a very personal decision only you can make.

Thinking about goals of care

Don't wait until you are ill or near the end of life to think about the essential question of quality versus quantity of life. It is important to consider your thoughts and emotions around illness, dying, and death when you are healthy and of sound mind. It can be hard to feel confident about what to do and what is right during a medical emergency.

Think of it this way: Any major storm potentially coming your way, like a hurricane, is better faced with advance planning. Anticipating and preparing ahead of time allows you to face a life-threatening event with calm. End of life is no different.

So start thinking now about what you may want — even if only hypothetically — just to begin opening the door to these topics. It may be uncomfortable or scary initially, but the more you consider these questions now, the better you'll know what you want when in a medical emergency, ill, or dying.

Deciding where you want to die

Another important question to ask yourself to prepare for end of life is:

Where would I like to die?

Did you know that you have a choice about this? This is a personal goal that's greatly affected by your goals of care, and vice versa.

For some people, it doesn't matter where they die. But for many people, it matters a great deal. When surveyed, a majority of Americans consistently say that they want to die at home. In 2016, a Kaiser Family Foundation survey on Aging and End-of-Life Medical Care found that 71 percent of people preferred to die at home. Not surprising. Home is familiar and comfortable. Home is where you are surrounded by the stories of your life. Home is your domain.

REMEMBER

You cannot completely control where you will die; for example, you may die unexpectedly or suddenly. Where you die is never guaranteed, but you can make decisions toward achieving that goal.

Where you will die is influenced by the goals of care you establish with your doctor or healthcare provider:

>> If you elect "to do everything possible to prolong your life," then you will likely die at the hospital. This is simply because the hospital is the place where the medical personnel, treatments, tests, equipment, and so on are located "to do everything possible" medically for you.

>> If you elect "to minimize treatments and procedures that might cause pain and suffering," then many more care options are available to you, including dying at home. I talk more about the care options at end of life later in this chapter.

It may be that you want to die at home *and* want everything possible to prolong your life. While you can be at home when stable, if you have a medical emergency or a complicating symptom, you will be taken to the hospital for treatment so that the full resources of the hospital are available for your care. This may occur repeatedly, or you may be admitted to the hospital long term. In the end, you'll likely die at the hospital. In this case, you must think carefully about what is more important to you and which acts as your primary guide in decision-making: where you want to die or your goals of care.

Again, there is no guarantee that any decision you make or goal you establish will happen exactly the way you want. Things can happen and are unpredictable. But what you can do is plan for your goals and make decisions in support of them. This increases the likelihood of end of life occurring as you envision.

Discussing your goals with others

When you have thought seriously for a long time about what you might want as your goals of care for end of life, share your decision with others:

>> Doctors and healthcare team

>> Family and loved ones

>> Healthcare proxy

>> Caregivers

It's essential that they also understand your wishes and preferences for end of life and are given the opportunity to discuss your motivation and reasoning with you. In this way, they are also given the time to understand and respect your thinking and decision. Even if they disagree with you, they will know that this is what you want. Communication avoids misunderstanding and conflict later on.

REMEMBER

If you decide that you want "to do everything possible to prolong your life," there is nothing else you need to do except talk with your family and loved ones. Medically, if you do nothing, all measures will be taken to try and save your life.

NEW

You may be thinking, why do I need to tell my family if what will be done medically is consistent with what I want? The reason — and it's a *big* one — is to provide peace of mind to your family. Letting them know what you want relieves them of the burden of having to make decisions for you, if necessary, without knowing for certain and releases them of the doubt afterwards. So give this gift to those you love.

If you decide that you want "to minimize treatments and procedures that might cause pain and suffering," then there is paperwork that you will need to complete to officially state this, legally and medically. I talk more about the relevant paperwork you need to complete in the next section.

REMEMBER

Whatever decision you make, a conscious decision about the end of life can make you feel more in control of your own life. And, at end of life, when so much is beyond your control, this can feel quite empowering.

Establishing Your Medical Orders

Under ordinary circumstances, all life-saving treatments will be used to try to save your life. If you want to minimize the treatments and procedures that might cause pain and suffering, you will need to specify the kind of medical treatments that you do and do not want at end of life.

One way to do this is to complete medical orders that instruct your healthcare team about your preferences. These are legal documents that are signed by your doctor or other healthcare provider. I discuss the common medical orders related to end of life here.

Another way to specify the kind of medical treatments that you do and do not want at end of life is through *advance directives.* Since these legal documents do not require your doctor or a healthcare provider to sign off, I talk about these documents in Chapter 4.

REMEMBER

You don't have to choose between medical orders and advance directives (ADs). Medical orders are usually only completed when you have a serious illness or anticipate being in the hospital. Advance directives cover you all the time in any situation, even when you are healthy. Complete your advance directives (as described in Chapter 4). When you become ill, supplement with medical orders that are consistent with your ADs.

Knowing your medical orders

All the medical orders discussed here are completed with your doctor or other healthcare provider. You typically encounter these orders upon hospitalization or enrollment in hospice.

TIP

Even if you completed these orders on a previous occasion, it's always a good idea to review the older form to see whether it is still accurate and represents what you currently want. In addition, forms are frequently updated, and newer forms may include additional options not on an older form.

TIP

Also, if you want to make a specific order that's not presented to you, please request the form from your provider.

DNR

DNR = Do Not Resuscitate

A *DNR order* means you do not want any life-saving measures if your heart stops beating. The "R" in DNR refers to "resuscitation" and applies to the treatments used to restart the heart, which include cardiopulmonary resuscitation (CPR), defibrillation, and intravenous medications, such as epinephrine.

There are pros and cons to attempting resuscitation, and it isn't always successful. Your doctor can tell you more about the risks and benefits. Please talk with your doctor about DNR and how it relates to you and your specific condition.

Ideally, a DNR order is set up before an emergency occurs.

DNI

DNI = Do Not Intubate

A *DNI order* means you don't want to be put on a ventilator if you are having difficulty breathing or cannot do so on your own. The "I" in DNI refers to "intubation" and is a procedure in which a breathing tube is placed down your airway, into the lungs, and is then connected to a life support machine.

Intubation is almost always a part of the CPR process and is either performed while the patient is receiving CPR or immediately afterwards if the CPR successfully restarts the heart. As a result, DNR and DNI often go hand-in-hand.

But a DNI order can be separate from a DNR. It prevents you from being put on a ventilator when your heart is still beating, in situations outside of cardiac arrest. You may choose a DNI to avoid the possible complications of having a breathing tube placed and the potential for becoming dependent on a ventilator long-term.

Out-of-hospital DNR

Usually, DNR and DNI orders are completed when you are in need of hospitalization. If you would like to establish these orders outside of hospitalization, there are special DNR orders that are effective outside a hospital setting. These are called "out-of-hospital," "pre-hospital, comfort care," or "no CPR" orders.

You may also include these orders in a POLST (described later in this section) or in your advance directive (described in Chapter 4).

DNAR

DNAR = Do Not Attempt Resuscitation

A *DNAR order* is the same as a DNR, but you may see this term used instead. The acronym was introduced in 2005 by the American Heart Association to clarify the order. The clearer language references a resuscitation attempt and reduces the implication that resuscitation is likely to succeed.

AND

AND = Allow Natural Death

An *AND order* means not interfering with the natural dying process. An AND is the same as a DNR and DNAR, but in even clearer language. Instead of focusing on what is not done, the order focuses on what is allowed for the patient. Comfort measures are allowed in a natural death.

The AND term is used at some hospitals as an alternative to the more traditional DNR order. While it is the preferred term, AND is still not universally used by all hospitals and care facilities.

POLST

POLST = Portable Medical Orders

A *POLST* is an out-of-hospital order that specifies the medical treatments that you do and do not want, and your goals of care. It is more comprehensive than a DNR.

The POLST form is designed for people who are seriously ill or have advanced frailty, and is not intended for people who are healthy.

A POLST travels with you and instructs medical personnel in whatever care setting you are located. If you transfer from one facility to another, such as a hospital to a nursing home or hospice, or even to home, the POLST is still effective.

POLST is a word of its own and means "portable medical orders." It is no longer an acronym; originally, it stood for "Physician Orders for Life-Sustaining Treatment." Depending on the state you live in, it may be called something else, but it means the same thing. These names are interchangeable and include:

>> MOLST = Medical Orders for Life-Sustaining Treatment

>> COLST = Clinician Orders for Life-Sustaining Treatment

>> POST = Provider Orders for Scope of Treatment

>> MOST = Medical Orders for Scope of Treatment

>> TPOPP = Transportable Physician Orders for Patient Preferences

There is a national POLST form, which some states have adopted. However, many states have created their own state version of POLST, adapted from the national form. So check to see what your state does.

To improve consistency of process, the National POLST Office is working with all states to adopt national standards and the national POLST form.

Completing medical orders

For any of these medical orders, you will need to meet with your doctor and discuss your medical condition, prognosis, and treatment options. Your doctor will review the form with you and explain any medical terms and treatments so that you fully understand what they are and how they relate to you.

Then, you will complete the form together. Your medical order only becomes valid once you and your doctor or healthcare provider sign it.

Make copies of the completed form and share it with all members of your health-care team, your family, healthcare proxy, and caregivers. If you live at home, keep a copy in a visible location, such as on the refrigerator.

Changing your mind

You can change your mind at any time about any medical order. All medical orders are reversible and can be withdrawn at any time.

If you think you want to change your mind about your preferences, talk to your family, healthcare proxy, and healthcare team. Your doctor can answer any questions and concerns you have. They can also make the change in your medical record. If you're not able to speak for yourself or are having difficulty in getting your medical order changed, your loved ones and healthcare proxy can advocate for you.

Understanding End-of-Life Care

There may come a time when you change your goals of care to minimize treatments and procedures that might cause pain and suffering. This is common when the pain and suffering you are experiencing outweigh any potential benefits of the treatments and procedures of illness. Or, it may be that viable treatment options are no longer available. Nothing more can be done.

When this happens, the illness is allowed to run its natural course. The goals of care are to minimize the pain and suffering of illness and offer comfort measures until death.

These goals of care at end of life are at the center of the hospice concept, a community model of care based on compassion. Hospice began only in the mid-1960s, and modern hospice today continues to evolve with increasing public demand for better ways to die. It is important, then, to understand what hospice is and what it offers at end of life.

Touring the origins of hospice

The word *hospice* derives from the Latin *hospes,* which means both "guest" and "host." This guest–host relationship was highly important in ancient

Indo-European society, in which it represented a bond of trust between two people based on ritual and hospitality.

The Latin *hospes*, a person who receives guests, is the basis of the Old French word *hospital*. Hospital was originally a place of lodging or an inn, then a lodging for those in need, and then a place where people in need could receive care. Eventually, "hospital" came to mean a place where people receive medical care. And in contrast, "hospice" came to mean a place where the aged and terminally ill receive care at end of life.

The first modern-day hospice was founded in 1967 by Dame Cicely Saunders, a social worker turned nurse then medical doctor, in south London, England. The first hospice in the United States, The Connecticut Hospice, was established in 1974 by Florence Wald, former Dean of Yale School of Nursing.

Since then, there has been a steady increase in hospice services globally. According to the Worldwide Hospice Palliative Care Alliance (WHPCA), an international non-governmental organization focused exclusively on hospice and palliative care development, there is representation in over 100 countries worldwide. Despite the rapid growth of hospice services globally, WHPCA estimates that over 27 million people still lack hospice at the end of life, with over 20 million of those dying in avoidable pain and distress.

Knowing what hospice is (and isn't)

NEW

Now, hospice is not a place at all. Hospice has developed into a philosophy of care, which has become the standard of care at end of life. It is a shift in medical care to one that focuses on you as a person, not the disease.

Hospice care focuses on comfort and symptom management to alleviate pain and suffering. It is a holistic, compassionate approach to care, addressing the physical, emotional, social, and spiritual needs of patients, their families, and their environment. It considers the wishes and preferences of the patient, emphasizing communication as an important component to good care.

A hospice approach to end of life usually provides a symptom management plan; physical, emotional, and spiritual support; and education about care techniques, what to expect, and more. A hospice care team is assembled and comprised specially trained doctors, nurses, social workers, and other specialists who work together to provide care and support for your needs at end of life. I talk more about each member of the healthcare team and the role they play in the next section.

Where to get hospice

The majority of hospice care occurs in wherever a patient calls home. This includes houses, apartments, skilled nursing facilities, assisted living facilities, hotels, and more.

The focus of hospice care is for you to remain in your home, the place where the overwhelming majority of people say they would like to die. Field personnel come to your home. Essential medical and care equipment are provided to you. Medication and supplies are sent and delivered to your home. Therefore, hospice care helps you to stay in your home, the environment most familiar and comfortable to you.

While there are independent hospice houses and inpatient hospice units, they make up a small percentage of the places where people receive hospice care.

Eligibility criteria for hospice

Currently, in order to receive hospice care, you must enroll with a hospice service. Typically, the eligibility requirement is a terminal illness with a prognosis of less than six months to live if the illness runs its normal course. Usually, hospice is for those who no longer seek curative treatments for their illness.

However, it is not uncommon for a person to improve under hospice care. For example, once aggressive curative treatments, like chemotherapy, are stopped, the body has a chance to rest and recover. You may feel better, but this does not mean that the disease is reduced or cured. You, and the disease, may be in respite. It's possible that you may not die within six months. If that is the case, you may need to be recertified in order to continue to receive hospice care.

Knowing what palliative care is (and isn't)

Palliative care grew out of the modern hospice movement and was spearheaded by Dr. Balfour Mount, a surgical oncologist at the Royal Victoria Hospital and McGill University in Montreal, Canada. After studying with Dr. Saunders at St. Christopher's, Mount introduced the hospice concept to the hospital setting. He coined the term "palliative care" to distinguish it from hospice and expanded its approach to all patients facing life-threatening illnesses.

NEW

Today, *palliative care* is considered a specialized form of medical care that focuses on addressing the symptoms of serious illness and the quality of life for the patient. It is a branch of medicine, just like oncology, pediatrics, and orthopedics.

The focus of palliative care is to lower symptom burden. The concept of *symptom burden* is complex and multidimensional and is generally defined as the impact of multiple symptoms as a result of illness on you the patient. The impact encompasses symptoms — including those perceived by you — that produce negative physical, emotional, social, and spiritual patient responses. Some of these symptoms are pain, depression, anxiety, fatigue, shortness of breath, constipation, nausea or vomiting, loss of appetite, and trouble sleeping. Palliative care works on reducing the impact of these negative symptoms to improve quality of life for you.

REMEMBER

Palliative care is appropriate to and can benefit people *of any age and at any stage of a serious illness*. Palliative care is *not* just for end of life.

NEW

Contrary to common thinking, palliative care can be provided along with curative treatments. You can receive palliative care wherever you are located and in any setting, whether that be at home or in a hospital, assisted living facility, or clinic.

If you are living with a serious illness, ask to see a palliative care specialist. Living with illness can be challenging, and palliative care supports you to live a fuller, more comfortable life.

Hospice versus palliative care

Table 5-1 summarizes the similarities and differences of hospice versus palliative care.

TABLE 5-1   **Hospice versus Palliative Care**

Question	Hospice Care	Palliative Care
Who can receive care?	Any individual with a serious illness, with a life expectancy of <6 months	Any individual with a serious illness, regardless of age or life expectancy
Will my symptoms, including pain, be relieved?	Yes, as much as possible	Yes, as much as possible
Can I continue to receive curative treatments for my illness?	No, hospice care focuses on comfort, not cure	Yes, palliative care can be given concurrently with curative treatments
Who provides these services?	An interdisciplinary team led by the hospice doctor, usually in collaboration with the primary care physician	An interdisciplinary team led by the palliative care doctor, in collaboration with the primary care physician and specialists
Where are services provided?	Most care settings, except acute care facilities and clinics	Any care setting

(continued)

TABLE 5-1 *(continued)*

Question	Hospice Care	Palliative Care
How long can I receive care?	As long as the eligibility criteria for hospice is met	Not time-limited, but most receive palliative care on an intermittent basis
Does Medicare and/or Medicaid pay?	Yes, Medicare pays for all related costs. In most states, Medicaid does as well	Some treatments and medications may be covered
Does private insurance pay?	Most private insurers have a hospice benefit that pays all related costs	Some treatments and medications may be covered

Adapted from National Hospice and Palliative Care Organization, Palliative Care or Hospice? Informational Sheet.

Consult with your doctors, the hospice services in your local area, and your insurance company to find out the specific benefits and terms that apply to you and your situation.

A common pathway for those with a serious or terminal illness is to receive palliative care and then transition to hospice care when they near end of life.

Meeting Your Healthcare Team

You will likely have a team of healthcare professionals working to care for and support you, as shown in Figure 5-1. Some may come from hospice and some may be brought in privately by you. Regardless, they all work together with an aim to provide an end of life consistent with your wishes and preferences.

Some of the healthcare professionals will be with you throughout the entire illness journey to death. Others will only be involved for a limited time based upon your condition and needs. So be aware that your healthcare team will be in constant flux.

REMEMBER

As your healthcare team changes, it can be disorienting and exhausting to continually reintroduce yourself and adjust to new team members. Be patient with them and yourself. Know that every member of your healthcare team is there to support you to have the best end of life possible.

The doctor

If you are ill, you are likely to have a team of doctors. You may just call them all "doctors," but most doctors have extra expertise in a particular area of medicine. Doctors specialize, and there are hundreds of specialties and subspecialties.

FIGURE 5-1:
Your care team will be comprised various healthcare professionals.

Doctors will come and go as part of your healthcare team. Some doctors will only be involved for a limited time to take care of a particular issue or symptom. Very rarely will a doctor stay with you throughout your entire illness journey, and if so, it's likely to be your primary care physician or family doctor.

Unless you have a very involved primary care physician overseeing your overall care, it may be up to you to coordinate and manage all the medical information that describes the history, condition, and symptoms of your illness, given the variety and number of doctors who may come and go as part of your healthcare team. It's a huge job, so try to stay organized and enlist help.

At end of life, there are two other medical doctors who play an important role and may become part of your healthcare team:

» The *palliative care doctor* is a physician with additional training in hospice and palliative medicine. They support a wide range of patients with serious, chronic, or life-threatening illnesses.

» The *hospice doctor* is also a physician with additional training in hospice and palliative medicine, but who specializes in end-of-life care. They support patients nearing the end of life and typically work for a hospice service, facility, or unit.

Once you enroll with a hospice service, the hospice doctor will communicate with your primary care physician or other specialists regarding your plan of care. Or, you can elect for the hospice doctor to become your primary doctor and oversee your overall care. Either way, the hospice doctor will be the one to develop the plan of care, monitor the progression of your illness, prescribe appropriate medications, and coordinate care with the other healthcare team members. The hospice doctor is involved with you until the end.

The nurse

Nurses are an integral part of the healthcare team and often are the main point of contact for patients and their families. They bring a high level of medical knowledge, communication skills, and compassion to their work.

The *hospice nurse* is specially trained in assessing and managing a patient's physical, emotional, and comfort needs, including pain management. They remain in contact with the hospice physician to coordinate and address care — as changes occur — and are the ones on the ground in your home. They are the ones responsible for your overall care and needs.

The responsibilities of a hospice nurse include some of the following:

>> **Visit you in your home as needed.** On average, the hospice nurse visits once a week. When you begin actively dying, visits may become more frequent.

>> **Check vital signs and manage pain or other symptoms.** During visits, the nurse assesses your condition, checks vitals, evaluates medication, and talks with you and your caregivers about any issues. Outside of nursing visits, it is up to the caregivers to monitor your condition and notify hospice of changes.

>> **Communicate and coordinate services and care with other hospice team members.** The nurse addresses any issues or potential issues, identified or brought up by you with the hospice team. If needed, other team members will be brought in to visit you.

>> **Ensure you and your family's needs are met.** Don't hesitate to ask questions or raise concerns to your nurse. If your needs are not being addressed or met, you will need to speak up. You cannot assume that they know what's going on with you.

>> **Educate family members on how to best care for you.** The nurse can provide information and guide your caregivers on care practices and medication management. Please be proactive in communicating with the nurse about what you need or would like to know.

>> **Listen, comfort, and support you and your family members.** Hospice nurses are usually available day or night to respond to your needs; help can be just a phone call away.

You are likely to have several nurses involved in your care, but usually one nurse is your primary case nurse. Get to know your nurse and communicate your questions, concerns, and needs to them. If there is flexibility within the hospice service, try to be matched with a nurse that is a good fit for you and your caregivers.

I have worked with many hospice nurses and find them to be kind-hearted, but overwhelmed. It is a demanding, unappreciated job that comes with its own personal rewards. Hospice nurses are considered a special breed in the nursing field. They try their best to make sure that you are as prepared as possible to deal with your declining health needs at end of life.

The social worker

The *social worker* provides emotional and psychosocial support to the patient and family as well as addresses non medical concerns. A social worker is great in helping you cope and plan for the impacts of illness and aging, now and for the future.

Hospice social workers are skilled in helping you cope with the stress of dealing with a terminal illness. They are able to perform psychosocial assessments by evaluating the mental, emotional, social, and spiritual effects of a disease on patients. They can provide ongoing emotional support and counseling in times of crisis. Social workers usually have a friendly and listening ear.

Beyond the emotional support, social workers are well informed and connected to resources, organizations, and services within the community that can help you navigate through what might be a difficult, challenging, and emotional end of life. Social workers are available to help coordinate the logistics of your care, such as dealing with insurance companies or the Veterans Administration, taking care of financial and legal issues, and assisting with advance care planning and funeral arrangements. They are great at understanding, explaining, and helping you complete the necessary but onerous medical paperwork. Social workers are an invaluable resource that can save you time and effort in your own research.

TIP

Take advantage of having a social worker work for you and be your advocate. It alleviates some of the burden of practical matters that are no fun when ill and at end of life.

The end-of-life doula

The end-of-life doula is a relatively new professional in the field but is becoming an important member of the healthcare team at end of life. Given its emerging role, not many hospices or hospitals have end-of-life doulas on staff yet. It is worth engaging with an end-of-life doula privately, if that is an option for you. An end-of-life doula can make a big difference in the end-of-life experience for you and your loved ones.

An *end-of-life doula* is a non medical professional who companions, supports, guides, and educates a dying person and their loved ones through the transition to death. They offer individualized, compassionate care, which may include emotional, spiritual, informational, and physical support. End-of-life doulas bring added comfort and peace of mind to create a more meaningful experience during an emotionally difficult time.

End-of-life doulas can be involved from as early as initial diagnosis of a disease through bereavement post-death. It is common to engage with an end-of-life doula well before hospice becomes involved. In this way, a doula can smooth the transition to end of life, which makes it less stressful for everyone.

End-of-life doulas support in a variety of ways, including some of the following:

» Offer companionship to you and your loved ones

» Provide emotional support

» Be a calm presence and witness

» Serve as a sounding board for decision-making

» Facilitate unresolved issues or family dynamics

» Assist in life review and meaning-making

» Help with legacy work

» Aid in advance care directives and planning

» Explore rituals and ceremonies

» Provide vigil planning and support

» Assist with funeral and memorial planning

» Facilitate meditation and guided imagery

» Offer grief processing and support

» Provide respite

While some approaches and skills of the doula complement other members of the healthcare team, end-of-life doulas are often able to fill in the gaps of care that arise and do not fall within another's area of care.

TIP

If you're interested in having an end-of-life doula for additional support, try to find a local doula in your area. The National End-of-Life Doula Alliance (NEDA), a non profit membership organization, lists over 1,800 doulas in the United States and internationally. And many of the private doula training organizations also maintain directories of their graduates. You can also try searching online for an end-of-life doula in your geographic area. If you're still having trouble finding a doula, try inquiring at your local hospice or funeral home to see if they know of local doulas; they may have coordinated or worked with one in the past.

An end-of-life doula can be a valuable member of your care team. They offer more personalized and customized support throughout an illness journey. Doulas take away some of the unknowns and fears around the process of dying and offer support and presence in a positive, meaningful way.

The spiritual care counselor

A *spiritual care counselor*, also called a hospice chaplain, offers support for the spiritual issues that often arise as death nears. It is natural for people who are at the end of their life to be anxious or afraid, to search for hope and meaning, and to question their faith and beliefs. A spiritual care counselor helps you to explore and work through these questions and emotions.

TIP

The spiritual care counselor can be available to your family too, because it's natural for them to have similar feelings of anxiety and doubt, and question what is happening and why.

REMEMBER

It is important for the spiritual care counselor to understand and honor the spiritual and cultural traditions, values, and beliefs of you and your family, and to inform the other team members. In this way, the diversity in spiritual beliefs and backgrounds of everyone is honored.

The focus of care by the spiritual care counselor tends to be more spiritual in nature than religious and is nondenominational. However, the counselor may address religious issues with you if requested, particularly if the religion or faith of the spiritual care counselor is the same as yours. Otherwise, the spiritual care counselor can work with your specified clergy or faith leader. They can help arrange and set up rituals or ceremonies consistent with your spiritual beliefs or religion or cultural heritage, if requested and as needed.

The home health aide

A *home health aide* is a certified nursing assistant who provides hands-on support to help with the tasks of daily living. Home health aides are the team members who spend the most time with you, and hence, become the eyes, ears, and hands of the healthcare team.

The home health aide supplements the care provided by the nurses. Therefore, an aide may be the first to notice a small change in your condition, which could be a sign of a bigger problem. When that happens, your aide will alert the nurse or a more senior member of the healthcare team.

Hospice aides help in many practical and personal care needs. Duties of a hospice aide may include:

>> Communication and tracking of medical changes

>> Wound care

>> Bathing and dressing

>> Personal care, including hair, skin, mouth care, and nails

>> Help with toileting or incontinence

>> Light meal preparation

>> Light housekeeping

>> Companionship

>> Education on proper and safe care techniques

It can be difficult for you to adjust to asking and needing help from others. For the home health aide, the job is messy and challenging. It is not an easy situation for anyone, especially in the beginning. However, with regular visits and patience, aides can become a source of comfort, emotional support, and companionship for you and your family.

The bereavement counselor

The *bereavement counselor* offers support to address the different stages of grief you may be experiencing associated with declining health and imminent death. Bereavement counselors provide comfort, education, and support for both antici-patory grief and loss after death.

For you, a bereavement counselor is especially useful as a listening ear and compassionate presence for the overwhelming emotions — grief — you are experiencing as you age, are ill, or are dying. There are so many losses which lead to the final act of death. In Chapter 9, I talk about some of the losses of abilities and capabilities of a physical, mental, social, and spiritual nature that occur at end of life or in any serious illness journey. Having someone to talk to about what is happening and how you are feeling is essential to coping.

A bereavement counselor can also be of support to your loved ones, guiding them through grief before and after your death. If you are enrolled with hospice at death, your family will receive bereavement support through hospice for 13 months after death, which may include ongoing check-ins, support groups, grief education, and one-on-one visits. The first year after a death can be particularly difficult for your loved ones as they experience the milestones of the first year, such as first holidays without you and the anniversary of your death.

REMEMBER

It is essential that you have healthy outlets to express your grief. If not with a bereavement counselor, make sure that there is someone who can listen and support you in a nonjudgmental, calm, and compassionate way.

The volunteers

Volunteers are an important part of hospice. Volunteers offer the gift of their time to be with you, in whatever way you like, for anything that you may need.

A *hospice volunteer* is specially trained in hospice and end-of-life issues to provide compassionate companionship and support to the patient and family. Hospice volunteers are usually required to attend volunteer training at the hospice in order to learn about hospice, the rules and regulations, the duties and responsibilities of a volunteer, and how to be with patients.

Most of what a volunteer provides is added socialization for the patient. Sometimes that entails having a conversation about current events, or listening to your life story, or reading from a favorite book. Other times, it may simply be providing companionship by watching television together or holding your hand while sitting quietly bedside.

Depending on the hospice, volunteers are able to do more and assist in general tasks. For example, volunteers may be involved in documenting a patient's life story, running errands, or doing light housekeeping.

MY HOSPICE VOLUNTEER EXPERIENCE

I have been a hospice volunteer since 2018. It has been a true honor to be with so many people at the end of their lives. We have had deep conversations and shared intimate moments. We have talked, laughed, cried, and held silence together. I have learned so much about life and how to live fully from those who are dying. It has greatly impacted my life.

As a hospice volunteer, I have done jigsaw puzzles, listened to opera, had lively conversations about travel, cooked a meal together, read poems, looked at photos of your family, offered gentle massages, pushed you to the garden to admire spring blooms, meditated, chanted mantras, wondered with you about what happens after death, given an impromptu manicure, learned about Italian coffee, played board games, played video games, colored, brought you ice cream, held the phone by your ear as a loved one spoke to you, and lastly, listened to your hopes, fears, and dreams of living and dying.

Thank you to all my patients for sharing your precious time, stories, and feelings with me at the end of life. It was an honor.

Other support staff

In some cases, there may be other therapists or specialists as part of the health-care team. They may be involved for only a limited time, as needed. Other support staff may include:

>> A physical therapist

>> An occupational therapist

>> A speech therapist

>> A wound care specialist

>> An art and/or music therapist

>> A nutritionist

If you think you could benefit from any of these additional services, inquire with your hospice to see whether they are offered or bring in an independent specialist privately.

IN THIS CHAPTER

» **Focusing on yourself**

» **Celebrating yourself**

» **Sensing the end is near**

» **Planning for a vigil**

Chapter **6**

Expecting Death: Pre-Death Planning

While this book prepares you for end of life and is forward-thinking about death, you may still feel death as far-off, sometime in the future. The time will come when you feel death is close. That's when you should do this part of physical preparation. You can still prepare for end of life by doing all the other things in the rest of this book — other physical preparation and the emotional, social, and spiritual preparation — but the preparation in this chapter is so influenced by how you feel when death feels close.

Read this chapter so you can see what's coming in the pipeline. And if you have been doing all the other preparation in the rest of the book, you will be better prepared mentally and emotionally to do this pre-death planning. The concepts, ideas, and preparation that you have done prior influence your perspective on what's to come.

In this chapter, I focus on how to celebrate yourself at the end of life, how death can go at the end, and how to prepare for the actual event of death itself — to make it the most positive, meaningful, and comfortable for you.

Finally, It's All About Me

When death feels near, if you haven't already, begin focusing on yourself. This is the time to bring more attention to yourself. Because death is an intense, impactful, emotional event regardless, for everyone involved, why not make it all those things and positive, not all those things and negative.

NEW

Why shouldn't you celebrate death? Just like when we celebrate other age milestones in our life, such as Sweet Sixteen or turning 50 years old, we can celebrate our death too. In fact, the end of life deserves celebration as the culmination of your life.

At the end of your life, be proud of having made it this far, however old you are. You have lived a unique life with its own unique story. Congratulations! You are a pretty darn amazing individual, and if you don't believe it, please read Chapter 12 to understand how incredible you are.

For the purposes of this chapter, I am assuming that by the time you need to do this pre-death planning, you will have done some of the emotional preparation for end of life and realize that you are worth celebrating. So let's get on with this assumption and begin planning your death, which is all about you.

Celebrating Your Life

Many people realize that they won't be attending their own funerals, but would like to hear what others are saying about them. We want to hear the stories of good times spent together and discover which ones stand out as memorable. *Oh, I had forgotten about the time we did that together . . . .* We all want to laugh, smile, and remember.

Celebration of Life gatherings, also known as living funerals, have become hugely popular. Family and friends gather while you are still alive, and you get to see everyone too! Celebrations of Life tend to be less somber affairs and more celebratory. The gathering focuses on you, your life, your personality, and the impact you've had on others. There are usually memory-making activities, storytelling, and just good ol' fun.

You can think of it as just a party, but remember, part of the reason for this gathering is for you and others to see each other one last time. The party doesn't have to turn into a sad affair, but understand the meaning and significance of this party. Decide how you would like your guests to be present at this event — the rules of engagement — and make them known.

Figure 6-1 shows an example of a light-hearted, positive invitation focused on sharing memories for my Celebration of Life.

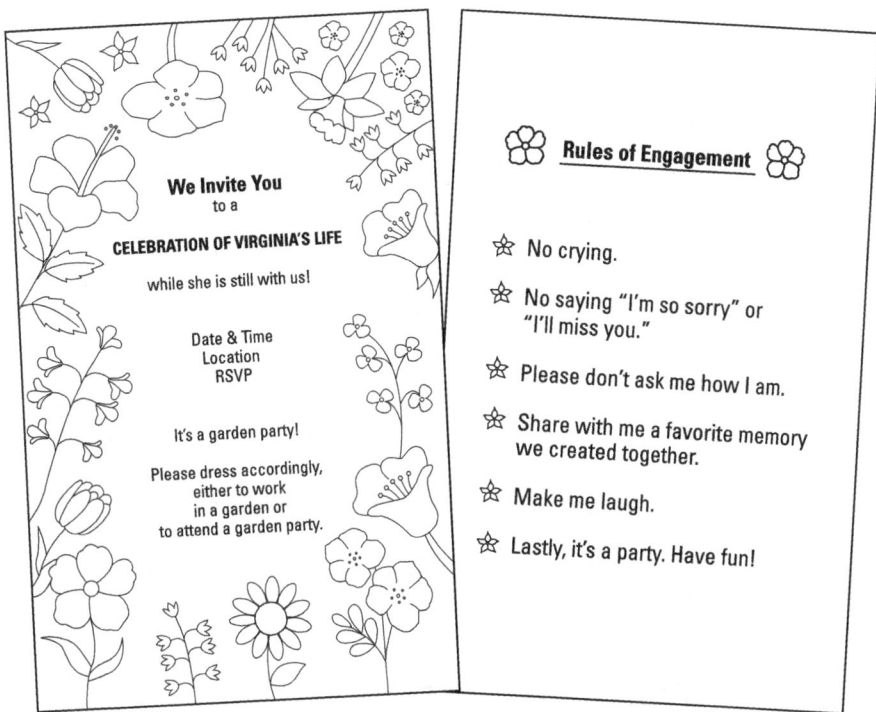

We Invite You
to a

CELEBRATION OF VIRGINIA'S LIFE

while she is still with us!

Date & Time
Location
RSVP

It's a garden party!

Please dress accordingly,
either to work
in a garden or
to attend a garden party.

Rules of Engagement

☆ No crying.

☆ No saying "I'm so sorry" or "I'll miss you."

☆ Please don't ask me how I am.

☆ Share with me a favorite memory we created together.

☆ Make me laugh.

☆ Lastly, it's a party. Have fun!

FIGURE 6-1:
My Celebration of Life invitation to a garden party.

TIP

Make sure others are planning the party for you. Certainly, you should be providing input and making all the important decisions, but let others do the heavy work of organizing and managing the party. Be like the queen or king — sitting in your royal recliner — making proclamations and letting others carry them out.

Lastly, take it very easy in the days leading up to the party. Store up energy so that you are more able to engage and participate. Enjoy seeing and spending time with everyone, especially those you haven't seen in a long time. Have fun.

Sensing Death Is Near

Death can occur at any time. However, you may feel death especially close if you are old or have a serious illness. Having more thoughts of your mortality then is common.

NEW

There are many things you can do to retain autonomy in the remaining time you have that will allow you to feel more in control of your life. One important thing you can do in expectation of death is to set up a *vigil plan.* This means thinking more about the event of death and how you would like it to go. Your wishes and preferences can be set forth in a vigil plan.

Before I discuss the vigil plan, I explain the situations a vigil plan would apply to. When you are expecting death and feel it close, you can plan for the event.

The exception: Sudden death

Sudden deaths account for approximately 10 percent of all deaths. This includes fatal accidents and sudden, unexpected deaths from illness, such as cardiac arrests and ruptured brain aneurysms.

Sudden deaths are tragic in that they are unexpected and catch everyone unaware and unprepared. I hope that you will have done some physical, emotional, social, and spiritual preparation in advance to ease some of the burden on your loved ones so that they can focus on their grief.

Given the suddenness of death, there is no planning for the event. It happens by factors beyond your control.

Natural death

The remaining 90 percent of deaths occur naturally, from either illness progression or old age. In these situations, you may get a sense that death is approaching.

In the case of illness, it could be a matter of months or years. You will either die from the illness itself or a complication of the disease. Since declining health due to illness is so closely monitored by the healthcare profession, usually, you will get a sense of death approaching, particularly if the doctors tell you no more can be done medically.

In the case of old age, it may be a time frame of years over which your health will gradually decline until death. This is *frailty,* a medical term that describes the deterioration of multiple physiological systems of the body. This breakdown results in increased weakness, instability, fatigue, and weight loss. These symptoms result in your body not being able to get through and recover from illnesses and injuries. Frailty is a normal part of the aging process.

Planned death

With advancements in science and medicine and better personal health habits, we have significantly increased our life expectancy, far beyond our caveman days. However, what we have given ourselves is more time at the end of life when we are sick and old, not when we are healthy. As a result, we are living prolonged lives at the end of life.

We dream of a quick and peaceful death, but more and more, that does not happen. The old and sick are faced with the daunting question of quality versus quantity of life (for an extended discussion of this topic, please see Chapter 5). Consequently, many people are searching for better options to hasten death.

Medical Aid in Dying

Medical Aid in Dying (MAiD) is a modern name for an ancient idea of hastening one's death to a time of one's choosing.

According to Compassion & Choices, *medical aid in dying* is "a trusted and time-tested medical practice that allows a terminally ill, mentally capable adult with a prognosis of six months or less to live to request from their doctor a prescription for medication they can decide to self-ingest to die peacefully in their sleep." MAiD is a patient-centered process that gives terminally ill patients control over their end-of-life options.

There are many arguments in favor and in opposition of MAiD that are beyond the scope of this book. However, factors cited by MAiD-eligible patients include loss of independence, loss of dignity, loss of the ability to engage in meaningful activities or daily life, severe pain, and intolerable physical or emotional suffering.

In my experience as an end-of-life doula, what I know is that no one wants to die, but that which makes life unbearable for any one person is a very personal and individual decision.

MAiD ELIGIBILITY CRITERIA

To be eligible for MAiD, you must meet the following criteria:

>> Be at least 18 years old

>> Have a prognosis of six months or less to live

>> Demonstrate mental capacity to make your own healthcare decisions

>> Be able to self-administer the medication

If you believe that you are eligible for MAiD and live in one of the authorized jurisdictions (listed in the next section), begin a conversation with your doctor or healthcare team.

WHERE MAiD IS ACCESSIBLE

In the United States, MAiD is authorized in 12 states and the District of Columbia, as of December 2025. These include:

» California

» Colorado

» Delaware

» Hawaii

» Illinois

» Maine

» Montana

» New Jersey

» New Mexico

» Oregon

» Vermont

» Washington

» Washington, D.C.

Each state has different legal eligibility criteria and safeguards in place, so please check out your state's requirements if you live in one of the listed jurisdictions.

WHAT MAiD IS AND IS NOT

MAiD has been referred to as "physician aid in dying," "assisted dying," "death with dignity," and "right to die." These terms generally refer to the same concept but have nuanced distinctions from MAiD in terms of its legal definition, location, or public connotation.

Medical Aid in Dying is not suicide, assisted suicide, or euthanasia. These terms are misleading and factually incorrect.

Dying with dignity abroad

"To live with dignity — to die with dignity"

—motto of Dignitas

There is no one term, worldwide, used to describe the right to die at a time of one's choosing with assistance. While it is still illegal in most countries, some countries have legalized assisted dying, and many other jurisdictions are considering some form of legislation. What is clear is that support and access to dying with dignity is expanding across the globe.

There are variations in laws on assisted dying worldwide, which include different legal requirements and eligibility criteria. In some countries, assistance in dying is not restricted to the terminally ill and allows for intolerable suffering. Canada delayed expanding its MAiD laws to include those suffering solely from a mental illness, and in the Netherlands and Belgium, assisted dying for mature minors is legal.

Access to some model of assisted dying exists in the United States, Canada, some countries in Europe, Australia, New Zealand, and a few countries in Central and South America. Switzerland has the longest history of a legal practice in this, and currently, has no residency requirement.

WARNING

The landscape of the right to die changes rapidly. Please, always seek out the most current status on right-to-die laws where you live.

Voluntary Stopping of Eating and Drinking

Voluntary Stopping of Eating and Drinking (VSED) is a lesser known, available option to hasten one's death to a time of one's choosing. It is a legal method in all 50 states of the United States.

Theoretically, if we do not eat or drink, then the body will die. The body cannot sustain itself without nutrition. Yes, this is possible, but it is not easy under normal circumstances. In a healthy person, overcoming the urges of the body to live can be difficult. It can be a terrible, agonizing process. For a person near the end of life, however, the body is already in decline. The body is in a weakened, deteriorating state due to illness or old age. The body may have already lost its desire for sustenance; this is a common and natural part of the dying process. In fact, in a weak and dying state, eating may cause additional pain and discomfort to the body. Yet, to die by VSED is still not easy, but it is easier, especially with good palliative support.

For sick people with a serious illness, it can take from four to ten days or even longer for the body to die. For a healthy adult, it can take up to thirty days. That is a month of accelerating the dying process of the body.

REMEMBER

VSED is not without challenges. While VSED is completely under the power and control of the dying person, it is not easy mentally. It requires effort, conviction, and discipline.

TIP

Fortunately, many symptom-related challenges can be anticipated and usually managed with good advance planning and support from your healthcare team. *Do not attempt VSED alone.* If you are interested and believe you are capable of VSED, begin a conversation with an end-of-life doula or a healthcare professional.

Creating a Vigil Plan

In the situations of natural death or planned deaths, creating a vigil plan ahead of time is recommended. The *vigil plan* helps you, and your loved ones, in the transition of dying and details the conditions and environment that are most positive, meaningful, and comfortable for you. Having a vigil plan isn't necessary, but it's a good idea.

The vigil plan is an important personal plan that you make for yourself. It doesn't involve doctors, nurses, attorneys, or a tax accountant. This is a very personal plan that honors you and gives you autonomy in your life up until the last moment of breath.

Realizing the benefits to a vigil plan

The vigil plan sets the conditions and environment for the last days and moments of your life. More than likely, you will be nonresponsive and your body will be in the physical process of shutting down. You may be thinking, "Why should I create a vigil plan if I won't even be conscious during this time?" Good question. The answer is *peace of mind*, for you and your loved ones.

Having a vigil plan gives you peace of mind *going into* the process of dying. You can know how it is going to go and what it is going to be like, having predetermined and preestablished, ahead of time, the conditions that you can control. In this way, you have done the best for yourself by setting an environment that is supportive and positive for you in the work of dying. If you're feeling uncertain about what dying will be like, set up a vigil plan. Because this is it! Your moment, your death. Make it good.

NEW

Having a vigil plan often changes the experience of death from one that is full of sorrow, stress, and chaos to one of calm, reverence, and sacredness. It's a gift for everyone involved.

For your loved ones, a vigil plan helps them be the most supportive for you. By leaving these "instructions," you give them a guide as to what will make you most at ease during your dying days and your death. I can tell you from my experience being with many family members and friends in those last days leading up to death that all they want for you is to be calm, comfortable, and at peace — to be surrounded by their love in your last moments on earth.

Understanding the elements of a vigil plan

A vigil plan can be very detailed or simple and straightforward. It expresses your wishes and preferences, and incorporates your culture, traditions, spirituality, and life experience. It is a very personal reflection of you.

What are your choices in the dying process? Most people never think about what they would want during these last days. When you are dying, you are doing hard work — yes! *Hard work!* Your mind and body are undergoing the physical process of shutting down and releasing. So think about what would be the most supportive and positive for you in doing this hard work. You can

>> **Choose who will be with you.** Among your family and friends, who will be the most supportive and caring for you while dying? Who will understand that this is about you and not about them? Also, consider whether you want young children and your pets to come in and out of the room freely to be with you.

>> **Determine where you want to die.** At home, in the hospital, or in another place. You can even choose which room you would like to be in — the bedroom, the living room, or the garden.

>> **Set the mood.** This is so important. This is your death, your event. For example, if you love the color pink, have everything in the room pink — pink sheets, pink blanket, pink flowers, pink decorations. If you are a big baseball fan, keep a game on in the background. If you love nature, face the bed

toward the window and keep it open to let in fresh air. Make everything about you. Think about the following:

- **Lighting:** Natural, lamps, candles

- **Sounds:** Quiet, music, nature

- **Smells:** Flowers, incense, essential oils

- **Space:** Clean and decluttered or filled with your familiar things, flowers, or cards

- **Attitudes of others:** Wish me well, think positive thoughts, talk about my favorite things

>> **Determine bedside activities.** For your loved ones, one of the hardest parts of the dying process is waiting for death to occur. They feel uncomfortable watching you or don't know what to do. It helps them if you specify a few bedside activities that would be supportive and comfortable for you. These may include reading (choose which books, poems, or letters), singing/humming, meditation, guided imagery, and even what people should be speaking to you about (for example, only fond memories, no griping!).

>> **Decide about touch.** Are you okay with being touched by your loved ones? Or do you prefer no touching? (This does not refer to the necessary touching involved in personal hygiene.) Touching can include hand holding, caresses, and massage by your loved ones. If you are comfortable with touch, you can even specify where on the body, such as anywhere or just my hands and face.

>> **Incorporate spiritual elements.** Your spirituality, faith, or religion may be very important to you and has guided you all your life. You may have a strong belief about what happens to you after death based on your religion. If so, incorporate your spiritual beliefs into your dying process. The beliefs of your faith have supported you all your life; let them support you now in your death. Ask for a priest to be present and give last rites, or arrange for Buddhist monks to chant while you are dying, or have Jewish prayers read to you. Play hymns or burn incense. Whatever is consistent with your spiritual beliefs.

>> **Incorporate cultural traditions and rites.** Similar to spirituality, your cultural beliefs may be very important to you and have guided you all your life. It is important to incorporate any important elements of your cultural heritage into your dying process, especially if your traditions have beliefs about what happens to you or your spirit after death.

>> **Lastly, determine the amount of presence you want.** Some people don't want to be alone at death and would like someone to be present at all times. Others prefer some alone time, especially in the last moments of life. It can be hard "to let go" while your loved ones are present.

REMEMBER

You may not care about some of the elements discussed here, and that's okay. You may feel strongly about certain elements, and those are the ones you should emphasize. Either way, you have the ability, freedom, and control to specify your wishes about these elements in a vigil plan.

Getting help for a vigil plan

If you would like assistance in creating a vigil plan, enlist the help of an end-of-life doula. They can talk you through the important elements of vigil, help you figure out what's most important during dying, and draft a plan of your wishes. A doula will encourage you to be as personalized and creative as possible in your plan, but a doula will also help determine what is realistic to implement.

TIP

An end-of-life doula can also facilitate the input of loved ones into your vigil plan. After all, it will be the responsibility of your loved ones to implement the plan when you are dying. If your loved ones are unable or unwilling to do so at the time, an end-of-life doula can be most useful. The doula can create the space and ensure that the vigil plan is implemented according to your wishes. This frees your loved ones to just be with you instead.

Chapter **7**

Making Post-Death Arrangements

P lanning for end of life may be way more complicated than you ever imag-ined, and making your post-death arrangements will be the last decisions you ever make for yourself.

The two primary areas of post-death decision-making involve deciding what happens to your body after death and how you want to be remembered by others in mourning. Both decisions are very personal. For the former, your physical body has served you all your life, and you can decide what happens to it after death. For the latter, people in your life coming together after death offers a space for their collective grief and keeps you alive in their hearts.

This chapter explains the available options on what to do with your body after death, helps you decide how you want to be mourned by others in remembrance and grief, and offers guidance on how to make all these post-death arrangements as personal and meaningful as possible.

Why Should I Bother? I'll Be Dead!

You may be asking yourself, "Why should I bother with planning for *after* my death? I'll be dead!" Yes, this is true; you will be dead. But it all goes back to the ideas of taking control of your death and making it about you — who you are and expressing yourself — even in death. It is about determining how you will be cared for and remembered after death.

NEW

Making your own arrangements for after you die can give you peace of mind *going into* the process of dying. You know how your body will be taken care of after death, what is going to happen to your body, and where your body will be in perpetuity.

Yet, some people don't care very much what happens to their body after death. They just want the easiest and cheapest method of disposal. And that's fine. However, many people care very much about their body after death. They have strong beliefs about the afterlife, and preparing their body in the proper way with rituals is an important part of the process.

NEW

You also have the opportunity to determine how, when, where, and if, people gather to remember you. An event about you should remind everyone of you and feel like you are with them in spirit. In that case, the gathering should reflect you as a person. Who knows you best but you?

TIP

Making your own arrangements for after death also relieves the burden for your loved ones. Instead of guessing what you would want and leaving it to them to make these decisions, your loved ones can just do what you wanted and focus on their grief. They will be in deep grief over your passing. Give them the gift of time and space to mourn you in a way that befits you.

REMEMBER

Lastly, when you predetermine and preestablish the after-death plan ahead of time, you have decided how you want to be cared for and remembered by others. This is your lasting — and last — memory of you that you can create. This is your death; make it as good as possible.

Deciding What Happens to My Body

What happens to your body after death is something you can determine and control. The first steps are to understand the options and choices, and then to document your wishes and preferences.

Plowing through paperwork

Two important legal documents come into effect after death. One is the death certificate, and the other is the body disposition form. The former, you do not fill out, but your loved ones will need to have it in order to take care of your estate and affairs. The latter, which you fill out while still alive, determines what happens to your body after death.

The death certificate

The *death certificate* is the official record of death. It identifies personal information of the deceased and the date, time, location, and cause of death. The death certificate is signed by the medical professional certifying the death, the funeral director completing the information, and the registrar authorized to receive the death record.

Only certain family members are able to obtain a death certificate when someone dies. This includes a spouse, siblings, and children. When a death certificate becomes public record, then it can be requested by anyone; this can be as long as 25 years or more after death.

A certified death certificate is necessary to take care of many of the personal and business affairs of the deceased. This includes executing a will, filing legal paperwork, dealing with real estate transactions, and submitting insurance claims. Some organizations require a certified copy of the death certificate, while many accept a photocopy of a certified copy of record.

TIP

The funeral director will typically ask you how many copies of the death certificate you would like sent to you from the government office. You should generally request between five and ten certified copies of the death certificate. A fee is charged for each certified copy.

The body disposition form

This is a little-known form, which has important implications for what happens to your body after death. This form provides another means by which you can control what happens to you — your remains — after death.

The *body disposition form* allows you to designate someone you trust, your agent, to take control of your remains. With this form, you can leave special instructions about what is to be done with your remains and entrust the agent to carry out your wishes. You may find slight variations in the naming of the body disposition form state-by-state.

The agent you designate has primary control of your remains and bypasses the state's hierarchy of control, which is usually the spouse first, followed by the children, parents, and then siblings.

REMEMBER

You give the agent the first priority and authority to make decisions about your remains. This is especially important and relevant if you want to designate someone outside the hierarchy of control, such as a chosen family member or a close friend. Other relevant situations are if you are estranged from your next-of-kin or you were never legally married to your partner.

REMEMBER

What is most important for you is to have conversations with any potential agent about what you would like done with your body and remains well before death. Make sure your agent understands what you want and you trust them to carry out your wishes.

WARNING

However, do not expect your agent to personally pay for your post-death arrangements, such as a costly funeral. If your arrangements become a burden to your agent, your wishes may not be carried out. Your agent is not obligated to carry out your wishes if they're highly impractical, illegal, or financially burdensome. Therefore, it's a good idea to think about what can reasonably be done after death, and then set aside funds to pay for any related expenses. Afterwards, you can rest assured about resting in peace.

Understanding body disposition options

Some people don't care very much what happens to their body after death. But others care very much about their body after death. Whether you do or don't care, what you choose to have done with your body after death is a very personal reflection of you and your beliefs about life and the afterlife.

We are lucky to be living in a time when more and more options are becoming available to the public. This is driven by the sheer numbers of people dying on this planet and the problem of disposing of so many bodies in a sustainable way.

NEW

I discuss the current and available methods for body disposition (see the upcoming sections), so you are informed as to your options. Some of the practices discussed here may be unfamiliar to you, so be open to new ideas. Take time to understand all these options to see if they align with your thinking. Also talk to your local funeral home to see what options they offer and whether they can coordinate with the organizations offering alternate body disposition methods, if you prefer one of them.

Organ and tissue donation

You can give the gift of life to someone in need by choosing to donate your organs, eyes, and tissue; see Figure 7-1 for examples of which body parts can be donated (it's quite a lot!). By signing up to be an organ donor, you can provide lifesaving organs to up to eight people. Through eye donation, you give the gift of sight, and through tissue donation, you can impact so many people in need and improve their quality of life.

What body parts can be donated?

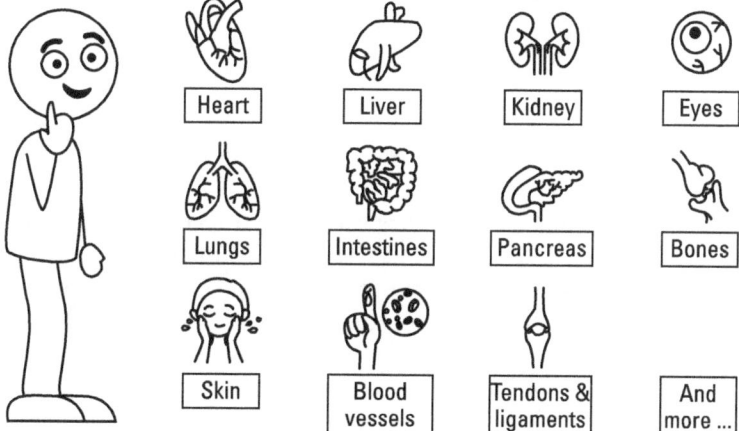

FIGURE 7-1: Becoming an organ donor can benefit multiple recipients.

The first step is to register as an organ donor. You can sign up with any of the nonprofit transplant organizations, your state's registry, or at your local DMV. All the information is sent to the national database (the Organ Procurement and Transplantation Network [OPTN]), which houses the candidate waiting list for organ donation and matching, and transplantation. The national registry records your legal consent to organ, tissue, and eye donation upon death. It does not cost you any money to register and donate your organs.

REMEMBER

For organ donation, dying at home isn't logistically possible. If you want to donate your organs, you must die in a hospital so that your organs can be maintained with oxygen. However, it is possible to die at home and donate tissue and eyes because these remain viable for several hours without oxygen.

Organ donation does not interfere with any of your post-death arrangements, such as a viewing or the funeral. A surgical team will remove the organs and tissue in the hours after death and close all cuts. Great care is given to your body since your donation is so appreciated and valued. Afterwards, your body is transported to the funeral home of your choice for personal post-death arrangements to follow.

Traditional burial

A *traditional burial* typically involves the embalming and dressing of the body, a viewing at a funeral home, and a funeral service either at the funeral home or a church. After the service, the body is placed in a casket, transported to the cemetery, and buried in the ground, typically in a concrete vault. Monuments and markers are placed on the plot as a memorial.

Traditional burial is the method of body disposition that we are most familiar with as a society. However, given the decreasing availability of land and environmental concerns, what was once the most common form of body disposition is now less in demand.

Green burial

There is a growing movement for an eco-friendlier burial than a traditional burial. A traditional burial carries serious environmental concerns, from the toxic embalming chemicals that eventually leach into the ground to the gross amount of concrete poured into the ground.

The goal of a *green burial* is to minimize the environmental impacts and to preserve the land. A green burial occurs shortly after death and involves a simple wooden casket or other biodegradable container, or shrouding of the body; and placement of the body directly in the soil to naturally decompose. Not all cemeteries offer green burials, so it is important to check before choosing your final resting place.

The ceremony and elements of a green burial are equally beautiful and reverent — if not more so — compared to a traditional burial, but have a very different feeling. A green burial is usually aligned with the deceased's worldview of the environment and nature. In some *greenfields* (undeveloped land), it is now possible to plant a tree on the grave, eventually turning the land back into a forest (as depicted in Figure 7-2).

Cremation

Cremation is currently the most widely used method of body disposition. *Cremation* is the reduction of the body to ashes through intense heat. The procedure takes a few hours at extremely high temperatures in a furnace. The remains, known as *cremains*, are then ground into a fine substance, which can be stored in a container or urn.

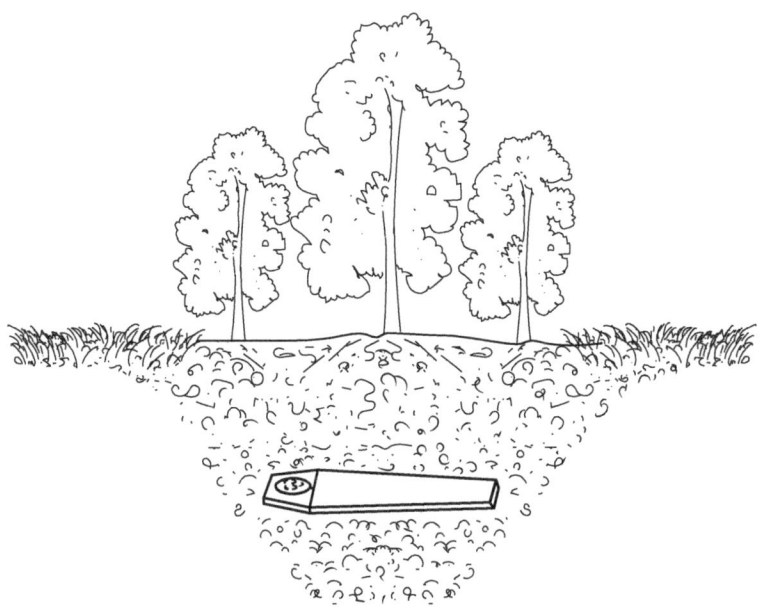

FIGURE 7-2:
A green burial can align with a person's respect for nature.

Most cremations today occur in indoor, enclosed facilities called *crematoriums*. The ancient practice of cremation on an open-air funeral pyre is still common in India and Nepal. The only public open-air pyre in the United States is in Crestone, Colorado, and is only available to Saguache County residents.

Cremation is not considered an eco-friendly option because of the high energy requirements of furnaces and the high carbon emissions from burning. However, cremation does not require land usage or harm, and in that respect, it is more environmentally friendly than traditional burial. However, some people are embalmed prior to cremation. In these situations, the use of toxic chemicals for preservation and the potential release of toxic air emissions are also considered not eco-friendly.

Alkaline hydrolysis

Alkaline hydrolysis, also called *water cremation*, is a new method of cremation that does not involve flames. According to Aquamation, the process uses 90 percent less energy than flame cremation and does not release any harmful emissions. It is an eco-friendly body disposition option.

The body is placed in a specialized, airtight container and filled with water and an alkaline solution (for example, lye). Heat, with pressure and gentle circulation of the water, is used to accelerate the natural decomposition of the body. The process takes hours to complete and results in bone fragments and a substance known as *water effluent*. The sterile effluent is discharged for recycling (as any wastewater would be), and the cremains are ground into a fine substance, which can be stored in a container or urn.

Alkaline hydrolysis is gaining acceptance and popularity as an alternative to traditional burial and flame-based cremation. Legalization of the method and availability to consumers are on a state-by-state basis. As of 2025, alkaline hydrolysis is legal in more than half of the states. Unfortunately, not all states where the method is legal have providers.

TIP

If you are interested in alkaline hydrolysis as a body disposition option, check first to see whether your state allows it. If so, look for providers in your state. If none are available, you can make accommodations with your local funeral home to ship your body to a state that does.

Natural organic reduction

Natural organic reduction, or also known as *human composting,* is an accelerated conversion of human remains to soil. The process returns the organic matter of our body to the earth and is considered eco-friendly.

The body is placed in a container along with organic materials like wood chips, straw, and alfalfa. Over a period of weeks to months, the microbial activity breaks down the body, transforming it into nutrient-rich soil. Only the bones remain, which are broken down and mixed back into the soil. The biological process of breakdown is similar to what occurs in forests as organic material decomposes and becomes topsoil.

One human body generates about one cubic yard of soil from the composting process. In most facilities, families can take some or all of the soil home once the process is complete and/or donate the soil to conservation efforts.

Natural organic reduction is becoming increasingly popular. Similar to alkaline hydrolysis, legalization of the method and availability to consumers are on a state-by-state basis. As of May 2025, thirteen states had legalized natural organic reduction as a body disposition method.

TIP

If you are interested in natural organic reduction as a body disposition option, check to see if your state allows it. If not, you can make accommodations with your local funeral home to ship your body to a state that does.

Body donation

Body donation means donating your body for medical research. This is a common choice for people who are interested in advancing science, particularly those who have a disease with no cure. Donating your body allows medical researchers and educators to train, practice, and continue to learn more about the systems of the body and how they operate.

TIP

For example, you can donate your brain for use in scientific research. Your brain may help researchers study Alzheimer's or other related dementias. Obviously, it is only possible to study the brain tissues and structure when you are no longer alive. With brain donation, you can donate your brain and die at home. To learn more about brain donation and sign up as a donor, go to the NIH NeuroBioBank, the national resource for brain tissue research.

TIP

For whole body donations, you can find information at the American Association for Anatomy website on guidelines, best practices, and reputable institutions that accept body donations.

Donating your body to science has been described as "the ultimate gift to future generations."

Remembering Me After Death

We all want to be remembered after we are gone. We hope to live on in the hearts and minds of those we love. We also live on in those whose lives we've touched in some way, whether we knew it or not.

NEW

If you care about how you will be remembered and want to have a say in it, read on. You may be surprised at all the things you can impact after death, if you plan for them before death.

Gathering together after death

One of the most difficult parts of death for the surviving loved ones is the realization of never spending time or making new memories with you again. That is why community grieving is so important to the healing of grief. These gatherings after death are opportunities to relive old memories, share in good times spent together, and discover new things about you in untold stories.

Funerals, memorials, and wakes offer us the time and place to gather after death to remember and honor you. These ceremonies also give us the much-needed support that is necessary to process death and to take the first steps toward healing.

Since the COVID-19 pandemic when large gatherings of people were discouraged and even prohibited, there has been a great "loosening" of the way things are done post-death, in terms of timing, place, and order. People have become very creative using technology, from creating hybrid models for remote participation to enhancing gatherings with visuals. Nowadays, almost anything is possible.

There are a number of terms for the ceremonies which can occur after death. I explain the terms, when they apply, and what typically happens. Then you can decide which you want and determine as many of the details as desired.

Wakes

A *wake* is a social gathering associated with death. Traditionally, a wake referred to the post-death vigil, when the family and friends would watch over the body until it was buried to protect it from evil spirits. In modern times, a wake is more of a social gathering where people reminisce about the deceased, share stories, and offer each other comfort. The body may or may not be present at the wake.

Beyond the general definition, there is little agreement on what else constitutes a wake. Some wakes are formal affairs, but many wakes are informal gatherings that are quite festive. There can be an abundance of food, drink, music, and celebration. Some wakes are open to anyone and attended by many people, while other wakes are restricted to family and close friends. Wakes can be held in the family home, a funeral home, or somewhere else. While wakes are typically held before a funeral, some consider a wake to be the reception after the funeral. Regardless of the details, a wake is when people come together to honor you, share stories, say goodbye, and support each other in grief.

Essentially all the components of a wake can be decided and planned by you before death. In this way, the mood and atmosphere of the gathering is consistent with who you are as a person. Besides, if you don't do it, your loved ones will have to. On the one hand, for you to plan the wake eases the burden for your loved ones; on the other hand, it may be helpful for your loved ones to plan the wake as part of their grieving process. It's up to you to determine how much input you would like to offer into a ceremony remembering you.

Viewings

A *viewing* is a wake with a casket or urn holding the remains of the deceased present.

If it is an open casket, there may be an opportunity to view the deceased. This would occur after the deceased has been prepared, embalmed, and dressed, by a mortician. The body is then laid out in a casket for viewing. Visitors come to pay respects and offer condolences to the family. Viewings are not services, so visitors come and go as they please. Viewings are typically held before a funeral.

If the deceased was cremated, a cremation urn may be present instead, usually with a selection of photos, in a lovely memorial display.

Funerals

A *funeral* is a formal ceremony to honor the deceased and is followed by either a burial or cremation. The funeral service typically takes place at a cemetery, funeral home, or place of worship. A procession from the venue to the gravesite at the cemetery, or to the crematorium, often occurs after the funeral service. Funerals generally take place within a week after death.

A funeral is typically much more formal and procedural than a wake. The service typically has a structured program that may include prayers, readings, eulogies, music, and often a tribute video or slideshow. Food and drink are not common at funerals, although there may be a reception afterwards.

A funeral may follow religious or secular traditions. If religious, a faith leader often leads the service and the program may more closely follow that of a religious service.

NEW

A current trend in funeral planning is a move away from funerals being dark, somber affairs to ones of celebration and beauty. Many contemporary funeral homes are bright and light-filled spaces, filled with soft colors and modern accents. I have seen funeral spaces transformed into indoor gardens and candle-lit beaches. It is now possible to personalize your funeral to such a degree that you may even look forward to resting there.

TIP

If you are active in planning your own post-death arrangements, please take time to visit funeral homes in your area to find one to your liking.

Home funerals

A *home funeral* is community-led death care. According to the National Home Funeral Alliance, this is "when individuals who are not funeral directors decide to provide some form of after-death care and it allows time to honor the life of the departed."

Home funerals represent a return to the way people of all cultures and society have always cared for their dead — within the community. In the past century and a half, we have moved away from this model of care with professionalization and growth of the funeral industry. It is now more common to hire professionals to do the work of after-death care.

NEW

More recently, there is a growing movement aligned with the positive death movement to care for our own dead. What better way to say goodbye than with this *last act of care* — that is what I call the after-death care service I offer to my clients as an end-of-life doula. After all, the deceased is your loved one. After-death care allows a last opportunity to express your love to your just departed.

The main benefits to a home funeral are more time, privacy, and engagement in the last hours or days that you will see your loved one. Too often, the first action that is taken after a death is to call the funeral home. Transport comes, and the body is whisked away. I have seen families left stunned and bereft, with a great feeling of emptiness. The transition of death from a living person taking their last breaths to an empty home is abrupt. A home funeral, or even just some after-death care, slows down time, honors the transition of death, and allows space for a new reality to set in. It offers a meaningful process of saying goodbye.

KATHLEEN'S STORY

Whenever I am present at a death, I am always prepared to offer the Last Act of Caring. It is my after-death care service, and it differs for every person, depending upon who they are, the setting, the level of family participation, and what feels right in the moment. Even if the family does not want to be involved, I always do it for my client. Dying can be such a messy business. It is important that every person in my care leave their home looking like themselves, clean, and dignified. It leaves the loved ones with a positive impression of the death experience.

Kathleen was 76 years old and dying from lung cancer that had metastasized to the brain. When Kathleen died, it was peaceful with her husband and two adult daughters bedside. We agreed to perform the Last Act of Caring ritual; I would guide and facilitate the husband and daughters as they cared for Mom one last time.

I scented a large bowl of warm water with lavender and a hint of mint, aromas that we knew Kathleen loved, and prepared soft washcloths for the task. The husband washed Kathleen's face with such great tenderness, all the while murmuring words of love to her. He washed her hands, gazing lovingly as he wiped each finger. The daughters washed Kathleen's feet and broke down sobbing. I helped with the rest of her body; it was hard work as her body had given off a lot of secretions. But the daughters and I did it together, calmly, laughing and crying occasionally, with candles, soft light, pleasant smells, and opera music. Then, we dressed Kathleen in clothes she had chosen prior, and laid her out beautifully on her bed.

Afterwards, each family member spent private time with Kathleen, while we waited for her best friend and sister to arrive and say their goodbyes. When everyone felt emotionally and physically ready for Kathleen to depart the home, I called the funeral transport to come take the body.

Afterwards, one of the daughters told me how nervous and uncertain she had felt prior, when thinking about being with her mom's dead body. But she said the ritual "helped me a lot. I understand now that my mom is really gone."

The husband was even more transformed. About his wife, he was pleasantly surprised and remarked on how peaceful and calm Kathleen looked. "It was much better than I expected." About a year later, the husband contacted me and said he often thinks of the time spent being with Kathleen after death for solace in his grief.

The elements of a home funeral include the following:

>> Completion of paperwork, including the death certificate and transport permit

>> Transportation of the body

>> Body care

>> Celebration and ritual

>> Laying in honor

>> Making, buying, or renting caskets, shrouds, or urns

>> Disposition of the body

You can plan your own home funeral and undertake one, some, or all the tasks. Some families opt for being involved in the after-death care and the rituals of washing, preparing, and dressing the body, while others may include the laying of the body in honor and celebration. The creative possibilities and personalization of a home funeral make it truly feel like a special event.

NEW

I understand if thinking about after-death care makes you feel squeamish. As a society, we are not comfortable thinking about or dealing with death. And that's okay. It can be hard to change your ideas and ways about how you think things should be done. Just know that other options exist if you wish. I appreciate your openness to new ideas and your reading of this book.

TIP

If you want to hire someone to help you, find a home funeral guide to assist. There are many funeral directors, end-of-life doulas, and celebrants well-versed in home funerals and after-death care. Ask your local funeral director or end-of-life doula, or check out the directory on the National Home Funeral Alliance website.

REMEMBER

It is legal to care for your own dead in every state. In most states, families can take care of everything that is necessary on their own without hiring a funeral director. However, in some states, having a funeral director involved is required, usually to provide transportation and complete the paperwork. Check out the legal requirements in your state or work with a home funeral guide familiar with the regulations in your area.

It could be that the last hands that touch your body are those of the people who love you.

Memorials

A *memorial* is an event to honor a person's life. It is similar to the funeral service but without the casket or urn present. It's also similar to a Celebration of Life gathering that occurs after the death (see Chapter 6 for a discussion of Celebration of Life gatherings before death).

Unlike wakes and funerals, memorial services can take place days, weeks, months, or even a year after the death. Sometimes, a memorial is held on a milestone or meaningful date to the deceased, such as the next birthday or the first day of spring.

Factors to consider when planning a memorial are:

>> Structured versus flexible

>> Formal versus casual

>> Religious versus secular

>> Small and intimate versus large and welcoming

Memorials do not usually occur at a funeral home or graveside. Memorial services typically take place at a location that has significance to the deceased, such as a park, beach, or favorite restaurant. For large affairs, a community gathering place or hotel is a suitable venue. For small gatherings, families can invite people to their home. Wherever you choose to hold the memorial, consider the décor, catering, music, or audiovisual needs for the event.

REMEMBER

A memorial service is about remembering the life of your loved one. Therefore, make it a personal, unique, and intimate experience. When your loved one is brought into the hearts and minds of everyone at the memorial with love, laughter, and meaning, then the memorial is a success.

Writing your own obituary

Very few people write their own obituary, but it is the ultimate in deciding how you want to be remembered. You choose exactly what you want people to remember about you and your life. It is your words.

Today's obituaries, printed in the local newspaper or online, tend to be dry summaries of a person, reading more like a resume. While they may serve the purpose of informing a community of a person's passing, they are often without personality or humor, lacking the qualities that constitute a person.

As an end-of-life doula, I often engage my clients with writing their own obituaries. From my perspective, it serves two purposes.

The first benefit is that writing your own obituary provides an opportunity for you to "set the record" on how you want to be remembered since you get to select the information to be included. A typical obituary usually has the following elements:

>> **Factual data:** Name, age, date, and place of death

>> **Biographical data:** Date of birth, where you've lived, education, career

>> **Family data:** Genealogy, surviving family members, important relationships

>> **Service details:** Date, time, and location of any funeral services or memorials open to the public

>> **Acknowledgments and donations:** Gives thanks to particular people, such as caregivers or medical personnel, and asks for donations be given to selected charities in lieu of flowers

>> **Photo:** A formal photo or a snapshot of you

If you are writing your own obituary, you may include all, some, or none of the preceding information in your obituary. Since the obituary becomes one of the most read remembrances of you, this is a chance for you to say more about yourself and include other stuff about who you are. You may want to include the following:

>> **Personality:** Who you are as a person and how you would like to be remembered — for example, as kind, funny, or competitive.

>> **Values:** What is important to you. For example, loving others, a good joke, or caring for the environment.

>> **Accomplishments:** What you are most proud of. For example, running a marathon at 70, building your own home, or starting a business.

>> **Hobbies and passions:** What you loved while living. For example, your family, being an avid tennis fan, or loving to travel.

>> **Legacy:** Others you have impacted. For example, being a teacher, volunteering at the soup kitchen, or rescuing stray animals.

Finding the words to best describe your life in a few short paragraphs is not easy, but doing it really makes you take a hard look at what you want to say about yourself — and that's the second reason for writing your obituary: It crystallizes the question of *How do I want people to remember me?* If there is something you don't like about yourself or the way you are living, and you've exaggerated the opposite, your obituary becomes a joke. Instead, you still have time — while you're still alive — to change yourself and your life to reflect what you would like your obituary to say about you.

NEW

I hope that you are living the kind of life that is reflected in your obituary. By writing your own obituary, it reveals a lot to you about yourself and the life you are living. It is an amazing self-growth exercise.

Lastly, if you don't write your own obituary, the task will fall to your loved ones. And writing the obituary for someone else is never an easy one. There is a lot of pressure and emotion in writing the lasting record of somebody else.

TIP

If it should become your responsibility to write an obituary for someone else, don't do it alone. An obituary should not be a personal reflection of the person you loved. Gather other family members and close friends and write it together.

Personalizing Post-Death Arrangements

For any post-death ceremony, ritual, or gathering, you'll want it to reflect who you are, your life, and what was most important to you. Therefore, it is important for you to consider your beliefs and values, whether they're rooted in religious or cultural traditions, and include elements from those traditions into any post-death arrangements you make. Your death doesn't have to be generic!

Religious

Every faith's perspectives on death, community, the physical world, and the afterlife are reflected in its traditions and practices. This is especially the case at end of life, when religions have very specific rituals and customs at death to prepare the dying for transition, and post-death, to support its followers through the process of death and grief.

If you are a religious person, it is important to incorporate the ceremonies and rituals of your religion into your post-death arrangements. If your family is not religious but you are, it becomes even more critical, while you are still alive, to have conversations with your family members and also specify in writing your wishes and preferences for post-death arrangements. Any ritual, ceremony, or gathering should acknowledge and respect the religious beliefs and practices you held in life.

For example, in Islam and Judaism, the use of embalming chemicals is antithetical to their beliefs, and hence, viewings are not held.

At a Catholic wake, family and friends gather to pray for the deceased. It is more like a prayer service that a priest may preside over. However, Irish Catholic wakes can be quite rousing, celebratory affairs with food, drink, and music. At intervals, the rosary may be recited.

If you are attending a religious ceremony or gathering for a deceased person, you may want to read up ahead of time as to the applicable rituals and practices, so as not to be caught unaware or do something accidently inappropriate.

Cultural

People of all cultures experience death and grieve the loss of people they love, but they may show it in different ways. It's important to be culturally sensitive to how others experience, show, and honor death and grief.

It may be that your culture and cultural heritage are very important to you. Maybe it doesn't appear that way on the *outside* to others, but *inside*, you hold your cultural beliefs and traditions close to your heart. This is common for many immigrants, who strive to be Americans and assimilate into American culture, but hold very dear the values and traditions of their homeland.

When you are facing the end of your life, you want to die as who you are and who you know yourself to be. You want to be true to your identity, culture, faith, beliefs, and values of life.

It is similar to a person, who is a nonpracticing Catholic and lives a secular life, yet asks for last rites on their deathbed. I was with a Chinese man who reverted to speaking only in Chinese in his last months. He wanted to feel strongly his identity as Chinese and hear his native tongue; this behavior confounded his children. It was the same for a German woman I tended to as her end-of-life doula.

REMEMBER

Therefore, it's important to incorporate the ceremonies and rituals of your culture into your post-death arrangements as well. Even if your family, in particular your children, don't hold close the same culture, it becomes critical, while you are still alive, to have conversations with them and also specify in writing your wishes and preferences for post-death arrangements. Any ritual, ceremony, or gathering should acknowledge and respect the beliefs and practices of your culture.

For example, white is the color of grief and mourning in China and many other Asian countries. White symbolizes purity, innocence, and rebirth. These ideals are firmly rooted in the spiritual beliefs and traditions of Buddhism and Hinduism. Therefore, at many Chinese funerals, wearing white is customary.

You may go to a funeral and see some women crying dramatically over the deceased. You are shocked at their behavior and excessive display of crying. Oops! You forgot that the deceased was a proud Irish. *Keening* is a raw, vocalized lament of sorrow, which provides a space for emotional release and expresses the collective grief of mourners. It was a common practice and an integral part of Gaelic funerals, but keening was banned by the Church in the 1950s. There are now modern efforts to revive the practice.

In contrast, the jazz funerals of New Orleans are particularly upbeat and joyous affairs. This festive tradition celebrates life at the moment of death. In a traditional jazz funeral, a brass band accompanies the mourners in a procession from the funeral service to the burial site. On the way to the cemetery, the mourners are solemn and slow, somber hymns are played. After burial, the band begins to play up-tempo music and people begin to dance, filling the streets with joyful music and dancing. The significance of this shift symbolizes a "cutting loose" of the body of the deceased as well as the mourners "cutting loose" — to celebrate the deceased and life itself.

TIP

If you are attending a funeral or post-death service for a deceased person, do not expect to know what it will be like, even if you knew that person for a very long time. It may be that the wake, cremation service, or burial includes cultural elements. Be open to observing. Respect others' way of honoring the dead no matter how unfamiliar their practices may be to you.

3

Emotional Preparation

Create ease with your fear of dying.

Adapt to losses at end of life.

Discover the power of grief to transform life and find out how to live with it.

Take care of the emotional baggage that weighs you down.

Know how special you are by doing a life review.

Understand the importance of caring for and loving yourself first.

Chapter **8**

Facing Aging, Illness, and Death

ondering about the issues and concerns of aging, illness, and death is natural. Everyone gets sick at some point in life. I have been sick many times with many different illnesses, and I am certain that you have too. We all age. We feel the passage of time and question ourselves at the major milestones. I am in my late middle years approaching my elderly years. You could be at a different stage of life — young adult, middle-aged, or elderly — and be thinking about the years ahead. And everyone has seen death. Maybe not in a fellow human being, but death exists all around us in the plants and animals and in the cycle of the seasons. Aging, illness, and death are part of our living world.

So why, when we are faced with aging, illness, and death in ourselves, do we resist? First, aging, illness, and death are characterized by uncertainty. We don't know what to feel, what will happen, or how long it will last. We want — *need* — to know. We don't like living with uncertainty.

The uncertainty of aging, illness, and death can lead to the second reason we resist. We become afraid. Fearing things we don't know is natural. We are taught to be cautious and approach things warily until we are more certain. And we are certain that we do not want to die. So the fear combined with the uncertainty amplifies our worries. In addition, aging, illness, and death are associated with the more difficult emotions of sadness, grief, guilt, and regret. Therefore, we resist even more.

In this chapter, I continue to explore the fear surrounding the issues of aging, illness, and dying, how to develop a relationship with these concepts, and how to find more ease in life by embracing our fear.

I'm Afraid of Dying

In this part of the book, I talk about the emotional preparation for end of life. Thinking about the end of your life can be scary. Thinking about dying can even be frightening. You may feel anxious thinking about getting a disease that will cause your death. And incredibly sad to even think about leaving your loved ones and not being a part of their lives anymore. Maybe you can't imagine no longer living and leaving this world. All these statements may be true, and some of them may already be a part of your current reality. It's all right to say that you are afraid of dying.

I'm not here to tell you not to be afraid or fearful or uncertain or worried when you think about death and dying. Whatever you are feeling, it's okay. I acknowledge and accept that that is the way you feel about death and dying. And I want you to acknowledge and accept your feelings too. Right now, in this moment, reading these words.

You may have a multitude of reasons why you are afraid of death. Maybe you had a less than positive experience with the death of a grandparent or a pet when you were young. Maybe a close person in your life died, such as a parent or a best friend, and you never got to see them before death or at death to say goodbye. Maybe you experienced a trauma and nearly died once before. All these experiences can contribute to a fear of death.

Even if you can't identify a past negative brush with death, it is perfectly natural for you to be a bit — or even a lot — scared of dying. In fact, we are all conditioned to fear death. We live in a society that denies death. Look around at your community. Are we talking about death, dying, aging, and illness honestly and openly? No. Are we talking about these subjects in hushed tones, dismissively, or even worse, like it is a reflection of failure in our own lives? Yes, more than likely. Our society and Western culture emphasize health, strength, independence, and resilience. We only talk about positive attitudes and positive attributes — as if these are the things that we should be striving for all the time. Living life and denying death. As a result, most people don't talk about preparing for the end of life.

Ariès, Phillipe, a French cultural historian, researched and created the field of study on the history of attitudes to death and dying. He calls the time period in which we are now living, beginning from the mid-19th century to present day, "Forbidden Death." An ominous title that seems very appropriate to our times. As Ariès describes it, the truth of death is challenged. Societal attitudes about death and dying become more remote as the subjects of death and dying are no longer discussed and become taboo. The exhibited emotions are fear and ignorance.

Our denial of death perpetuates it as an unknown. And remember that what is unknown frightens us. Is this what you experience when with your family and friends? Even if you are not afraid of death and dying, it seems everyone else is. Every time you bring up the subject, people either brush you off or shut you down. There is no interest in speaking about death, aging, or illness. There is no one to talk to.

Or maybe you are afraid of dying and would like to address this fear before the time comes. It takes courage to do so because a fear of death can impact your physical and mental processes of dying in a negative way.

ANDRE'S STORY

Andre was terrified of dying. He had been having a recurring nightmare about dying; sometimes, these nightmares occurred every night. In almost all the dreams, there was a demonic, foreboding figure of death beckoning Andre. He would try to turn away and couldn't. Sometimes, his deceased mother was present and couldn't save him. Andre became increasingly distressed by these dreams and developed an overwhelming fear of his impending death and what awaited him.

Andre was only in his mid-50s, but he had had heart disease for many years. Death was coming soon for Andre. He now lay on the bed, completely nonresponsive, with loud "death rattle" breathing. Shouts of anguish and moaning filled the room. His body flailed in violent spasms, as if chasing away the specters of death. Andre was dying a distressing death.

(continued)

(continued)

Andre's aunt, a petite older woman, was quietly crying bedside. Lydia's greatest fear was that Andre was scared and afraid while dying right now. She feared that he was mentally suffering, and his fear of dying was the reason that he was holding on.

As an end-of-life doula in the room with Lydia, I asked myself, "What's missing? How else can I promote calm and peace?" In my experience, some of the emotional distress experienced by family members stems from the helplessness and powerlessness they feel as they watch their loved one die. They don't know what to do, what they can do, or what they are allowed to do, just that they are willing and want to do something. The desire for the family member is *to not be a bystander*, but to help their loved one in a time of great need. This is not only emotionally comforting, but empowering.

I softened the lighting in the room, turned off the TV, and put on Andre's favorite music — all to create a soothing, peaceful atmosphere. I then turned to Lydia and said, "Speak to Andre."

Lydia needed no more encouragement than those three words. She went to Andre's side and began to stroke his arms and hands. She began to speak words of love and courage, reminding Andre of his mother waiting for him in the warm and beautiful light. Lydia became an active participant in support of Andre's dying process.

After some time, Andre showed signs of physical easing. There was noticeably less tension in his body, and the spasms ceased. Whatever fear Andre had, he carried it with him to death. Yet, with Lydia's active, gentle, and loving support, he died peacefully, and calmly, four hours later.

REMEMBER

Your mental state and a fear of death can impact the way you die. That is why so many people talk about having "peace of mind" when preparing for end of life and entering the dying process. Better to address your fear rather than carry it with you into dying when you are no longer able to do anything about it and have it possibly affect the way you die.

Becoming Friends with Death

So now you want to overcome your fear of death and you don't know how to go about it. Acknowledging this feeling within you is important because it's the key to moving forward: the desire to change the way you think. In fact, you always have a choice about what to think and how to respond. If you are afraid of death today, it doesn't have to be the way you feel tomorrow or one day in the future.

You have taken the first step. You want to know more about death and preparing for the end of life. You want something different for yourself. You are curious. You are reading this book. Thank you.

In this section, I talk about how to create and develop a relationship with the concepts of death and dying. And hopefully by the end, you will begin to think of Death more like a friend rather than an enemy.

Acknowledging death

Fear can rise out of ignorance. So the more information you have about death and dying, the better prepared you will be emotionally, physically, socially, and spiritually.

TIP

Find out how to be prepared, what the dying process is like, and what to expect. Preparing for end of life is a process. So the more you prepare, the more ease you will have going into the process knowing that everything is taken care of. Isn't that the way with most things in life?

While you can continuously prepare for end of life, the event — death — only occurs once for you. There is no going back and learning from death and then getting it right the second time. You will die only once. Your family and friends are the ones who may gain insight from your death experience and decide to be better prepared for themselves. But there is no going back for you.

You cannot avoid or outrun Death, so don't waste your energy trying. You will only experience death once, so try to make it a good one.

If you can't beat them, join them

A well-known proverb says, "If you can't beat them, join them." You've probably heard this saying. It's often used in the context of facing a powerful opponent and then realizing that your efforts are futile. In that situation, it would be better to stop fighting the opponent and be on their side. In more general terms, the phrase means, "When facing an insurmountable challenge, the best course of action is to accept the situation and work with the other party rather than continue to fight against them." This is a pretty good approach to how you should face death and prepare for end of life.

Death is an insurmountable challenge or unbeatable opponent. There's no getting around it. It's going to happen.

So according to the saying, the best course of action is to accept the certainty of death and work with rather than against it. Maybe you think that you accept this fact already, but do you *really* accept it? Maybe you just hold this fact in your brain like book knowledge, but it is not internalized into your heart and being. Or do you accept that you will die, but think that it is a long time away? This is also not necessarily true. Death can happen suddenly. So, accept that death exists and can happen any time.

The latter part of the action clause, working *with* death, means allowing our acceptance of the existence of death to be a part of our life. Letting the awareness of our mortality to influence the way we operate — work — in this world. Because if we truly want to live, and live fully, we have to acknowledge that Death walks hand-in-hand with Life, which is a nice image to have in mind about these two entities, as shown in Figure 8-1.

FIGURE 8-1:
Walk hand-in-hand with Death to live fully.

And lastly, with regard to the final part of the proverb's meaning of working with rather than fighting against an insurmountable enemy, remember that there is no fighting or winning with death. In fact, don't even think of death as a game that you are playing. It is not a race, a challenge, or an opponent. There is no winning or losing. Death just is.

Embracing Death

Like most fears, we can't overcome a fear of death by avoiding, suppressing, or denying it. We have to face our fear full on and realize that there is nothing to be afraid of.

So bring death close to you. This is an important realization: to know that bringing death close to you won't make it happen. You will not die just by thinking about death.

In fact, those of us working in the deathcare space, such as end-of-life doulas and healthcare workers in hospice and palliative care, are not accelerating our own deaths because we see dying every day. Instead, we care for those who are dying and facing death. And because of our work, we feel that our own lives are more precious. We see how short and fragile life can be. Hence, we appreciate life more and are grateful for what we have. The effects are positive. And for me, it is a big reason why I continue to do the work of an end-of-life doula — it has a positive effect on my life. So bring death close.

But how do you go about bringing death close? If you are afraid of death, it can seem hard, challenging, and maybe even intimidating. What do you do? How do you even begin? I propose that you create and develop a new relationship with the concepts of death and dying — embrace Death in a mental sense, as shown in Figure 8-2. Essentially, become friends with Death. And like any good friend, you will find that your life is enhanced, richer, or fuller for bringing them into your life.

When beginning any new venture or relationship in life, whether it's working out or joining a knitting club, it always helps to have companionship, support, and accountability. Hence, you don't have to do this alone.

First, see if there is anyone in your circle of family and friends who can support you in this new relationship. Someone with whom you can share your thoughts, questions, and doubts. Someone close enough that you are comfortable sharing your feelings and who won't talk you out of speaking about death and dying. Someone who can listen and be kind.

If no one comes to mind, or you don't feel comfortable speaking on these subjects with a close friend or family member, find an end-of-life doula who can support you in this new relationship. End-of-life doulas are comfortable with the topics of death and dying, and are skilled in listening and being supportive with these difficult topics. And it may be easier for you to speak with someone not too close to you. Someone who can be neutral and nonjudgmental.

Taking a daily mortality vitamin

According to the National Cancer Institute, a vitamin is "a nutrient that the body needs in small amounts to function and stay healthy." Sources for vitamins mostly come from a balanced diet, but supplementing with pills of essential vitamins and minerals is an option. To bring death close, I propose that we take a mortality vitamin on a daily basis — in other words, that we think about death once a day.

Psychology research studies have shown that just thinking about death once a day has significant positive effects on living. It supports the concept of mortality awareness enhancing life. *When Death Is Good for Life: Considering the Positive Trajectories of Terror Management*, a study by Kenneth E. Vail III et al., concludes:

"The awareness of mortality can motivate people to enhance their physical health and prioritize growth-oriented goals; live up to positive standards and beliefs; build supportive relationships and encourage the development of peaceful, charitable communities; and foster open-minded and growth-oriented behaviors."

Psychology researchers in terror management theory (TMT) have studied how the fear of death influences human thinking and behavior. According to TMT, the awareness of our mortality terrifies us. As a result, we either avoid thinking about death at all or adapt to confer our lives with self-esteem, worthiness, and sustainability. We want to believe that we play a role in a meaningful world.

On the one hand, this worldview can lead to troubling behavior by an individual, having negative, and even deleterious, consequences for society. For instance, one path to addressing death anxiety is by establishing self-importance through being part of important groups. The desire to belong and to feel important, unfortunately, often leads to displays of prejudice and superiority.

Much of the early research in TMT focused on how the awareness of our mortality and our efforts to buffer against it led to negative and unsavory behaviors in individuals. Unfortunately, these findings fueled an association of an awareness of death with negative outcomes and pushed mortality awareness further into the shadows.

On the other hand, terror management efforts can contribute to personal growth and enriching experiences. More recent studies in TMT have brought to light the more positive and beneficial, personal and social, outcomes from an awareness of death. TMT research has shown that mortality awareness can also have positive trajectories for life. The researchers noted,

"When being consciously aware of death, people may make deliberate evaluations of their attitudes and behaviors and, if perceiving a way to better prevent or cope with death, adjust their behavior and attitudes accordingly."

Thinking about death once a day, people are in less depressed moods, engage in healthy behavior, strive more toward living positively, and show greater acts of kindness and compassion toward others. These are powerful outcomes that can contribute to positive living.

TIP

This is not like going on a diet or spending thousands of dollars going to therapy. This is just *thinking about your own mortality once a day*.

So take a mortality vitamin once a day. It can have a powerful effect even in small doses. In the next few sections, I look into ways in which this works.

Living healthier

The conscious awareness of death motivates change in people's behavior to reduce the connection between health risks and death. People are motivated to improve their health in order to avoid death.

In research studies, people were shown to engage in more health-enhancing behaviors. They exercised more, smoked less, and were even shown to use sunscreen. These outcomes are remarkable in shifting attitudes and modifying behavior of people toward more healthy living.

WARNING

The key is to not wait until you become unhealthy and sick before assessing the way you live. Too many people only change their diet or start exercising after they are diagnosed with heart disease, diabetes, or some other illness that will shorten their lifespan.

Start now. Adjust your lifestyle now. Take your daily mortality vitamin and let it start affecting the way you live.

Prioritizing what's important

Fearing death is more probable when the likelihood is that you will not die well. Unfortunately, many in our society are not dying well. So, the issue becomes knowing how to die well. The first thing you can do is prepare. So thank you again for reading this book.

The second thing you can do is make death personal. When a death is personal — embodying and reflecting who you are as an individual — then death can feel comfortable and right, even good. You may have heard of the term a *good death*. A good death is different for every single person. What a good death is for me is not the same as a good death for you. Why? Because what is personal and important to me is not the same as what is personal and important to you. Therefore, only you can determine your own good death.

Most people at the end of life want to be living their last years, months, weeks, and hours in a way that is important and meaningful to them while being surrounded by the people they love. With limited time left to live, it boils down to these essential questions:

>> What is most important to you?

>> Who is most important to you?

Only you can answer these two questions. By answering and incorporating these important elements into your dying process, you make death personal. When we as a society begin to break down the ongoing depersonalized, assembly-line approach to death that currently exists and replace it with love, care, and meaning at end of life, then death can feel good.

What is most important to you? Not surprisingly, it is not money. As my good friend and fellow end-of-life doula Diane Button says, "The dying are not clutching hundred-dollar bills on their deathbed." More often, what is most important in life are simple things: ideals, values, beliefs, or faith. These can be things like love or honesty, music or nature, and religion or your spiritual practice.

Who is most important to you? I have found in my work as an end-of-life doula that the dying want to spend their time with the close people they love. The ones who "get" them. The ones who love unconditionally and show up in times of need. These are the people who matter most. And more often than not, they may be close friends and chosen family, not necessarily biological family. That's okay.

Research supports that a conscious awareness of death is correlated with improved relationships with family, friends, and loved ones. People are found also to be more engaged and caring about their community and the environment.

TIP

So after you have identified what and who are most important to you, start living life that way. Don't wait until you are given a terminal diagnosis to start living the "good life" so you can have a "good death."

Begin now. Take your daily mortality vitamin and let it start affecting the way you live.

Appreciating the now

Mortality awareness works by putting our life, role, and purpose in perspective. Our priorities begin to shift with respect to personal relationships, work, finances, and leisure time. Simply, and most importantly, we appreciate being alive.

"Every day, think as you wake up, 'I am fortunate to be alive. I have a precious human life. I am not going to waste it.'"

—His Holiness the 14th Dalai Lama

His Holiness the 14th Dalai Lama is the most prominent spokesperson on the values of compassion and gratitude. In fact, he identifies them as being necessary components toward a life of happiness. (In Chapter 20, I talk about the value of compassion as it relates to the end of life.)

My purpose here is not to teach you about gratitude or how to instill more gratitude in your life. There are countless books, podcasts, methods, life coaches, and spiritual teachers on the subject of gratitude. The Dalai Lama himself has spoken and written more than 140 books to date on helping us to live better lives through compassion and gratitude.

I am here to make you aware of the value and importance of gratitude in addressing a fear of death and becoming more at ease with dying.

Research also supports that living with gratitude and compassion have been shown to be positive motivators toward positive living. Again, if it leads you to a happier life — the "good life" — then you are more likely to have a "good death." So why not do it?

I am not an expert on gratitude nor even on practicing gratitude. All I can do is *try*. I try to live a life of appreciating the small moments, the people around me, and the gifts that I am given. You can also *try* to ask this much of yourself too.

NEW

How you go about instilling more gratitude in your life is something for you to figure out. Only you know yourself best and what new ideas/methods/practices will work best for you in your daily life. It can be as simple as reciting the saying of the Dalai Lama when you wake up every morning: "I am fortunate to be alive. I have a precious human life. I am not going to waste it." Or it can be more extensive, such as adopting a meditation practice and learning to meditate on gratitude. However you go about it, it is more about your desire to incorporate more gratitude into your life and being consistent.

So take your daily mortality vitamin. Start living life with gratitude, not taking life for granted.

Chapter 9

Losing Who You Once Were

Change is hard. Change as a result of loss is even harder because of the swirling emotions associated with the loss. Yet change is part of our evolution as a society and individuals. It is a natural part of the process of living and dying.

What we lose at end of life or in any serious illness journey are our abilities and capabilities of functioning and being in this world. And I don't mean "losing" in the context of misplacing something and finding it again. That would mean the loss is temporary and that upon "finding" it, the ability would be restored. No, I mean "losing" as in, the thing you have or know to be a certain way is not the same as it was before. It has changed, transformed, or is gone — then it is considered a loss. And at end of life, there are so many losses which lead to the final act of death.

End of life is filled with so many losses of abilities and capabilities of a physical, mental, social, and spiritual nature. Finding out more about these losses will only make you better prepared for the changes to come.

In this chapter, I explore the different aspects that define who we think we are, some of the many types of losses we can experience at the end of life, and how to adapt to a new you as a result of loss and change.

I'm Scared of What's Happening to Me

In this chapter, I continue the discussion about emotional preparation for end of life that I introduce in Chapter 8. It can be scary — very scary — to think about the changes and losses you will undergo at the end of life. We spend our whole lives discovering and becoming who we are, and to begin to "lose" parts of ourselves can be very disconcerting.

Most people go through a kind of "identity searching" as young adults. Others only feel comfortable in their own skin when they are middle-aged or elderly, after decades of searching. In fact, people grow and change throughout their whole life. It's a continuous, evolving discovery of self. Then, at the end of life, we begin to lose so much of who we have worked so hard to become. In a short span of time — years or even months — we lose so many of our abilities and capabilities. It can be devastating and frightening to think about losing who you are at the end of life.

This may sound scary, but realize that you have been facing, coping, and dealing with loss your whole life. We experience small losses every single day, yet we have the ability to acknowledge, cope, and move on from these small losses. For example, we strain our back. As a result, we have to change what we do and rest more until we feel better. We had a fight with our best friend and miss their company until we make up. Or our favorite coffee place closes down and now we are stuck with drinking bad joe. These "losses" are so minor that we may not even register them as losses. After a brief moment of sadness, we change our behavior and move on with life.

It is only when the losses get bigger in magnitude and impact that they can evoke a strong emotional response. For instance, we actually say, "I lost my job." Losing a job disrupts the stability of our life and affects great changes, and with this loss, there can be a lot of emotions. Or moving to a new place to live can be a traumatic experience. There is the loss of home, familiarity, routine, and community. Starting over in a new location can be filled with uncertainty.

Other major losses include divorce, breakup of a relationship, or even a death of a loved one. We grieve intensely the loss of someone we love. The experiences are emotional and painful. Yet with time, love, and kindness, we heal and begin to live joyfully again.

Even greater than the major and minor losses I mention here is the loss of who you thought you were. You feel adrift and unmoored from the person whom you have always seen yourself as being. It's like looking in the mirror and not recognizing yourself anymore. And those who are near the end of life or have an illness that has brought bodily change may truly no longer recognize themselves in the mirror.

Being confronted with so many changes and losses is hard and challenging in itself. Although how you choose to cope and deal with them is a choice in your end-of-life journey; just be aware of the consequences of your attitude.

You can choose to fight the changes, and initially, this is a common path for many who are ill and aged. Yet in the end, you will not "win." Unfortunately, what is happening to and within your body cannot be overcome. Fighting losses may feel good and spirited for a time, but at end of life, the fight can also lead to much frustration, disappointment, and anger.

NEW

If you would like to have more grace at end of life, think of it as a process of losing, adapting, and letting go — which is kinda the process you use automatically when facing a minor everyday loss. In this way, you face each change, choose your mental response to it, adapt, and then move on with living. In this way, you stay focused on you and life, instead of what age or the disease is doing to you.

TIP

It's important to stay focused on yourself during this time. Nourish and nurture yourself. Take care of yourself physically, mentally, emotionally, socially, and spiritually. I talk more about self-care in Chapter 13.

Dying, like living, is a process of loss and change. You, like everything else on this planet, can never remain exactly the same forever. So, who you are is also changing and transforming, like our character shown in Figure 9-1. You are not losing who you were — you are transforming to a new and different you.

FIGURE 9-1:
We are always transforming, hopefully for the better.

Who Am I?

First, there isn't just one definition of who you are. You are not defined in just one way or by one thing. Your identity is multifaceted. You are so much more than you may realize.

Second, you've been changing your entire life, and you will continue to change up until the moment you die. While some changes in life occur from wins and adapting to success (desirable), changes at end life are a result of losses you are experiencing, and more often, are changing you in a way that you do not want (undesirable). These changes are usually not within your control and are forced upon you. However, what *is* within your control is how you will respond to these changes.

Last, try to see yourself anew. Learning, developing, and defining who you are is a lifelong process up until you die. You can't remain who you were, so let yourself see who you are becoming.

Pause at this moment and check in with yourself to see your current identity. Ask, "Who am I?" Identity is broadly defined as the set of roles, beliefs, traits, appearance, and experiences that characterize a person. Together, all these components contribute to a sense of who you are.

Understanding who you are helps you acknowledge your positive qualities, find meaning, and determine how you want to be in the world. I have an exercise you can do to figure out who you think you are at this moment in time.

The following are five categories that broadly define a person's identity. For each category, please list up to five things. If you can't think of five things, list those that come to mind. If you can, try to list things that are related to your current situation, so that you can get a sense of your current sense of identity. Take your time and be thoughtful.

Name five roles that you have played in life.

Examples: mom, student, coach, salesperson, husband

1. _____

2. _____

3. _____

4. _____

5. _____

Name five skills or things that you are really good at.

Examples: organizing things, carpentry, listening, tennis

1. _____

2. _____

3. _____

4. _____

5. _____

Name five physical qualities or body parts that you value.

Examples: my eyes, height, hair, dressing style

1. _____

2. _____

3. _____

4. _____

5. _____

Name five personality traits that are your strengths.

Examples: honesty, loving, thinking of others, calm

1. _____

2. _____

3. _____

4. _____

5. _____

Name five values and beliefs that are important to you.

Examples: kindness, nature, your religion, justice

1. _____

2. _____

3. _____

4. _____

5. _____

TIP

It's great to do this exercise now so you have a snapshot of who you are at this moment in time. Keep the information as a reference. It can act as a baseline for comparison when losses and changes occur later in life. Then, you will be able to see how you have changed as a result, which may affect your perception of yourself in that future moment.

Navigating Dimensions of Loss

When we age or are seriously ill or near the end of life, we lose many of our abilities and capabilities of a physical, mental, social, and spiritual nature. Many of these losses occur naturally as a part of aging. For some diagnosed with a serious illness, these losses begin as a result of the disease and the medical treatments. And for all at the end of life, we lose everything and then die.

In the following sections, I review some common losses that people experience. I have not listed all possible losses that a person may encounter. Perceiving something as a loss is a personal reaction to how it affects you. Some may not be bothered by a particular loss of ability, while others are greatly affected. I talk about some of the usual or universal losses experienced at end of life so that you can be familiar with, anticipate, and prepare for what's to come.

Physical loss

Physical losses seem to impact people the most because we are a very active society. Our life is full of action, running from place to place, as we survive, live, and thrive. We are not a society based on quiet contemplation. We are go, GO, GO!

No longer being able to do something physically can be devastating and require a big adjustment. Being aware and planning for these losses will ease the changes associated with them. Asking for help and letting others in for support are discussed in Chapter 14.

Working

Stopping work is probably one of the first major losses that happens as a result of age or illness. When this happens, it can be devastating to our personal being. This is because working and our role in our job can be so much a part of our life and identity.

Yet, a time comes when you are no longer able to do the job or perform the job successfully, or doing so is unsafe for yourself and others. Whether that's work in an office or at a construction site, or at home as a caregiver or homemaker. It becomes impossible to perform the job satisfactorily. You are forced into retirement.

When your physical ability no longer allows you to work and forces you to stop, you can feel angry and frustrated because you know that you could do the job "if only I didn't have this disease!" Stopping work is a bitter pill to swallow because it is not your choice, even when we know that many people can make successful transitions from working to retirement.

Many people try to continue to work for as long as they possibly can. Whether you continue to work or not is your choice for the time being until it becomes impossible. Just think about whether working is how you really want to be spending your time.

PETER'S STORY

I once supported a man who had esophageal cancer that had metastasized to the lung, liver, and brain. Peter was in his 50s and knew that he would not last the year. He was very active in his care and well-attuned to his body.

When Peter got his diagnosis, he immediately stopped working even though he was in good shape and probably could have continued working for some time. Without a job, he dedicated his "free" time to full-time management of his cancer and health.

Peter never had that period of idleness that occurs between stopping work and engaging in something else. He immediately used all his time, energy, and resources to research his cancer and manage his care. Even though his prognosis was dire at the time of diagnosis, surprisingly, Peter managed to live another seven years.

From my perspective as his end-of-life doula, Peter's active management of his cancer and health resulted in a much smoother dying process for him. He was able to anticipate, adapt, and cope with losses and changes as the illness progressed.

Roles

We have many roles throughout our lives. We have roles related to our family life, such as daughter, father, grandparent, brother, or wife. We have roles related to our work and career, such as doctor, police officer, teacher, manager, or actor. We have societal roles that we may play, such as friend, advocate, neighbor, or community leader. We have roles related to the important activities in our lives, such as runner, artist, gardener, or juggler.

In the "Who Am I?" section, I ask you to "Name five roles that you have played in life." I bet that once you started thinking, you found it hard to limit it to five. Maybe you realized that you play many, many roles in life and had to choose the five most important to you.

Each of us takes on multiple roles, and they change all the time based on our circumstances in life and how we see ourselves. Don't get stuck seeing yourself in the same roles all the time or feeling like you have to be in the same role as before. Life's circumstances change us, and illness, in particular, impacts the roles we play in life. Don't focus on the roles you have to give up; rather, see yourself in terms of the roles you are able to fulfil now.

Physical appearance

Changes in physical appearance are another distressing aspect of loss in illness and aging. Anything that alters our physical self can be traumatic. This loss in our perception of our physical self — what we look like — is also accompanied by many intense emotions, including grief.

Think of past times when you got a bad haircut and how upset you were. Now imagine if you lost your hair due to chemotherapy treatment. For many people with cancer, this is a common reality and a dramatic adjustment to how they view themselves. Or you could be struggling with a loss of a body part or have a significant disability from surgery. Any of these occurrences due to aging or illness are major losses for your physical body.

I once met a woman who had breast cancer and had undergone a double mastectomy. She loved her breasts and felt they were part of what made her a woman. She told me that after her surgery, she stood naked in front of the mirror every day. In the beginning, all she did was sob. She could only see the scars and the breasts that were no longer there. But she continued to stand in front of the mirror every day trying to find a way to be comfortable with what she saw. Eventually, her crying became less and she began to be curious about this new body. Now, her breasts don't define who she is. She regards herself as a new woman, and she is a lovely woman indeed!

But not all changes in physical appearance are obvious or as major as a loss of a body part. Some losses result in subtler or more nuanced changes in physical appearance that are just as significant in a person's psyche. For example, some women are horrified at their physical appearance when they can no longer go to the beauty salon for a proper haircut and style. I've heard the same disgust from women who don't have on their makeup and lipstick. While these examples may seem trivial, for these women and others like them, the loss of personal grooming habits is major.

Changes in your physical appearance are not easy to adapt to. It is challenging. Yet, it comes back to defining who you are and how you see yourself. Don't hate your mirror. It doesn't reflect the image you expect, but maybe it's a portal to seeing yourself anew. It's not about who you were, but about who you are becoming with loss.

Mobility

At some point, life will slow down. Or should I say, you will be forced to slow down. Whether because of age or illness, you will move more slowly. It could be for a variety of reasons, such as pain, breathlessness, weakness, or inability.

The loss of mobility is a hard loss to adjust to in our fast-moving world, but fortunately, a lot of assistance and accommodations are available. We have the disabled community to thank for their ongoing advocacy and activism for rights, accessibility, and inclusion.

At some even later point, you will need assistance. For example, you may have to use a cane or a walker. *Ugh!* you think. *Now I have a visual aid that tells others I can't walk on my own.* It is at this point that many people become self-conscious and worry about how they are perceived and received by others.

As you age or your illness progresses, there may come a time when your legs are no longer able to bear your weight. You need a wheelchair. At this point, your ability to get around becomes severely restricted. Mobility requires another person to assist you in and out of the wheelchair and to push you. And a vehicle to accommodate it. Everything takes more time and more energy. It becomes a bigger deal, so you start not going out as much.

Eventually, the time comes when you simply lie down in bed and don't get up again. You are too weak and unable to hold yourself up. Some people are bedbound for months or years before they die, while others only lie down shortly before they die.

What I hope you realize here is that the loss of mobility is a progression. It's not sudden. It usually occurs slowly over the course of an illness or age. Consequently, you have the advantage of time. You have the time to adjust and prepare for how to manage — so that you can live fully within your abilities.

Energy

Similar to the loss of mobility, the loss of energy occurs as a progression. Initially, you may feel little to no loss of energy and resume your usual life. What you may notice is that it may take you more time to recover. You are more tired at the end of the day, or a particularly strenuous activity really wears you out when you used to be able to do it without a problem.

The time comes when deciding to do something requires more energy than you have, or once you do it, you need much more time to recover. Then, each decision to do something can seem momentous. Not only does it impact you physically, but it also impacts others who may be involved. You balance the feelings of determination and desire with disappointment and frustration. It's not easy. It's never easy.

What I tell my clients at the end of life is this: Protect your energy. Only do the things that you really want to do. Only do things that give you joy. The upside of doing something *must* outweigh the downside of doing it (see Figure 9-2).

FIGURE 9-2:
Consider which activities bring you joy and which ones exhaust you.

Instead of using your energy to meet the expectations and desires of others, use your limited, precious energy on yourself. Always ask yourself: Is this how I want to spend my energy?

Appetite

For many people, eating is a simple joy in life. For others, it's simply necessary to function; they find joy in other ways. Whatever your relationship is with eating and food, be aware of its potential to change as you approach the end of life.

Here are some common changes in eating:

>> Your sense of taste changes.

>> You lose your sense of taste.

>> You crave certain flavors.

>> You eat less.

>> You don't feel like eating.

>> You have difficulty chewing or swallowing.

If you are trying to buy yourself more time in life, then you probably want to watch your diet. However, if you are terminally ill and on a path toward death, then in my opinion, eat what you want. Do not deny yourself whatever pleasure you get from eating the foods you enjoy.

WARNING

As you near the end of life, your physical body begins the process of shutting down. The digestive system slows down and eventually stops working. This is a natural process of the body. At this point, food in the body is not processed, broken down, or eliminated. This can result in great discomfort.

REMEMBER

So be aware of what your body is telling you. If you are hungry or thirsty, eat and drink. If you don't feel like eating or drinking, that's okay too. And don't let anyone encourage or force you to eat or drink if you don't want to.

Going to the bathroom

Okay, I admit this is a tough one. There is nothing for me to say about this loss and the resulting changes. It's pretty straightforward. You need help going to the bathroom. It's no longer a private matter. Eventually, combined with your limited mobility and "accidents," you begin wearing diapers (or more politely known as incontinence or adult briefs). Someone else is changing your diaper and wiping your bottom.

Instead, I leave you with this cartoon so we can at least think about this humorously.

Mental loss

Mental losses are a result of changes in the brain. Because the brain is the master controller of all systems in the body, any change in the brain can have great impacts in the way our body functions and our mind thinks.

The losses in this section are related to the changes in our memory, thinking, and reasoning, which are a natural part of aging or may be associated with a disease's progression. I discuss the common symptoms of loss of cognition, forgetfulness, confusion, and mood swings.

I am not addressing mental health illnesses nor the large class of brain disorders, such as dementia or Alzheimer's.

Forgetfulness

Many people become forgetful as they age. You forget things more often. It takes more time to think of a word or remember someone's name. You may misplace an item or not remember what you are doing. It is common and natural to experience memory issues as you age or if you have an illness that is affecting that part of your brain.

Forgetfulness can be frustrating and aggravating, but do not waste your emotional energy on negative feelings. If your brain can't remember, you can't remember. Instead realize that this is your new state of being and adapt. Many tips and techniques can help you deal with forgetfulness. Here are just a few:

>> Follow a routine.

>> Use notes, calendars, and to-do lists.

>> Repeat aloud as you write something down.

>> Check off items as you complete them.

>> Put items in the same place every time.

>> Limit distractions and focus.

>> Get enough sleep.

Mild forgetfulness usually doesn't interfere with your usual activities. If your memory problems become more serious and start affecting your daily life, please see a doctor.

Confusion

Confusion can be a result of forgetfulness. For example, if you forget where you're going, you may become confused. Forgetfulness is forgetting initially, but then remembering your destination; confusion is not knowing when, why, or where you are. Therefore, confusion is a broader term for disruptions to not only your memory, but also your ability to think, focus, and be aware.

According to the Cleveland Clinic, confusion is a symptom that disrupts your ability to control what you think, do, and say. Therefore, you don't recognize that you're confused. You think you're fine, but others tell you that you're not. Your close friends and family play an important role in identifying confusion. And suspecting confusion in your loved one can be very scary.

Serious confusion is not a normal part of aging and usually is a result of a disruption of brain function. Confusion happens because a part of your brain is not working as it should. Many medical conditions and diseases cause confusion. Please see a doctor to find out what is going on.

Cognition

When you begin to lose cognitive function, memory, language, and judgment are affected. The memory issues are usually more serious than forgetfulness. Communication becomes challenging; it is difficult to follow a conversation or find the right words to say. Judgment in evaluating things becomes poor. It is common and natural to experience mild cognitive loss as you age or if you have an illness that is affecting that part of your brain.

According to the Mayo Clinic, mild cognitive impairment is the in-between stage between typical thinking skills and dementia. You may or may not be aware of the mental changes. Your close friends and family play an important role in identifying when changes become serious enough to go see a doctor.

If your cognitive loss is related to a specific brain disorder, many professional organizations can help you, such as the Alzheimer's Association or the Lewy Body Dementia Association. It's important for you to get information, resources, and professional and community support.

Mood swings

It's natural to experience mood swings when you experience any loss or any major change in life. Because aging and illness lead to many losses, experiencing mood swings then is natural. In age and illness, people lose so much independence and autonomy over their own lives, they deserve a break if they're cranky!

No, seriously. Mood swings can result in negative emotional responses, such as depression, apathy, or irritability. Mood swings are difficult for everyone. It takes a lot of grace, patience, and compassion to deal with mood swings — whether you're the one experiencing them personally or a loved one is.

If you're aging, ill, or near the end of life, give yourself grace, be patient with yourself, and offer yourself self-compassion. The losses and changes you are experiencing are not easy to handle, but anger won't help, and in fact, makes the situation worse for everyone. Be kind and forgiving to yourself. It's not easy.

If you are caring for someone who is experiencing mood swings, again, it takes grace, patience, and compassion. Here are two tips to help you through a challenging time of caring for someone with mood swings:

>> **Know it's not about you.** In other words, don't take it personally. I know it can be hard to think this way when anger or irritation is directed at you, but don't respond to negativity with negativity. If it becomes too much for you, try to find creative solutions and get help.

>> **Get support for you and the person with mood swings.** You don't have to do this alone. There are social services, support groups, other family members and friends, and even neighbors who may be willing to help if you ask. Reach out; you'll be glad you did.

Severe mood swings may be a sign that something more serious is going on. In this case, please go see a doctor.

Social loss

The social component comprises the relational aspects of life relating to family, friends, and society. Therefore, social losses are related to the changes in how we interact with others. They're not given a lot of attention but are very impactful and equally devastating to an individual.

Support at the end of life depends upon others to help and assist in every aspect of living. So, it's good to be familiar with the more common losses and changes that will arise, so as to be prepared. I discuss the loss of our ability to communicate well, changes in relationships, and the eventual withdrawal from society.

Communication

If you are able to speak well until you die, you are lucky. Our ability to communicate our thoughts, wishes, and preferences is our lifeline to the outside. When communication becomes difficult, it can become very scary and isolating. There are many diseases that affect our ability to communicate.

I am working with a woman who recently said to me, "Living life is communication." She is 93 years old and once was an avid reader and conversationalist. Now, both her eyesight and hearing are nearly gone. She senses that others do not want to sit with her or, if they do sit with her out of pity, she feels left out of the conversations. She feels that she has lived a long, good life and is ready to die.

Again, the key is anticipating and adapting to the loss of your ability to communicate. Many tools and aids are available to help you interact with others and maintain an active social life. It starts with a willingness to adapt and to set your expectations within your current reality.

Relationships

The effect on your relationships, in particular your friendships, is one of the most profound changes people experience socially. Who your friends are and how you interact with them may change dramatically.

If you are diagnosed with a serious or terminal illness, you are likely to see immediate changes in your relationships — everything from genuine concern and surprising gestures of support to awkwardness and uncomfortableness in being with you. You may even find yourself ghosted. The most unfortunate aspect is that the loss of friendships is usually beyond your control. Friends — even good friends — may not be able to cope themselves with what is happening to you and no longer know how to interact with you. For this reason and possibly many others, a friend may decide they can no longer be your friend. I talk more about losing friends in Chapter 16.

Therefore, love the people who choose to remain in your life. They are showing up for you and supporting you as you are with all your difficulties, needs, and cranky moods. Let them love you . . . and love them back . . .

NEW

While you will lose friends, you will also gain new friends. If I were to meet you as a new client, I wouldn't know the "old" you; I'd only see the current "you." I'd see you new and fresh, for who you are now. And let me tell you, you are pretty darn amazing! So please, let new people into your life. Don't focus on the losses, but instead on what you gain.

Withdrawal

There will come a time toward the end of life when you'll spend more time in quiet. This is natural, and this is good.

Initially, you may find yourself not doing much with lots of idle time as you may not be working or as active as you once were. In general, you need more assistance doing things and have less energy. These are the times when unpleasant feelings, such as frustration, restlessness, and boredom may arise. You may get easily irritated with yourself and others. You may be thinking, *Hey, I'm not dead yet! What is everyone else doing?*

Maybe you have relied on others for most of your life to distract and keep you occupied — not surprisingly given the interconnectedness of social media. Maybe you need others to entertain you and validate your existence.

NEW

Preparing for end of life is about being comfortable with yourself by yourself. Yes, I mean feeling good on your own just the way you are.

At end of life, you will spend increasingly more time by yourself in quiet time. You can lie there and be angry that nobody is paying any attention to you, or you can spend that precious time learning to love yourself. When you love yourself, then you can start cultivating a path toward inner peace. This will help you stay grounded and calm at the end of life. I talk more about this concept in Chapter 13.

A former client of mine, now deceased, said to me near the end of his life, "I didn't know that I could give so much joy out into the world and never leave my bedroom." You too can share your joy with others. Find a way to live not by doing, but by being . . . joyfully.

Spiritual loss

For some people, their spiritual or religious beliefs act as a source of comfort and strength in dealing with life's ups and downs. Their beliefs are an emotional support system helping them to stay grounded and hopeful during difficult times.

It's common to question *Why me?* or to feel tested by your faith when diagnosed with a life-threatening illness. And it can be hard to stay positive and hopeful about life and the future when you feel disconnected from your faith or spirituality. When your beliefs are shaken or in doubt or discarded, you can feel lost. I discuss some of these spiritual losses because they affect your emotional state and can contribute to a sense of fear. And by being aware of these losses, you can then prepare.

For the purposes of this section on spiritual losses, I use the term "spirituality" to refer to both religion and spirituality. In Chapter 18, you can find a more in-depth discussion on the distinction between religion and spirituality.

Disconnection

If you're part of a religious or spiritual community, think about how it helps you and in what ways.

Being surrounded by your spiritual community and doing things in line with your spirituality reinforces your belief in yourself and the divine. Perhaps you go to church regularly, volunteer in the activities of temple life, or hike in nature. Maybe you sing in the church choir, work in the food pantry for the homeless, or replant trees for reforestation. All these activities serve as spiritual reminders.

Has being sick or the circumstances of your current situation affected your ability to do the things that help you spiritually? It can be especially difficult when you are no longer able to physically participate in the activities or life of the community. The loss of your spiritual community is a heartbreaking one experienced by many who are ill or dying.

TIP

Therefore, it's important to stay connected to your spiritual practices and community. Reach out to your spiritual leaders, clergy, rabbis, imams, wise teachers, and shamans. Share what is going on with you and seek guidance. Many faith leaders and spiritual counselors will come to you if you are in need.

TIP

Stay connected with your spiritual practices. You may need to be creative here and find new ways to express and connect with your spirituality. For example, if you had regularly attended religious services, you may now try attending online services. Or perhaps try to explore a deeper internal practice of spirituality through prayer or meditation.

Don't just ignore and dismiss the loss of spirituality wrought by disease or age. If anything, these are the times when you need it more in your life. Your spirituality can give you strength, hope, and comfort in difficult times. So, anticipate, prepare, and adapt. Whatever happens, stay connected.

Uncertainty and doubt

Sometimes a disconnect from your spiritual practices can spur a doubting of your spiritual beliefs. This is understandable. There are already so many losses and changes in your life due to aging and illness; it can be hard to know what to believe anymore.

Staying positive and strong is easier when your belief system is supported and reinforced. When you lose or are disconnected from your beliefs, uncertainty, doubt, and other negative feelings may arise. You may experience fear, anger, and abandonment. This can lead to a sense of "me against the world" and isolation.

A common question that comes up for people diagnosed with a serious illness is *Why me?* Many people don't understand why a terrible life-threatening illness has befallen them. *Why did I get cancer? Why am I going to die?* These questions can evoke feelings of despair, anger, and confusion.

If you have a relationship with God, feelings of abandonment are also not unusual and can be deeply painful and confusing. What was once a source of love and strength may feel like betrayal or abandonment; you feel betrayed by God and turn away. You doubt God's love for you.

You may worry about what happens to you after death. If your faith believes in an afterlife, such as heaven, you may wonder or question whether you are deserving enough to get there. Naturally, you may begin to look back at your life and recount the good and bad deeds you've done. Which way does the balance of your life tip? Believing in some sort of an afterlife — heaven or something else — can be a source of great comfort to you in preparing for the end of life. However, if you're uncertain of the balance of your life, a fear of hell can lead to angst and distress. Or perhaps you believe that nothing exists or happens to you after death. Or maybe you just don't know. After all, death is still one of the greatest mysteries of our existence.

It's good to ask these questions and explore the conflict between your beliefs and what is happening in life. Humans have struggled with these spiritual issues since the beginning of mankind. You are not the first. Since man first looked up at the night sky and wondered if the stars were the souls of their deceased, the unknowns of spirit and nature have existed. Perhaps the process of asking the questions and the inherent struggling within reveal something to you about who you are, your life, and your beliefs.

So don't give up your spiritual beliefs if you get no satisfactory answers. Instead, rely more on your spiritual practices, spiritual leaders, and spiritual community. They have always been there in life; lean into them more in the truly difficult times, such as preparing for the end of life. You don't have to make this journey alone. Stay connected.

Hope, meaning, and purpose

In your illness journey or as you age, you will experience some or many of the losses described in this chapter. You may even experience some losses that I haven't discussed. Anticipating everything that may happen to you based on your age, health, illness, and circumstances in life is impossible. What you can do is *try* to prepare.

REMEMBER

By trying, you are staying active in caring for yourself and in managing the illness. So try to anticipate, acknowledge what is happening, adapt, and let go of losses.

Even in this process, it's natural at times to feel a loss of hope, meaning, or purpose in life, especially if an illness progresses slowly over the course of years. On the one hand, you have more time to adapt and adjust to the loss and changes in life; on the other hand, it may be difficult to remain positive about life for such a long time in the face of so many challenges.

If an illness progresses rapidly, it may be difficult to adapt at all. You have no time to adjust to the new changes physically and mentally. And then one day, in a moment of clarity, you wonder who you are anymore and what you are doing in life. It can feel like life has no meaning or purpose anymore because you are spending all your time, energy, and resources in fighting the disease instead of living life.

REMEMBER

To remain hopeful about life, do all the things in this book. Love fiercely. Do a life review. Get your paperwork in order. Create a legacy. Ask for help. Stay connected to your communities. Prepare for end of life.

It's okay to occasionally lose hope or question the meaning or purpose of life, but if this loss stays with you for an extended period of time, seek help. Find an end-of-life doula or spiritual care counselor who can help you explore what is happening and find ways to stay connected to who you are. You don't have to do this alone.

Seeing Yourself Anew

You are a person with loss. You have successfully anticipated, acknowledged, and adapted to loss. You have changed and transformed. You are re-engaged with life. Congratulations!

As you travel this journey of illness or age, this is where the hard work of living lies. This constant process of anticipating, acknowledging, and adapting. It is part of the evolution of who you are. It is a process of becoming, of constantly seeing yourself anew.

Who are you now?

The last step is letting go and not letting the losses hold power over you. You've worked so hard, brought so many resources to bear. You may have adapted to a new way of life, but are you still living in the past? I hear so many people say, "I just want everything to be normal." What is normal? The past? *Now* is the new normal.

You are no longer the person you were before illness or aging. Who are you now?

If you are questioning who you are, this is the time to redo the identity exercise offered earlier in this chapter. This exercise can help you figure out who you are in this moment in time, as a person with loss. Understanding who you are will help you acknowledge your current positive qualities, find meaning, and guide you to how to be in the world as a person with loss.

For example, suppose you were a teacher, but because of illness, you had to stop working. This is a loss of role and job. As you do the following identity exercise, you may be asking yourself, *Am I still a teacher?* You can list "teacher," especially if that past role strongly informs your current self. However, you do not have to list "teacher" because you no longer teach; instead, you could list "education" as a value that is important to you.

Again, please list up to five things for each category, but if you can't think of five things, list as many that come to you. If you can, try to list things that are related to your current situation, so that you can get a sense of your current sense of identity. Take your time and be thoughtful.

Name five roles that you have played in life.

Examples: mom, student, coach, salesperson, husband

1. _____
2. _____
3. _____
4. _____
5. _____

Name five skills or things that you are really good at.

Examples: organizing things, carpentry, listening, playing sports

1. _____
2. _____
3. _____
4. _____
5. _____

Name five physical qualities or body parts that you value.

Examples: my eyes, height, hair, dressing style

1. _____
2. _____
3. _____
4. _____
5. _____

Name five personality traits that are your strengths.

Examples: honesty, loving, thinking of others, calm

1. _____
2. _____
3. _____
4. _____
5. _____

Name five values and beliefs that are important to you.

Examples: kindness, nature, your religion, fairness

1. _____

2. _____

3. _____

4. _____

5. _____

Sitting with loss

The "Who Am I?" exercise is a good way to see yourself anew in your current circumstances. To help you understand how, I use the teacher example from the "Who are you now?" section.

Suppose you were a teacher for most of your working life. You loved teaching and were devoted to the children. Teaching affected and influenced not only who you were but how you saw the world. In an earlier "Who Am I?" exercise, you may have filled it out with things like "teacher," "caring for children," "patience," "fairness," and "honesty."

NEW

But now, you've been diagnosed with cancer, you've quit work, and you're undergoing chemotherapy. If you filled out the "Who Am I?" exercise now, you might put down things like "mentor," "friend," "reading," "good listener," and "education." Instead of focusing on what you can no longer do, see yourself for what you can do. Your roles, strengths, and values have shifted. You are evolving, through loss and change.

REMEMBER

The losses you experience at end of life are scary and sad, but these emotions should not take away from the joy of discovering who you are becoming. I understand that it may be hard to find the joy, but be patient and kind to yourself. Give yourself time to sit with what is happening to you. Sit with your losses and think about how you can see yourself anew. Remember life is full of opposites, and living fully is about having both.

Chapter **10**

Being in Grief

Preparing for end of life is about learning how to live with loss. So now you are a person living with loss. Grief is the natural response to loss. Therefore, you are now a person in grief.

I know that grief is such a big, intense emotion. However, grief is not just one emotion, but many different emotions occurring singularly and simultaneously with others. Grief is complex. It's a journey that you go on and move through when you experience any loss. And you respond to a loss with grief because you loved the thing or person. So you see, grief is very much a part of living and loving.

In this chapter, I discuss the concepts of grief and mourning, how to acknowledge grief within yourself, and how to companion your grief to a new reality of living.

I'm So Sad

In this part of the book, I talk about emotional preparation for end of life. Do you begin to feel sad when you think of dying? It's okay. Allow yourself to feel sad; do not suppress this emotion. In addition to feeling afraid, feeling sad is a natural and common response to death and dying.

Right now, take a moment to pause and breathe. Open yourself to the possibility of dying. *I am going to die.* Allow yourself to be sad, if that is one of the emotions that arises. Allow yourself to be in touch with this intense, cleansing feeling.

REMEMBER

Sadness is a natural response to the thought, *I am going to die.* Sadness is a vulnerable human emotion. It feels raw and honest.

Whether or not you are currently sick, old, or dying, you will be sad when preparing for end of life. You will be sad for yourself and your life. Especially when you are alone in the quiet moments of the day or late at night lying in bed. If you feel an overwhelming wave of sadness wash through you, it's okay. It's okay to be sad and to cry.

TIP

It is important to give yourself outlets to be sad. Time to be sad, places to be sad, memories to be sad in. Just allow yourself to be sad and feel grief. I talk about all the different ways that grief can feel and be expressed later in this chapter.

Maybe you are the type of person who doesn't want to show your sadness to others. This can be for a multitude of reasons. Maybe you are not comfortable being sad or showing your sadness to others. Maybe you are protecting them, not wanting to frighten or concern your loved ones more than they already are. Maybe you worry about how others will respond. Either they are awkward with your sadness or they try to cheer you up. So, if you are with a person who is sad for whatever reason, do not immediately start trying to cheer them up or deflect them from sadness. If you want to be a good friend, allow them to be honest with their emotions and feel sad. After a good cry, then you can cheer them up. They will appreciate you even more because you gave them the time, space, and companionship to be with them in their sadness.

And this leads to the upside of grief: It can evoke such immense feelings of love and gratitude. How many times have you been with people who were intensely sad, began recalling a story of a past time, got to the extremely funny or happy moment, and then started to cry again even harder? This is what healthy grief can look like. This is what life is about. Full of happiness and sadness, laughter and tears, love and loss. Life is full of opposites, and you need both to live fully.

Grief and Mourning

What is grief? *Grief* is the inward response to loss. It is what you think and feel on the inside. When experiencing any major or minor loss in life, you respond with grief. And at end of life, there are many, many losses. I talk about the different kinds of losses that occur at the end of life in Chapter 9.

The response to loss is grief. Call it grief. Do not diminish what you are feeling by dismissing it or calling it something else. I know that grief is such a big, intense emotion for such a small word, but it is appropriate to call it what it is. Call a spade a spade.

What is mourning? *Mourning* is the outward expression of grief. When you experience a loss and feel grief, you express the grief to others by mourning (see Figure 10-1). Typical mourning behaviors associated with grief are crying and wailing. Less recognized mourning behavior is sitting quietly staring off into space or keeping yourself intensely busy. Both these actions are ways to mourn. However, keep in mind that others may not recognize these behaviors as mourning. Because you are not crying, others may think that "you're okay" and treat you as such, when in fact, you are far from okay. I talk about all the different ways of experiencing grief later in this chapter.

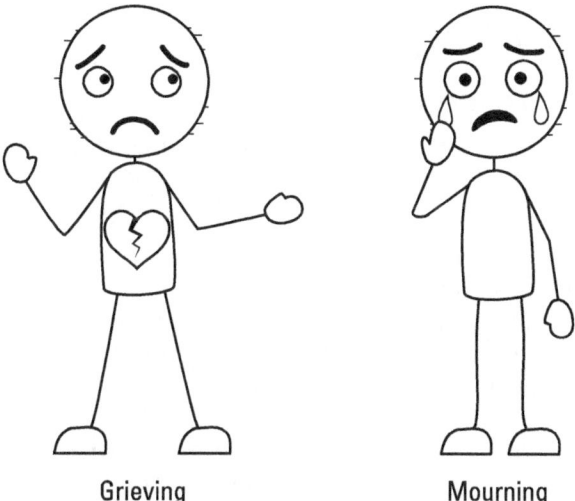

FIGURE 10-1:
The difference between grieving and mourning.

Grieving   Mourning

Grief and mourning are the natural human responses to loss. We experience loss every day in small and big ways. Similarly, we grieve and mourn in small and big ways too. Grieving and mourning are necessary. Giving space and time to move through these natural processes of loss leads to healing.

Anticipating grief

Grief doesn't occur only after a loss. Grief begins from the moment you hear the news and interpret it as a loss in your life. *Anticipatory grief* is responding to a loss before the loss has actually occurred. It is the grief you feel *in anticipation* of the loss.

Here's an example of anticipatory grief. You receive bad news of cancer from your doctor. The prognosis for this cancer is poor, and you can expect to live only a year or two more. From the moment you hear this news and understand that you will die from the cancer, you experience the swirl of emotions that constitute anticipatory grief. Everything that you feel that evening after hearing the news, and in the weeks and months to come — the sadness, the anger, the denial, the depression, and more — is anticipatory grief. You haven't even started chemotherapy and lost your hair yet or stopped working, but you already feel *so much*. And you are allowed to feel all that anticipatory grief. It's okay.

Unfortunately, experiencing anticipatory grief does not necessarily make the grief you experience at the time of loss any less. As you will discover, you just don't know how you will feel in grief. It's unpredictable.

Anticipatory grief is also very much like experiencing grief at loss. So grieving and mourning can feel nonstop — like a continuous, ongoing process.

Experiencing grief

"There is no correct way or time to grieve."

—Elisabeth Kübler-Ross and David Kessler,
On Grief & Grieving

We owe much of our current understanding of grief to Dr. Elisabeth Kübler-Ross, a Swiss-American psychiatrist and pioneer in near-death studies. She completely changed our understanding of the way we die and grieve, and she developed the theory on the five stages of grief, introduced in her seminal book *On Death and Dying* (Macmillan).

In 1969, Kübler-Ross saw that 75 percent of the population was dying "very lonely, miserable, angry, isolated, alienated . . . and we are doing this to them." She asked, "Why?" Out of this simple question has come a vast new understanding of death and dying, one that is patient-centered and based on deep listening. This personal, compassionate approach to death has eventually come to define end-of-life care.

When Kübler-Ross first described personal grief, she outlined The Five Stages of Grief (see Figure 10-2).

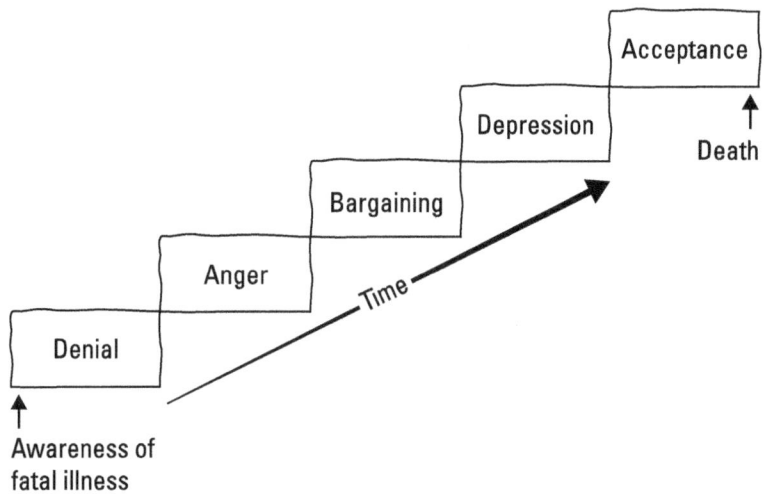

FIGURE 10-2:
The Five
Stages of Grief.

The five commonly known stages include denial, anger, bargaining, depression, and acceptance:

>> **Stage 1 — Denial**

Denial is usually the first stage of grief. In this stage, you are in a state of shock and disbelief. "How could this happen to me?" and "I feel fine" are common reactions. You are not ready to fully process the reality of the situation and take on only as much as you can handle.

>> **Stage 2 — Anger**

When you finally comprehend the situation, it's common to feel anger. "I don't deserve this" and "Life is not fair" are common reactions. The anger can be expressed in many different ways. You may even seek someone or something to blame for what is happening to you. Anger can be directed at yourself and/or others.

>> **Stage 3 — Bargaining**

This stage occurs when you try to delay or change the outcome. It entails bargaining for more hope. "If I do [this], will I have more time to live?" and "If I had just gone to the doctor sooner, . . ." are common reactions. Bargaining is about negotiating with yourself and others, like your doctor or God, for a different outcome if you change your behavior or beliefs.

>> **Stage 4 — Depression**

This stage occurs when you feel sadness, fear, guilt, regret, and many other negative emotions. It is a realization that you are going to die accompanied by hopelessness and despair. It is a low point in your illness journey and in life. It may seem endless with no way of moving forward or any reason to do so.

>> **Stage 5 — Acceptance**

Acceptance is about accepting the situation and what is happening. It is *not* about "liking" the situation or "feeling good" about what is happening. You may never feel all right about the situation, and that's okay. Acceptance is more about not resisting change and finding a new reality to exist in. You begin processing loss and grief for yourself and your loved ones.

By 1974, Kübler-Ross asserted that the stages were not meant to be linear. She went on to explain that several stages might occur simultaneously, be skipped, or not occur at all. Rather, the concept of the five stages was merely a starting point for discussing the elements of the grief journey.

Grief is so many emotions

We now know that grief is not one emotion, or even five. Grief is a range of emotions encompassing a wide span of human feelings. Because of this, it may be hard to recognize that what you are feeling is grief.

NEW

You can feel one emotion or many at the same time. You can transition from one feeling to another and back again or to a completely different emotion. You can be steady and feeling one emotion intensely, like depression, or you can be seesawing wildly all over the place. Grief is so many different emotions.

Here are some common emotions that you may feel in grief, in addition to the ones mentioned in the Kübler-Ross model:

>> Sadness

>> Anger

>> Fear

>> Depression

>> Disbelief/denial

>> Shock

>> Guilt

>> Regret

>> Longing/yearning

>> Helplessness/powerlessness

>> Confusion

>> Despair

>> Numbness

>> Relief

As you can see, grief encompasses a huge range of emotions. And most of the emotions listed, except for the last one — relief — are difficult, painful emotions to feel.

REMEMBER

Grieving is hard. But allowing yourself to feel these emotions will lead to healing.

TIP

So, when you feel any of these grief emotions, *don't do anything.* Don't push the emotion away. Don't suppress or ignore it.

WARNING

If you try to suppress the grief, it will only come back later and be more intense. Suppressed grief can eventually develop into prolonged grief and be even more debilitating later in life.

Instead, sit with your grief. Be with it and allow yourself to feel. Cry too. If you are in a public place and you feel comfortable doing so, just sit down and be with your grief. Feel and breathe. If you cannot give yourself this pause to be with your grief, acknowledge it and put it mentally to the side, but come back to it later in the day when you have time, space, and privacy to face it.

REMEMBER

Allowing yourself to feel grief is an expression of your love for the loss or loss to come. Honor that and yourself.

Grief is different for everyone

We now know that grief is different for everyone. How you grieve and mourn is unique to you. It will not be the same as your spouse, a family member, or your best friend. Just as there are so many different emotions you can feel in grief, there are so many different grief journeys.

In 1969, when Kübler-Ross first published her ideas on and approaches to grief, she used a linear model. Eventually, she moved away from a linear understanding of grief to one that acknowledges the complexity of grief. In 1978, she published a graphic depicting the stages as overlapping circles. Kübler-Ross described the grief journey as cyclical, with stages overlapping or repeating in response to evolving aspects of change, which is known as the Kübler-Ross Change Curve.

In the past half century, extensive research on grief has led to our knowledge of grief as complicated and complex. It is unique. Each person's grief journey is so personal. Figure 10-3 shows various images that you may find more relatable to your own grief experience.

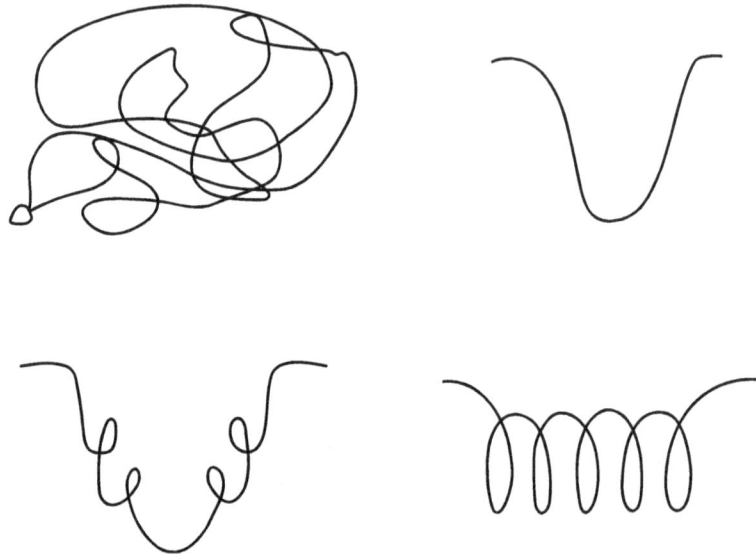

FIGURE 10-3:
Each person's grief journey is unique, taking its own path.

REMEMBER

A graphic can't tell the whole story of a person in grief. You can't know when someone else is grieving because you don't know their expression of grief. You don't know what their grief journey is like and where they are in it. If anything, assume they are in grief. Treat them with kindness and compassion.

And if you are in grief, treat yourself with kindness and self-compassion. You deserve to be good to yourself.

Grief in community

Grief is so much sadness. When you are feeling sad for yourself and the situation, you just want to bury yourself in a deep hole. You want to be alone in your darkness. You can't be bothered by the world, petty concerns, and your family and friends always trying to cheer you up. You have no energy or desire to engage with others.

It's okay to want to be by yourself for whatever reasons.

First, you probably need to rest. Grief can be tiresome and exhausting. You have been and are going through a lot. A grief journey carries tremendous weights of a physical, mental, social, or spiritual nature. It takes a lot to carry those weights.

Second, being alone is an opportunity to be with your thoughts and feelings about what is happening. *What do I think and feel about this loss?* Check in with yourself and sit with your grief. In this way, you begin to process grief.

REMEMBER

I have just given you two reasons why it's okay to be alone in grief, but being in community with others in grief is also a very important part of the grief journey and a step toward healing. So when in grief, spend some time alone but also spend time with others.

First, allow others to care for you. When you're grieving, it's not the time to be strong, resilient, or independent. Let go of your defenses, your habits, and self-judgment. Allow the people who love you into your space and life. Allow them to cook, clean, and care for you. This is good for the following reasons:

>> **It is a way for them to show their love for you.** Don't worry; you will have a time in the future to reciprocate your love. When a friend or family member has a future crisis and needs to be cared for, show up for them.

>> **It is a reminder of gratitude.** Be grateful that you have people in your life willing and able to show up for you. Even in loss, there is so much to be thankful for in life.

>> **It gives you the luxury to be with your grief and to begin processing it.** We live in a society that doesn't give us any time to grieve. We are expected to "get over it" and get back to work immediately. Use this gift of being with your grief.

A second reason to be in community with others when in grief is remembering. You are grieving because you lost something or someone that you love. Yes, it is painful and full of such sadness, but you don't have to spend all your time in pain and sorrow. Grief is also about remembering the love you had for that thing or person.

Imagine that someone you loved died. One component of healthy grief is recalling memories and storytelling about the deceased: close friends and family getting together, crying and laughing over stories of crazy times, shared adventures, and tender moments. It reminds us of the gift of love and friendship of having had that person in our life.

And if you are the dying person, it may give you comfort and pleasure to know that your friends and family will gather to tell stories about precious times spent with you — that you will not be forgotten but remembered with love and laughter.

Grief takes time

Grief stays with you forever. But with time, it lessens in intensity and changes form. It never goes away. Grief finds a place in your heart — your heart is big enough — and you begin to live again.

In the beginning, grief takes up your whole existence. You feel such big emotions, which are overwhelming, intense, and painful. It feels endless and bottomless. With time though, the pain will be less. You begin to live again and find happiness too. Maybe, you feel guilty for feeling happy or deny yourself happiness because you don't think you should feel good or better, but you can't deny the grief process. You are beginning to heal.

I know that we live in a society that doesn't give us time to grieve. Many of us can't get time off from work to even attend a funeral. Or we move for a new job and must begin work immediately. Or we have medical emergencies occurring one right after another and never have time to adjust to the changes and trauma. Too often, we are simply not given the time to adapt to what is happening before we must face the next thing.

TIP

If you are not given the luxury of time, you must create your own time to process your grief. Find quiet time in the evening or on the weekend when you can be with your grief. Do this repeatedly. Even when you think you are better, continue to check in with yourself. Honor your grief and the loss.

With time, you will heal from grief.

Letting grief transform

REMEMBER

Grief is an expression of love. You have lost something or someone you love, so of course, you grieve. Or you are anticipating losing something or someone you love, so you grieve. The grief reminds you of the loss and the love. It is a good grief. It may not feel good — even for a long time — but feeling grief is good.

To be immersed in your grief journey is to be open to feeling grief in whatever form it takes. It is to think about and feel the loss, acknowledge the thoughts and emotions, and allow yourself to be impacted by them. Out of the grief, you shift, and healing begins.

Making grief your companion

You live with grief all the time. Grief occurs because of the loss of someone or something, and its loss affects you. So, open yourself to feeling grief and mourning its loss. It is an expression of your love.

Therefore, let grief reside in your heart alongside love. Grief and love are like companions. You cannot love without the risk of loss. With loss, there is grief. Therefore, love and grief go together, as depicted in Figure 10-4.

FIGURE 10-4:
Grief and love can live inside your heart together.

Do not deny yourself the happiness and joy of loving something or someone because of the risk of losing. Some people believe that they cannot bear the pain of grief so they try not to love again. Life is about opposites and living fully is having both.

REMEMBER

You will heal from grief. Time, love, and kindness will help you heal. Keep your heart open.

Living a new reality

There is no going back to before the loss. That reality no longer exists. Loss has occurred. You have lost your job, you are divorced, or someone you love has died. There is no going back to the previous reality and having everything be the same. So, stop wishing for something that cannot be.

NEW

To heal from grief is to exist in a new reality. It is to find life without that person or thing in your life. You learn to live again in its absence.

Yet, learning to live with loss is not about existing in sorrow all the time. Healthy coping with loss is acknowledging, recognizing, and even honoring the loss in your new reality. It's about letting a memory awaken the love in your heart. It's about letting a memory make you feel sad and smile. It is about letting a good memory make you laugh and be grateful. These are also expressions of grief and are healthy ways to grieve.

Eventually you will smile and laugh about new things in life unassociated with your loss and grief, and that is the beginning of re-engaging with living. That's good, and it's okay too. You've been down for a while and now you are coming up into the light of living again. You are finding your new reality.

Chapter **11**

Takin' Care of (Unfinished) Business

You may be familiar with Bachman–Turner Overdrive's popular song, *Takin' Care of Business.* In life, we often feel we have plenty of time to take care of our business, or should I say, our "unfinished" business. *Unfinished business* includes the unresolved issues in our lives that we haven't taken care of and healed from. These are past experiences associated with negative emotions which live in the shadows of our lives.

Examples of unfinished business can be things like a breakup in a relationship that was bad for both of you, or being estranged from members of your family, or having done something wrong earlier in life and never feeling good about it. You have these unsettled feelings within you and figure that you will have time — one day — to deal with them. But the time never seems right, and you procrastinate. Then, one day, you get sick instead.

The things that weigh you down in life will weigh you down in death. It's no different. In fact, the emotional weights of your unfinished business can feel quite heavy. Even worse, now you have less time and energy to deal with them. To prepare for end of life is to take care of your unfinished business so that you can face death with peace of mind.

In this chapter, I further explore the concept of unfinished business, describe some of the different kinds of unfinished business that exist, and show you how to start taking steps toward having peace of mind.

I Want to Be at Peace

In this part of the book, I talk about emotional preparation for end of life. When people think about how they would like to be at death, I often hear the words "peaceful" or "with peace of mind." This sounds so wonderful. To be able to face death with an inner calm and contentment. To feel at ease and peace with your time, place, and purpose in this world. To not be troubled or worried about what is happening or what you are leaving behind. How lovely!

To face death with "a peaceful state of mind," you must come to the end of your life with as little baggage as possible, as in the "Good death" scenario depicted in Figure 11-1. If you are carrying heavy baggage of an emotional, spiritual, social, or physical nature, you cannot feel peace of mind. This baggage will weigh on your mind and spirit.

FIGURE 11-1: Dealing with your emotional baggage can help you enter end of life more peacefully.

Eventually, these weights will cause worry, anxiety, and possibly even distress. Facing death with these weights does not set up good conditions for a peaceful death. In fact, you may be setting yourself up for an emotionally difficult, and possibly distressing, death. And when you are lying on your deathbed, there is little to no time, energy, or ability left to do anything about it. You have made your bed and are now lying in it.

So, it's important to have as little baggage as possible when at Death's doorstep.

But here's the catch: You don't know when you will die. You could die at any moment. You could die today, tomorrow, or soon. You won't necessarily die only when you are old or get a terminal illness. You could die at any time. You could be hit by a car when you walk out the door. This means in order to have as little baggage as possible at Death's door, you must live life with as little baggage as possible. Because you never know when death will happen.

So now you see that preparing for end of life means preparing now. Not at the end of life when you are possibly sick, weak, scared, or unable. Preparing for end of life occurs now while you are still healthy, young, able, and cognitive. And I assume that some of these words describe you, plus you have the desire to prepare for end of life, and that is why you are reading this book. So thank you.

Preparing for end of life is a journey of shedding your bags. If you are carrying too many bags beginning this journey, don't worry. There is still time to "unpack" and leave some behind. Carrying as few bags as possible — while living and dying — gives you freedom. A mental freedom called *peace of mind*.

Investing in a Peaceful Death

Think of it this way: Preparing for end of life now is an investment in your future death.

We will all die. Unlike other major life events and milestones, this is an event that will happen to you, me, and everyone on this planet. Not everyone gets married. Not everyone reaches 50 years of age. Not everyone becomes a parent. But for certain, everyone will die.

We live not to just live. We all live to die. Death is the one event that we are all moving toward in life. It is the last event each of us will face individually in our own way. We live now to have death at the end.

When we die, it's over. Death is such a final act. It only occurs once. There is no going back and getting it right the second time around. You have only one chance at death, so do what you can to make it "good" the first — and only — time around.

REMEMBER

If you feel that I am hammering this message into you, I am. I can't stress enough how important it is to not just understand this message, but to internalize an understanding of death too.

Just like any goal you set in life, if you want something, you make a plan. You set actions and change your behavior, all in support of the goal. You invest whatever it takes to achieve it. For example, say your goal is to buy a home. So you make a budgeting plan, buy fewer extravagances, and start saving money in the bank. You research houses and neighborhoods, figuring out what features and elements you want and don't want in a future home. You invest time, money, and resources, all for the goal of hopefully one day owning your dream home.

The same applies if you want a peaceful, good death. It takes the same kind of foresight, planning, and dedication to achieve this goal in the future. Therefore, invest now — in yourself — to get the kind of peaceful death that you would like later by preparing in the present.

Shedding Emotional Baggage

There are many kinds of emotional baggage that we carry in life. Baggage from our childhood, baggage from our school years, and baggage from our adult years. Baggage from our relationships, and baggage from the way we treated ourselves and others. Baggage from the decisions we made, and baggage from things we did or didn't do. There is so much baggage. What have you been doing with all this life baggage?

We all carry baggage. The baggage is in the form of experiences from our past that are associated with a negative emotion. They weigh heavily on our mind and spirit. They exist in the shadows of our life. They pop up from time to time, reminding us of times when we didn't act well or when others were hurtful to us. And because of the pain and unpleasantness of remembering these negative experiences, we only suppress them more and push them further into the shadows of our being.

REMEMBER

Addressing your emotional baggage is important to having more peace of mind at death.

I can't tell you how or what the best way is to address your emotional baggage. I don't know you and the experiences and trauma you may be carrying. But if you want to lessen the negative power that these experiences hold over you, look for help. You don't have to do this alone. Therapy and counseling services are available in most communities. Specialty support groups exist for every kind of trauma. Even more services are available to you if you are able to go online.

TIP

Or, perhaps to start, just bring the baggage out into the light. Acknowledge it. Give it some air. Begin by first verbalizing what happened to you in the past. Find an end-of-life doula or a kind person to listen to you — advice I offer multiple times throughout the rest of this section because it's a beginning, a first step to shedding some of your emotional baggage. And if you are at the end of life, it may be enough.

I now talk about three common classes of emotional baggage that we carry with us throughout life: regrets, guilt, and shame. I discuss how these emotions can negatively affect our end of life. So shed as much baggage as possible. The less baggage you come with at death, the more peace of mind you'll have.

Regrets

What is regret? *Regret* is a negative emotion in which you blame yourself for an outcome. You feel bad because you did/didn't do something you believe you should/shouldn't have done.

You know this feeling of regret. We all experience regrets in life. We regret something we said. We regret something we did. We regret a missed opportunity that we didn't take advantage of. We regret not doing something that we should have. There are many regrets in life, small and large.

What you do with the big regrets from past decisions can impact you later on. If you do nothing about your regret and continue to self-blame, the regret can turn into a mental weight in your mind resulting in stress, depression, and possibly more. And at end of life, there is little time to address or seek help for such heavy weights.

In her best-selling memoir *The Top Five Regrets of the Dying*, Australian author Bronnie Ware recounts her years of caring for dying people and the wisdom she received from those experiences. As a palliative carer, Ware questioned her patients about any regrets they had or anything they would do differently. From those conversations, she described five common themes of regret that emerged at end of life:

1. **I wish I'd had the courage to live a life true to myself, not the life others expected of me.**

   Bronnie notes that this was the most common regret of all. When people realize that their life is almost over and look back on it, they clearly see how many dreams have gone unfulfilled due to choices they did or didn't make.

2. I wish I hadn't worked so hard.

This regret was expressed by every male patient that Bronnie nursed. All the men deeply regretted spending so much of their lives on the treadmill of a work existence. While women also spoke of this regret, many of the female patients had not been breadwinners.

3. I wish I'd had the courage to express my feelings.

Many people suppress their feelings in order to keep peace with others, but carry bitterness and resentment as a result. It is important to speak honestly even if we can't control the reactions of others.

4. I wish I had stayed in touch with my friends.

There were many deep regrets about not giving friendships the time and effort that they deserved. Many had become so caught up in their own lives that they had let special friendships slip by over the years. Everyone misses their friends when they are dying.

5. I wish that I had let myself be happier.

This was a surprisingly common regret. Many did not realize until the end of life that happiness is a choice. They had stayed stuck in old patterns and habits, fearing change and pretending to others, and themselves, that they were content. When you are on your deathbed, what others think of you is a long way from your mind.

Adapted from Bronnie Ware's The Top 5 Regrets of the Dying

Interestingly, psychology research has reported that regret is one of the highest rated negative emotions that can lead to positive behavior. Evaluating our regret can motivate us to corrective action, meaning the pain of regret can result in *now* choosing a different path. So begin addressing your past regrets now. Find an end-of-life doula or a kind person to listen to you. It is never too late to look at past regrets and make better choices for the future. Or to choose to live the kind of life we want now so that there will be no regrets at our death.

Guilt

What is guilt? *Guilt* is a negative emotion associated with committing acts of wrongdoing that you perceive as morally wrong. The acts of wrongdoing may be things you did that you shouldn't have done, or something you did not do that you should have done.

Guilt is an emotional response to the harm caused by you to another. While guilt is a feeling about yourself, it is socially relevant because it involves others. You worry not just about yourself, but also about the harm you may have caused to others. You feel guilty because your decisions or actions have negative repercussions to others.

Mistakes are a part of life. So feeling guilt after a mistake is normal and natural. Fortunately, guilt can be often remedied by making up for whatever pain or offense is caused. Therefore, guilt drives us to act. The most effective way to reduce or eliminate guilt is to apologize, correct, or make up for a wrong, and behave responsibly. So even though guilt is a negative emotion, it can be a positive motivator.

Guilt, like regret, is a negative emotion that can lead to positive corrective action. Therefore, guilt, if addressed, can be a powerful learning tool for personal growth.

Be aware that not everyone feels guilt over the same wrongdoing. The degree to which people feel guilt varies, so don't expect that your level of guilt is what others feel in the same situation.

Also be aware that your perception and subsequent guilt of a wrongdoing may be perceived differently by the harmed person.

NEW

Addressing your guilt is an action you are doing for yourself, not for the other person. You can't control another person's reaction to a wrongdoing or apology. The harmed person may not want to hear your apology or may not be ready to forgive you. Instead, you are addressing the guilt for yourself — to give yourself peace of mind over your past action. I talk more about forgiveness in Chapter 16.

WARNING

Living with chronic or persistent guilt can be detrimental to your mental health. Guilt that is not addressed has been linked to anxiety, depression, and other mental health disorders.

You don't want to be carrying guilt or chronic guilt with you as you face the end of life. A lot of time near the end of life is spent in reflection on the life you have lived, so the guilt embedded in certain memories may arise. It may be difficult to put your guilt to rest at such a time, especially if you have not addressed it before. Emotional weights such as guilt can lead to emotional suffering at end of life. This is not a path toward peace of mind at death.

So try to come to the end of your life with as little emotional baggage as possible. Try to take care of your unfinished business before facing the end of your life. Find healing for the guilt you carry while you still have time. A good place to start is to talk about your guilt over past wrongs. Find an end-of-life doula or a kind person to listen to you. Bring out from the shadows the guilt you carry into the light. Just talking about it may be enough to ease some of the guilt you feel. But, if you need to do more, reach out, make amends, and seek forgiveness for yourself and others. If you need additional guidance, seek help from a therapist or counselor. You don't have to do this alone.

Shame

What is shame? *Shame* is believing that something is wrong with you as a person. It is believing that somehow you are unworthy of love and connection.

We have all felt shame at one point or another. It's a universal emotion. Remember the times when mean or uncaring people said something about you — the way you look or dress, your weight, your race, or saying you're stupid — and you felt bad about yourself. We may start to believe these hurtful things that others say, especially when we are young. If so, we then start to believe we are imperfect and unworthy. We feel ashamed and begin to behave accordingly.

Shame is a negative emotion that festers and grows. Shame is much more of a destructive emotion and results in low self-esteem. Shame can also lead to anxiety, depression, and other psychological problems.

Unlike regret and guilt, shame is not a helpful or productive emotion and does not lead to positive corrective action. Consequently, shame is much harder to overcome.

Interestingly, psychology research in the United States has studied how prone people are to experiencing shame by age. Not surprisingly, adolescents are most prone to feeling shame. The identities of teenagers and young adults are not completely formed. As they struggle to find their identity and define their place in society, they are exposed to the criticisms and expectations of others. Young people are highly likely to feel some shame about themselves. The propensity for shame then decreases, through to middle age when people's personalities become more set and they are less likely to be affected by other people's expectations of them. However, as we enter old age, we begin to feel self-conscious again. We worry about the declines in our body, appearance, and abilities, from all the losses that I talk about in Chapter 9. We perceive that others are looking at us and treating us differently. Shame is quite prevalent among the elderly.

Not feeling shame is about accepting yourself just the way you are.

REMEMBER

NEW

The antidote to shame is the practice of self-compassion. It involves understanding how to forgive yourself, to be kind to yourself, and to not judge yourself negatively. Self-compassion quiets our inner critic and provides space within to improve the way we see ourselves. I talk more about compassion in Chapter 20.

Resolving past shame may be challenging, so seek help. A good place to start is to talk about the past shame you felt or current shame you feel. Find an end-of-life doula or a kind person to listen to you. Offer yourself forgiveness for how hard you are on yourself. Just talking about it may be enough to ease some of the shame you feel. If you need additional guidance, seek help from a therapist or counselor. You don't have to do this alone.

Sadly, if you are near the end of your life, you may be feeling shame about who you are now and your circumstances. You may not be in a safe environment and may not be treated with love and compassion. I acknowledge how challenging it may be to maintain a positive self-image.

WARNING

Know that a strong feeling of shame is associated with a perception of being a burden to others at end of life, which in turn is linked to a desire to die.

So, if you are a caregiver, please be aware of how your attitude and actions toward patients and those in your care are making them feel. Your job is so important. Yet you may not be recognized enough for your efforts nor feel appreciated. I understand that these conditions do not make your job easy and make it even harder for you to maintain a positive attitude. So, I thank you for all that you are doing.

All I can ask is that we try to be together with love, kindness, and compassion and without judgment of one another. Now and at end of life.

Chapter **12**

Reviewing Your Life

There can be so much value, meaning, and purpose in taking time to reflect back on our lives. It's not just about recalling the past but understanding and appreciating who we are now *because* of the past. You may be thinking, "The past is past. Why should I think about the past? I can't change the past. I should live in the now or look to the future."

While these statements are true, the past informs the now — and the future. This is true for us as a society and ourselves as individuals. Thinking about our past offers us an opportunity to think about how we would like our future to be. Because one day, the near future will be the near past. Do you like how the near past happened? You can't change what happened after it's past, but you always have the opportunity to shape the future. So you see, thinking about the past is thinking about the future. This is called doing a life review.

But doing a life review doesn't necessarily have to be about shaping the future. Life reviews are great for taking stock of where you are now in life and appreciating how you got to this point.

In this chapter, we continue to explore the importance of doing a life review, how it can be meaningful and revealing to you, and what methods are available to conduct your own life review.

I Am Pretty Darn Amazing

In this part of the book, I talk about emotional preparation for end of life. As people approach their death, it's natural for them to reflect back and assess what they did with their life. One of the feelings I have often seen in people who are sick or dying is a feeling of low self-worth. I hear this feeling stated as, "My life was insignificant" or "My life had no meaning." It is very sad to feel this way when there is very little time left in life to do anything about it. Or maybe you feel this way now and you are not sick or dying. I acknowledge that that is a possibility, and you're in luck. Keep reading. This chapter is for you too.

First of all, a life review is comprehensive and takes time. It's impossible to look back on your life — and all the years that you have lived — and sum it up in a flash moment.

Second, humans are complicated. Any one thing or any one person that is complicated can't be summed up in a simple word or sentence, like, "I had a good life." Or maybe you've thought of other words to describe your life or yourself, such as happy, difficult, challenging, or okay. These words are too general and don't really say anything about who you are as a person. There is so much more to you than you realize or remember.

I believe that you are an amazing individual. In fact, I believe that every single person on this planet is amazing. Does this make us all the same, if we are all amazing? No. This planet is made up of approximately 8 billion amazing individuals.

You are amazing because of your unique life's journey. It is about acknowledging that you have a unique story, unlike the other 7,999,999,999 individuals alive on this Earth. Your story is made up of the events of your life, the people you knew and the relationships you had, the places you've been, the things you've heard, and all the emotions you have ever felt. All these components over the course of your lifetime make up a unique story of you.

You are the only person who knows your story; no one else does. Others may tell parts of your story, but it is their interpretation or their perspective from the outside. No one else can tell your story from the inside. Only you know your *whole* story. This is why you are pretty darn amazing!

Looking Back at Your Life

You may find it difficult to think about yourself and your life in a useful or positive way. I offer two alternate ways or metaphors for you to think about yourself and your life. These metaphors may provide you with some ease or a new way of thinking about yourself and your life in the past, present, and the future.

The tapestry of you

Think of yourself as a tapestry, a rug woven of many threads. Each thread is one memory. Together, all the threads — all your memories — weave into a tapestry telling the story of who you are (see Figure 12-1).

FIGURE 12-1:
The tapestry of you is uniquely yours.

NEW

If you look closely at your tapestry, you can see all the separate threads — their color, thickness, shape, and placement in the tapestry. Seeing each thread alone, and then how it weaves with the other threads, allows you to see and understand the overall picture. Similarly in a life review, recalling memories of important events and people in your life helps you to understand who you are and see the broader picture of yourself — that you are made up of so many individual threads.

REMEMBER

Who you are at any moment in life is a result of everything in the past. *Everything.* All the good and the bad, and the humdrum of life in between.

Now step back and take a look at your tapestry from afar. Stand far enough back so that you can look at the big picture — the entire picture of you at this moment. What do you see in the tapestry? Try to look at yourself with curiosity and wonder. Try not to judge what you see or to say, "I like this" or "I don't like that." Just observe. At the very least, try to be neutral about what you see in your tapestry, and if you can, try to appreciate what you see — who you are right now. Aren't you amazing?

Now, take a closer look at your tapestry again. And ask yourself: Do you like what you see? Or do you mostly like what you see but would change a few things? Or do you not like what you see at all? You can't change this picture, but you have an opportunity to edit this version of your tapestry. You can choose to add a new thread, so as to revise this picture or create a new one. By adding a new thread, you can create a new tapestry of you, mostly still you, but something slightly different. Meaning, you have a choice about who you want to be in the future: the same or different. Hopefully a better picture, and not a worse one.

Most of the time, we aren't even conscious of who we are and whether we are staying true to who we want to be. We can become complacent about living life and being who we are in the moment. But also at every moment, we have the opportunity to change who we are, and a life review is one tool you can use to help you determine who you want to be.

KAREN'S STORY

I recently worked with Karen, a woman in her 70s who was in good health but keenly aware of her age and mortality. Karen wanted to be better prepared to face her advancing years. After doing a comprehensive life review with me, she had a better appreciation of who she was at the current stage of her life, and of the events and people in her past that had shaped and influenced her. And as we began discussing what the end of life could look like for her, Karen realized that *she didn't want to die the person she was now.* Wow! What a wakeup call! Karen realized that if she had an accident the next day or got a serious illness, she would die the person she was now. But if she didn't die suddenly or soon, then she still had time to shift her life and become the person she wanted to be when she died. So that's what she's doing now. Living life to becoming the person Karen wants to be at death. How cool is that!

REMEMBER

Checking in with yourself occasionally is a good thing. Like Karen (see her story in the nearby sidebar), the benefits of a life review can impact your future years at any point in your life. You don't have to be imminently dying or terminally ill or even elderly. You can be healthy and young. It helps to take a look at yourself — to see your threads and determine the picture of who you want to be in the future.

The roller coaster of life

NEW

You are a tapestry, but your life is a roller coaster. Each person in their own car on their own roller coaster of life. You know what the track was like behind you, but you don't know what the track is like ahead. There are smooth straight bits on a roller coaster, but there are also twists and turns, and ups and downs. Life is like that too.

Remember that a roller coaster has ups and downs. If it were flat, it would be like riding a train. For taking a trip, trains are nice and safe, offering a pleasant, usually uneventful, experience. But don't expect life to be like a train. Life is more like a roller coaster (see Figure 12-2), and it wouldn't be a roller coaster if it didn't have ups and downs.

FIGURE 12-2: Like a roller coaster, life has its ups and downs.

Early in the ride, that first uphill is agonizing. The roller-coaster car slowly chugs up the slope with the clanks and rattling of the chains and cogs pulling you uphill. The anticipation of the downhill is killing you. At the top of the slope, it's either going to be terrifyingly exhilarating or terrifyingly "I'm gonna sh*!t in my pants!" You just don't know. You just don't know how you will react. You want to love it, but you don't know if you can. Right now, you are scared out of your mind, gripping the bar in front by the whites of your knuckles!

After that first hill, there will be more twists and turns and ups and downs. Life is like that. Some of the upcoming slopes will be smaller, and some will be bigger. You just don't know. You think that you are better prepared to face the second or the third or subsequent hills ahead. Maybe you are and maybe you aren't. Maybe you will have more ease or you see each hill anew. Either way, you will face each uphill ahead with a bit of fear, strength, resolve, and anticipation.

Once you get on the ride, there is no stopping until the end. By the end of the ride, maybe you are queasy to your stomach and glad to get off, or maybe you are screaming with delight with your arms raised in the air. Or maybe, you're like me, getting a little bit of a scare and a thrill out of life at the same time.

REMEMBER

However you feel on the roller coaster, however you feel about the life you've led . . . you did it! You've done it! You are doing it! You are on the roller coaster of life — congratulations! It takes a lot of courage to be on this ride.

So here you are on the roller coaster of life. Whatever age you are, however many years you've lived — congratulations! Your age is just a number that tells you how many years you've been alive. You could be 10, 25, 38, 52, 77, or 100 years. Whatever your age is, you've made it this far. You could be at the beginning of your life, the middle of your life, or near the end. You actually don't know. And the number of years you've lived is no indication of what stage of life you are in. You could be 86 years old, soon to die of old age, or you could be 22 years old and die suddenly from an accident. You actually don't know how long the ride will last. You do not know how many more twists and turns and ups and downs there will be on this ride. You don't know when your car will pull into the station to get off. All you know is that you are alive right now and on the ride of your life.

I don't doubt that you've done the best you could to live a good life, yet life is hard. You have faced difficulties, challenges, hurdles, losses — even black holes — in life. Yet I hope that you have also experienced some happiness, joy, kindness, and love too — because these are the thrills that make life worth living. Remember life is about having both.

Conducting a Life Review

Hopefully by now, you are thinking a little bit more about your life's journey and how you came to be where you are today. It may be a pleasant experience as you think back fondly on certain events or people that you knew from the past. This is a great start. You are beginning to unlock the part of your brain that holds memories by recalling your past. However, a life review can be so much more than simply remembering quietly in your mind. Reaping the long-term benefits of a life review requires time, patience, and honesty with yourself. If you are willing to be open and vulnerable, a life review can be impactful and transformative.

In the upcoming sections, I review some of the benefits of doing a more comprehensive life review and then discuss what life review methods are available to you to make it a more meaningful, and possibly life-changing, experience.

Benefits of a life review

A life review gives you an opportunity to take stock of the present moment. You gain a greater clarity of your present life by understanding where you are now in life and how you got there.

Even more importantly, a life review can instill a sense of gratitude for the life you have lived. Gratitude is such an important quality to incorporate into living. Being able to appreciate the moments and people that influenced your past and those who will shape your future can influence how you interact and behave in this world.

Lastly, a life review is also an opportunity to chart your path forward. It allows us to see not only where we've come from — the path behind — but where we might like to go — the path ahead. By taking the time to think about the past in a thoughtful and conscious way, you become more committed, aware, and appreciative of what comes in the future.

Some of the many benefits to doing a life review include the following:

>> Allows for deep reflection on our life story

>> Reaffirms a sense of identity and self-worth

>> Acknowledges the influential people and events in our life

>> Promotes a sense of meaning and purpose in life

>> Instills a sense of pride and worth in our life's accomplishments

>> Reminds us of who and what is important in life

>> Strengthens interpersonal relationships

>> Offers an opportunity to make peace with the past

>> Promotes healing and forgiveness with others

>> Increases acceptance and satisfaction with our life's situation

>> Leaves behind a legacy for family and friends

>> Enhances overall well-being

REMEMBER

Enjoying any of these benefits of a life review depends upon how much of yourself you are willing to bring to a life review. The more open you are to looking at your past, the deeper the reflections will be, and the greater the impacts will be for you in doing a life review. You will reap more benefits. In effect, the more honest you are with yourself, the greater the understanding of your life will be.

Methods of a life review

I show you three methods of doing a life review here; they vary in structure, time, and outcome. One method needs the assistance of another person, and the other two can be done solo. The life review method that requires another person can be done in a few hours. The methods that you do on your own can take weeks or months.

All three methods involve either writing or recording your life review. When you write down or give voice to your recollections — to make the recounting of your life more "real" — a life review can be a transformative and healing process. Seeing or hearing your own life story helps you acknowledge the twists and turns and ups and downs of life and even makes a commitment to which threads of your life's tapestry you may add or change in the future.

In addition, you can then have a *legacy product* — a concrete physical object or process that is an outward expression of meaning of a person — created from your writings or recordings. Having your story preserved and sharing it with those you love can be an incredibly meaningful experience. I talk more about legacy in Chapter 17.

I recommend that you choose the method that is most appealing to you and for which you have the time and resources to accomplish it. Obviously, for the first method of Dignity Therapy, if you are unable to find someone to assist you, don't choose that method.

The method you choose isn't as important as what you bring to the life review. You need a willingness to be honest and go deep with an open heart.

Dignity Therapy

Dignity Therapy is a brief intervention that gives people an opportunity to share the moments that shaped their lives. It was developed by Dr. Harvey Max Chochinov, a distinguished professor of psychiatry at the University of Manitoba, Canada. For the past 25 years, he has led a research team addressing psychosocial dimensions of palliation and has helped define core competencies and standards of upholding dignity in end-of-life care. He has written numerous publications and earned many honors recognizing him as a leader in palliative care.

Dignity Therapy gives people a chance to record the meaningful aspects of their lives and leave something behind that can benefit their loved ones in the future. It is a recounting of thoughts, ideas, and events that are particularly relevant and meaningful to you and that you can pass along to others. While it is not necessarily a historical recounting of your life, meaningful moments are often associated or connected to specific events that have happened in your life. So naturally, the outcome may become a recounting of your life. Yet the emphasis in Dignity Therapy is not on facts or chronology, but on meaning.

During a Dignity Therapy interview, you are asked nine dignity-related questions. The interview is recorded and conducted by a professional skilled in the practice of deep, active listening. It typically lasts between 30 and 60 minutes. After the interview, the contents of the recording are transcribed and edited, and a final legacy document is presented to you. The idea of the legacy document is to preserve your thoughts for the future and transcend your death. You are free to share it with whomever you wish.

The nine Dignity Therapy questions are:

1. Tell me a little about your life history; particularly the parts that you either remember most or think are the most important? When did you feel most alive?

2. Are there specific things that you would want your family to know about you, and are there particular things you would want them to remember?

3. What are the most important roles you have played in life (family roles, vocational roles, community-service roles, and so forth)? Why were they so important to you, and what do you think you accomplished in those roles?

4. What are your most important accomplishments, and what do you feel most proud of?

5. Are there particular things that you feel still need to be said to your loved ones or things that you would want to take the time to say once again?

6. What are your hopes and dreams for your loved ones?

7. What have you learned about life that you would want to pass along to others? What advice or words of guidance would you wish to pass along to your (son, daughter, husband, wife, parents, other[s])?

8. Are there words or perhaps even instructions that you would like to offer your family to help prepare them for the future?

9. In creating this permanent record, are there other things that you would like included?

Dignity in Care/https://dignityincare.ca/en/dignity-therapy-at-end-of-life.html

While contemplating these questions can be thought-provoking, the most effective way to get the most meaning out of these questions is to be interviewed.

Giving voice to the meaningful moments in your life can be a powerful personal experience. Forgotten impactful events may be recalled with greater understanding and clarity with the passage of time. Or remembering a close, intimate relationship can evoke strong feelings and reawaken the heart. In recalling the moments that shape our lives, many people connect to a deep sense of purpose, meaning, and gratitude.

I have used a modified, simplified version of the questions above with many people preparing for end of life. My aim was not to do a formal Dignity Therapy session, but to just get my clients thinking about the meaningful moments in their lives. It is that powerful.

TIP

It is important to find a listening-based professional (for example, a therapist) or an end-of-life doula in your area to help you. Many trained end-of-life doulas are familiar with Dignity Therapy.

REMEMBER

Note that you don't have to be dying or ill to partake in a Dignity Therapy interview. These questions are relevant at any age or stage of your life. It can be a good way to check in with yourself, to see the path you've taken in life and chart a path forward for the kind of life that you would like to live.

COMMENTS FROM DIGNITY THERAPY PARTICIPANTS

Following is feedback from patients and families who participated in Dignity Therapy, taken from the Dignity In Care website.

"It's helped bring my memories, thoughts, and feelings into perspective instead of all jumbled emotions running through my head. The most important thing has been that I'm able to leave a sort of 'insight' of myself for my husband and children and all my family and friends."

"Dignity Therapy was a lovely experience. Getting down on paper what I thought was a dull, boring life really opened my eyes to how much I really have done."

"This experience has helped me to delve within myself and see more meaning to my life. I really look forward to sharing it with my family. I have no doubt that it will be enlightening to them."

The Stanford Letter Project

The Stanford Letter Project grew out of years of research on care at end of life at Stanford University School of Medicine. Researchers conducted interviews and focus groups in multiple languages with people in the community and talked to numerous patients and their family members as well as health professionals. Their research has shown that people find it extremely difficult to discuss end-of-life issues both with their doctors and with their friends and family. While almost all doctors agree that having end-of-life conversations with their patients is important, most doctors struggle with these conversations. And while patients feel that it's very important for them to have end-of-life conversations with their doctors and their family members, patients don't know how to initiate these conversations.

Two letter templates were created by the Stanford University School of Medicine to help people write letters about their wishes for care in the future. For a life review, I recommend the "Who Matters Most Letter."

"The goal of the Who Matters Most Letter template is to help all Americans complete the seven vital tasks of life review while they still can. . . . Sadly, almost everyone forgets to do this or postpones it until it is too late."

—The Stanford Letter Project,
Stanford University School of Medicine

The Stanford Letter Project is a tool to help you identify the people who matter the most to you, appreciate key experiences in your life, and reflect on the important relationships you have cultivated. It is an opportunity to express the deep love, gratitude, and commitment you feel toward your friends and family. You can do it now before it becomes too late.

The seven Tasks of Life Review are as follows:

>> **Task 1: Acknowledge the important people in your life.**

It is very important to start the process of life review by identifying key people in your life. Take the time to express your pride in their achievements.

>> **Task 2: Remember treasured moments from your life.**

The second life review task is to recall the most special, meaningful instances in your life, including those involving your loved ones. These moments or events can range from important life milestones to simple family moments that you treasure.

❯❯ Task 3: Apologize to those you love if you hurt them.

In our experience, many patients worry about specific past instances when they have hurt the people they love. In doing a life review, it is important to take a moment to ask forgiveness from those you have hurt. Also, take this time to forgive yourself for any mistakes you feel you have made in the past.

❯❯ Task 4: Forgive those who love you if they have hurt you.

Now is the time to give solace to those who may have hurt you. Let them know that you acknowledge what they have done, but that you ultimately have forgiven them. This will give them a sense of release and peace. Successfully letting go of old resentments will also give you peace.

❯❯ Task 5: Express your gratitude for all the love and care you have received.

Thank your loved ones for their concern through the trying times in your life and for everything else that they have done for you. You may mention specific instances that you hold close to your heart.

❯❯ Task 6: Tell your friends and family how much you love them.

Sometimes it is hard to express your love for someone in speech, so take advantage of this opportunity to write to those you love and express how much you care about them.

❯❯ Task 7: Take a moment to say "goodbye."

The final life review task is to bid adieu to your loved ones. If you feel comfortable, take this time to ensure that you and your loved ones have a proper parting without any regret or guilt. In working with diverse Americans, some have expressed reluctance to complete the task of saying "goodbye" due to cultural taboos. If you are uncomfortable completing the "goodbye" task, it is perfectly fine to defer this for later.

Stanford University/https://med.stanford.edu/letter/friendsandfamily.html

TIP

Find a quiet space and a block of uninterrupted time when you can sit down and write a letter. You can choose to write a letter to a single person or to a group, such as your family. Or you can write multiple letters to several of the important people in your life identified in Task 1. To start, it may be easiest to write one letter to one person. Later on, you can write more letters to the other key people in your life.

REMEMBER

There is no right or wrong way to write this letter. Just come with an intention to be honest, a willingness to look deeply within, and an open heart. You may find yourself getting emotional while writing your letter; that's good. Allow yourself to cry.

You can also decide to share your letters to those you wrote to. You can share the letters with them now or at some future time. You can also leave the letters to be given to your loved ones upon your death. Or you can simply write the letters for your own personal growth and exploration.

REMEMBER

The letter you write is just a first draft. It can and should be something that you re-visit from time to time. It is an evolving document and can morph and change throughout your life. Similar to Dignity Therapy, this is a good tool for checking in with yourself and seeing how you are doing in life.

Storytelling

This is the most informal and least structured of the life review methods that I discuss. *Storytelling* is a simple form of recalling and sharing past experiences. Through storytelling, you relive experiences, share your wisdom, and reaffirm your sense of identity.

"We dream, plan, complain, endorse, entertain, teach, learn, and reminisce by telling stories."

—Deborah Schiffrin and Anna De Fina in *Telling Stories: Language, Narrative, and Social Life*

Doing a life review unlocks the place where you hold memories in your brain, and you will feel many emotions in recalling the past. It is important to give yourself time and space to reflect upon life. Do not rush! Be open and allow whatever memories you have to rise to the surface. Some memories will be happy and bring a smile to your face. Other memories will be painful or make you feel sad or wistful. Just sit with whatever arises. All these memories, positive and negative, are part of what makes you who you are today. Honor that.

I have compiled the following list of 20 questions or prompts to use in a storytelling life review to do on your own. These prompts are intended to help you remember different stages or specific events in your life and stimulate storytelling. The prompts touch upon people, places, events, dreams, hopes, struggles, challenges, and ideas:

1. What is the earliest memory in your life?

2. What was life like for you as a child?

3. What was your family like, your parents and siblings?

4. As a child, what did you want to be when you grew up?

5. Did you go to school and what was school like for you?

6. What was life like for you as a teenager?

7. What dreams and goals did you have for yourself when you graduated from high school?

8. What was life like for you as a young adult in your 20s and 30s? What did you enjoy doing?

9. What do you remember about the first time you fell in love?

10. What was your first job? What other jobs have you held?

11. What role has religion or spirituality played in your life?

12. Who did you have the most significant relationships with in your life?

13. What have been the main disappointments in your life?

14. What was the hardest thing that you had to face in your life?

15. What was the happiest period in your life and what about it made it so?

16. What things are most important to you now?

17. How have your friendships changed through the years?

18. How do you feel about growing old?

19. What's your best advice for living?

20. What would you like others to remember about you?

You can answer one prompt or a few at a time. I do not recommend trying to answer all the questions in one sitting. Because it may be an emotional experience, give yourself time to sit and recall the memories. And if you give yourself time, maybe you will recall even more or remember forgotten details. Take weeks, or even months, to complete a life review. It is more important that you do this process thoughtfully and with openness.

Record these stories if possible, to create a lasting record for you and your loved ones. You can write down your stories in a journal or notebook, or you can make audio clips speaking into a recording device, such as your phone or voice app. These recordings or writings will capture your life and thoughts at this specific moment in time and can be used to begin to build your legacy to future generations. Find out more about what you can do with these stories to create legacy projects in Chapter 17.

Chapter **13**

Deserving of Self-Care

G iving and receiving care is all about love. We give care because we love the other person. We receive care from others because they love us. We are all deserving of love and good care in our life.

Yet, many people describe themselves as "givers." They give, help, and can't say "no" to others in need, even if it results in more stress or is detrimental to their own health. Many givers admit to being bad receivers of help themselves. They don't like to ask for help from others even when they really need it. They also find giving love easier than receiving love. Does this describe you?

End of life is all about receiving care and love from others. You become the focus of all those around you, whether or not you like it. You may have tried to live a life taking care of others, but end of life is the time when others take care of you. Accepting this care — and love — graciously begins with loving yourself. You need to feel worthy of receiving this care.

In this chapter, I talk about loving yourself, explain why this is important at end of life, and share ideas on how to take better care of yourself in a whole-person way.

I Love Myself

In this part of the book, I talk about emotional preparation for end of life. Love is *the* big emotion at end of life. Everything that is happening and occurring is about love; it may be unspoken, but it's all about love.

You don't want to die because you love life so much. You worry about your family because you love them so much. You love the person who you used to be, but not enough the person you have become. You don't realize that when your loved one encourages you to eat, move, or pray more, it is because they love you too much and are afraid of your death. You are embarrassed by all the help and care you need rather than accepting it as an expression of love from others. Everything is about love.

NEW

Know that you deserve all the care and love you have received in life and will receive at end of life. To know that you deserve it, you must feel worthy of receiving it, and that begins with loving yourself first.

When we love ourselves, we not only love to give, but receiving love is also much easier. Loving ourselves comes from a place of wholeness. We see ourself, others, and the world around us with a sense of peace, contentment, and love.

The other good reason to love yourself is, at the end of life, you start spending so much more time with yourself. This happens for many reasons, including the many losses you experience, a need to conserve your time and energy, and the thoughts you have that are too big to share with others. For whatever reasons, you will spend more and more time with yourself as you approach the end of life. And as you spend more quiet time with yourself — being with that person all the time — it helps to love that person. You.

This is the wisdom that I have gained as I've accompanied others in their journey toward death. I see some people struggle, while others are more serene. I see some people who are not comfortable in the quiet space at the end of life, while others are content. One of the things that I have discovered is that when you have to spend so much time with yourself, you have to like who you are. And liking who you are is something you must work on while you're living, not when you're close to death. So, to prepare for end of life, ask yourself: Do you love yourself?

Caring for Yourself

"After me, anyone can come first!"

—Alexandra Jonsson, former President of Healing Touch Canada

Loving yourself means putting yourself before others. I learned this principle during my training as an end-of-life doula and now realize that I should have been doing this all my life.

When I am in a better place or mood, then I can show up better with others. I am kinder, more considerate, and happier. I feel stronger, less depleted, and have more resources to draw upon. My mind is clearer, open, and able to process things faster. I see the world through more joyful eyes instead of focusing on the negative side of things. And more importantly, I like who I am. When speaking, interacting, and reacting to others, I like how I am showing up. I even walk differently.

So, taking care of myself means that I am showing the best version of myself for myself and for others.

NEW

Self-care is not a luxury; it is a priority.

Caring for yourself is easy during happy, relaxed times, but much harder to do during busy, difficult times. Yet, it is the stressful times when you need self-care the most — when, say, a big due date is looming, you're working two jobs to make ends meet, or you're sick with the flu or worse. This is the challenge in learning to make yourself a priority.

So make yourself a priority *now:*

>> **Not after you get a diagnosis:** So many people start eating healthier or exercising after they become diabetic.

>> **Not after you retire:** So many people postpone their dream vacation or time with friends for when they stop work.

>> **Not after an accident happens:** So many people change their lives after trauma.

Instead, make yourself a priority *now!*

Taking care of yourself requires a whole-person approach. Many people think that doing some exercise, for example, going to the gym or for a run, is self-care. While that provides some physical and emotional self-care, it's neither enough nor balanced. It may keep you going for a while, but it doesn't sustain or fulfill the whole person.

Self-care, as shown in Figure 13-1, is about nurturing yourself wholly: physically, mentally, emotionally, socially, and spiritually. I discuss each of these separately throughout the rest of this section. And then in the section that follows, I share ways to better take care of yourself.

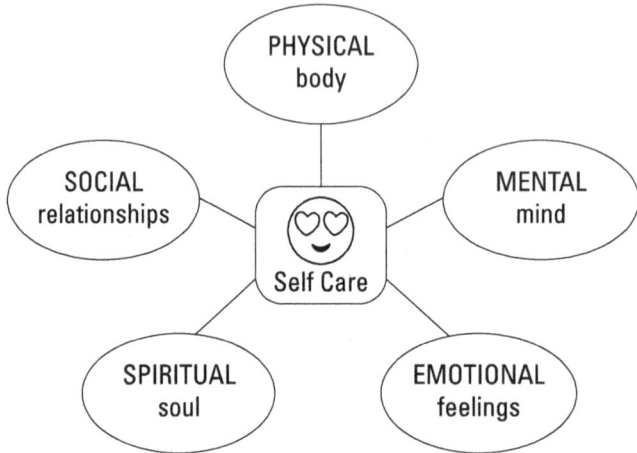

FIGURE 13-1:
As human beings, we are made up of all these components, so we need to take care of them all too.

And once you have developed good self-care practices, it will be easier to adapt your self-care as you age or when your physical abilities decline or are altered due to illness or end of life. It won't be such a far stretch or challenge to adjust your self-care expectations and practices. And you may find the need for care and support from others is an easier and smoother transition for you, your loved ones, and caregivers.

Physical self-care

This type of self-care is about taking care of your physical body. When you care for your body, it functions well, efficiently, and productively within your current health conditions. You think and feel better too.

Taking care of your physical body is about engaging in activities that enhance your physical well-being. Yet, physical self-care is not only about exercising; it's also about giving your body what it needs to be healthy and balanced. That means being active but also giving the body adequate rest and nutrition. The types of physical self-care you engage in depend upon the lifestyle you lead and your health.

When you think about the physical activities you do and the time available in your day, ask yourself:

» Am I getting enough sleep and rest?

» Am I eating a healthy diet to nourish my body?

» Am I exercising?

» Am I paying attention to my physical health with regular medical checkups and preventative care?

» Am I hydrating my body adequately during the day?

Set your expectations and practices within your current health conditions. At end of life, your self-care practices need to adapt to the declining abilities of your physical body. For example, you may need to change the types of exercises you do and rest more to recover rather than giving up on staying active. Think of physical self-care as a way to show up more alert and present in the best version of your current self for when you are with others later.

Mental self-care

This type of self-care is about taking care of your mind. When you care for your mind, it thinks clearly, is sharp, and is able to process information. With a healthy mind, you are able to learn, reflect, and grow as a person.

Taking care of your mind entails keeping it curious and inspired. It's about engaging in activities that fuel and feed your mind. Yet, it's not about constant stimulation; it's also about giving your mind quiet time to reflect upon your experiences, thoughts, and feelings. Mental self-care is also about cultivating self-awareness and positive thinking.

When you think about how much your mental state affects your daily energy and outlook on life, ask yourself:

» Do I feel stuck in a mental rut?

» Am I learning new things?

» Do I have a positive inner dialogue with myself?

» Do I listen to myself with kindness and compassion?

» Does my mind have enough replenishing, restorative down time?

Set your expectations and practices within your current health conditions. At end of life, mental capacity will likely decline, even if not a symptom of illness. Or you may feel like you exist in a brain fog state a lot of the time. Be aware of these changes and adapt expectations of yourself. Having strong mental self-care practices already in place helps with maintaining a positive attitude with all the changes at end of life.

Emotional self-care

This type of self-care is about taking care of your emotions and how you feel. It is about taking time to process your emotions and experiences in order to better understand yourself and your behavior. Healthy emotional self-care leads to loving and accepting yourself.

Emotional self-care is engaging in activities that help you acknowledge and express your feelings regularly and safely. It's about having ways to process your emotions, both positive and negative. And in facing hard or uncomfortable feelings, you begin to develop healthy coping strategies.

When you think about how you manage your emotions, especially during the difficult times, ask yourself:

>> Do I regularly check in with how I feel?

>> Do I have healthy ways for processing my emotions?

>> Do I have safe outlets for expressing my feelings?

>> Do I have strategies for emotionally recharging myself?

Set your expectations and practices within your current health conditions. At end of life, many people refrain from expressing their feelings about what is happening to them. Very often, they feel their emotions are too big and scary to handle and don't want to worry their loved ones more than they already are. Don't dam up your emotions! You may need to seek safe outlets for expressing your feelings around what is happening to you; find an end-of-life doula, someone who specializes in this type of emotional support.

Social self-care

Social self-care is about your relationships. It's about taking time to cultivate new relationships and nurture the close ones. A healthy social life involves putting time and energy into building social connections and then maintaining them.

Social self-care is engaging in activities that nurture your relationships with others. The problem is, oftentimes when life gets busy or crazy, the first thing we do is cancel plans and withdraw. While knowing when to say "no" and decline is important, social isolation can lead to loneliness. Therefore, be sure to understand your motivations behind isolating yourself. Never use it as an excuse to meet fulfilling a social need. Having regular social interaction is essential.

In our current world of remote work and social media, when you think about your social interactions with others, ask yourself:

>> Am I getting together with others in-person?

>> Am I proactively reaching out and making plans with others?

>> Do I have any relationships that are draining rather than fulfilling?

>> Am I able to set good social boundaries in response to my social needs?

Set your expectations and practices within your current health conditions. At end of life, having good social boundaries and self-care practices is essential. Because of your declining physical condition, energy, and attention span, you may find yourself being more selective about who you spend your time with and how. Large or loud social gatherings may be challenging and draining. Intimate gatherings become incredibly meaningful, allowing you to be more engaged. End of life does not have to be a socially isolating experience; you can adapt and remain connected with others.

Spiritual self-care

This type of self-care is about nurturing your spirit or soul — whatever you choose to call the inner essence that grounds as well as inspires you in life. This doesn't necessarily refer to religion; although for many, religion is the means through which they connect to a deep sense of purpose and to something greater.

Spiritual self-care is about engaging in activities that are meaningful to you, whether alone or in community. For the former, this can be about giving yourself time to meditate or pray. For the latter, this can be about doing something in support of your spiritual beliefs, such as volunteering in a soup kitchen or planting trees. It is affirming to engage in spiritual activities, which offer comfort, grounding, calm, and connection. Especially during difficult times, your spiritual beliefs can be a source of solace, strength, and resilience.

When you think about when and in what ways your spiritual beliefs and practices support you, ask yourself:

>> Am I doing work that feels meaningful to me?

>> Do I feel that I have a purpose in life?

>> Do I rely upon my spiritual practices in difficult times?

>> Do I find fulfillment in my spiritual practices?

Set your expectations and practices within your current health conditions. At end of life, your physical condition may prevent you from attending services or participating in the life of your spiritual community. If so, this is the time to reach out and let others in to support you wherever you are located. Also, spiritual self-care may shift to be more personal and introspective. Having a lot of quiet time, and alone time, at end of life is an opportunity to reinforce and strengthen your spiritual beliefs to give you comfort and courage to face the end of life.

Caring for Yourself Better

Hopefully, you now understand how important it is to love and take care of yourself, not just at end of life but every day.

At this point, you may be asking, But how do I care for myself better? First, I encourage you to figure out what you are currently doing in terms of self-care. Then, you can think about how to improve.

Doing a self-care assessment is a way of checking in with yourself and asking, "Am I prioritizing myself?" Many of us think that we are doing fine and are taking care of ourselves, but after we do an assessment, we can see that we aren't really or that we are imbalanced.

TIP

Therefore, it's a good idea to do a self-care assessment periodically. Check in with yourself and see how you are really doing. In this way, you become more aware of how to better nurture yourself physically, mentally, emotionally, socially, and spiritually.

Taking a self-care assessment

NEW

Self-care assessments help you evaluate what areas you are doing well in and what areas need improvement. Not only do these assessments help you identify areas that need attention, but they also give ideas for self-care that you may not have been aware of.

I share one here that you can do now. Among the many self-care assessments out there, this one is adapted from Saakvitne, Pearlman, and The Staff of the TSI/CAAP, *Transforming the Pain: A Workbook on Vicarious Traumatization,* Norton (1996).

Rate the following areas according to how well you think you are doing:

3 = I do this well (for example, frequently)

2 = I do this okay (for example, occasionally)

1 = I barely or rarely do this

0 = I never do this

? = This never occurred to me

Physical Self-Care

____ Eat regularly (for example, breakfast, lunch, and dinner)

____ Eat healthily

____ Exercise

____ Get regular medical care for prevention

____ Get medical care when needed

____ Take time off when sick

____ Get massages

____ Dance, swim, walk, run, play sports, or do some other fun physical activity

____ Take time to be sexual — with myself, with a partner

____ Get enough sleep

____ Wear clothes I like

____ Take vacations

____ Other:

Psychological Self-Care

____ Take a day off or a mini vacation

____ Make time away from telephones, email, and the internet

____ Make time for self-reflection

____ Notice my inner experience — listen to my thoughts, beliefs, attitudes, feelings

____ Take time to process my personal experiences

____ Write in a journal

____ Read literature that is unrelated to work

____ Do something I am not an expert at or in charge of

___ Decrease stress in my life

___ Engage my intelligence in a new area (for example, go to an art show, sports event, theatre)

___ Share different aspects of myself with others

___ Be curious

___ Say no to extra responsibilities

___ Practice receiving from others

___ Other:

Emotional Self-Care

___ Spend time with others whose company I enjoy

___ Stay in contact with important people in my life

___ Give myself affirmations, praise myself

___ Love myself

___ Re-read favorite books, re-watch favorite movies

___ Identify comforting activities, objects, people, and places, and seek them out

___ Allow myself to cry

___ Find things that make me laugh

___ Express my passion through social action, letters, donations, marches, protests

___ Other:

Spiritual Self-Care

___ Make time for reflection

___ Spend time in nature

___ Find a spiritual connection or community

___ Be open to inspiration

___ Cherish my optimism and hope

___ Be aware of non-material aspects of life

___ Try at times not to be in charge or the expert

___ Be open to not knowing

___ Identify what is meaningful to me and notice its place in my life

___ Meditate

___ Pray

___ Sing

___ Have experiences of awe

___ Play with children

___ Contribute to causes in which I believe

___ Read or listen to inspirational material (for example, literature, podcasts, music)

___ Other:

Relationship Self-Care

___ Schedule regular dates with my partner or spouse

___ Schedule regular activities with my children

___ Make time to see friends

___ Call, check on, or see my relatives

___ Spend time with my companion animals

___ Stay in contact with faraway friends

___ Make time to reply to personal emails and letters, send holiday cards

___ Allow others to do things for me

___ Enlarge my social circle

___ Ask for help when I need it

___ Share a fear, hope, or secret with someone I trust

___ Other:

Workplace or Professional Self-Care

___ Take a break during the workday (for example, lunch)

___ Take time to chat with co-workers

___ Make quiet time to complete tasks

___ Identify projects or tasks that are exciting and rewarding

___ Set limits with clients and colleagues

___ Balance my caseload so that no one day or part of a day is "too much"

___ Arrange workspace so it is comfortable and comforting

___ Get regular supervision or consultation

___ Negotiate for my needs (for example, benefits, pay raise)

___ Have a peer support group

___ Develop a non-trauma area of professional interest

___ Other:

Overall Balance

___ Strive for balance within my work–life and workday

___ Strive for balance among work, family, relationships, play, and rest

Other Areas of Self-Care that Are Relevant to You

___

___

___

Evaluating your self-care assessment

If you have completed your self-care assessment, congratulations! It doesn't matter if this is the first time you've done an assessment or if you think you are a pro at self-care. This exercise is a snapshot of your current approach to self-care and is meant to bring awareness to what you are doing well and what you could do better.

Look at your responses with the following in mind:

>> **Look for patterns in your responses.** Which areas have a lot of 2s and 3s? Which areas have a lot of 1s and 0s? Identifying these areas tells you which areas of self-care you are more active or attentive to versus the areas of self-care you neglect or ignore.

>> **Look at the ideas for self-care where you put a "1" or "?."** (An option in the assessment is a question mark indicating a self-care idea that never occurred to you.) Looking at these self-care items may lead you to ponder: What is my definition of self-care? Is it too narrow? Can I care for myself in a broader sense of my whole person?

REMEMBER

This exercise is not meant to make you feel guilty or pressure you to take better care of yourself. Hopefully, this exercise expands your thinking on what self-care is. Did you know that just giving yourself some quiet time or "down time" is self-care? Self-care is much more than you may have thought, and hopefully, you have some new ideas too.

WHAT I LEARNED ABOUT MY SELF-CARE

At the University of Vermont where I teach the End-of-Life Doula Professional Certificate program, all the students take a self-care assessment as part of the training course. Here are some of the comments from my students about their self-care practices:

"This exercise was oddly enjoyable for me. I typically shy away from any mention of "self-care" because I find the term is often misappropriated as a marketing ploy to sell women things they don't need under the guise of "wellness." But breaking self-care down into a highly pragmatic and literal list feels less like self-indulgent capitalistic bullsh*t and more like a disaster preparedness exercise, which was a fun change."

"I found the Self-Care Assessment Tool really helpful. It was a good holistic look at all the critical areas of self-care. It made me think and reflect on what I was currently doing and how I might do those things better or add new things in the future. It also made me reflect on my actions *over time*, not just in a single day or week. It was important for me not to just come up with new ideas, but to address potential barriers to those ideas, or at least to be realistic. With the hope of setting myself up for success, I also added quarterly dates into my calendar for reflection on adherence to my plan, and also to be able to make revisions as needed."

"I am a firm believer that we must put on our own oxygen masks before we can assist others. My greatest obstacle is trying to fit too many things into one day. I am making a concerted effort to not do this anymore and, instead, put scheduled time on the calendar to accomplish my self-care initiatives."

"I have always been a person that does mostly everything on his own, rarely asks for help. Even after a big knee surgery and a recent shoulder surgery, I do things alone at home, asking no one for assistance. I have a hard time asking for help because I do not want to be a burden to anyone. So after assessing myself with this worksheet, I see that I need to start letting people in, build stronger friendships by being vulnerable sometimes. I will make time to physically see my friends more often, bond with them in person, perhaps do activities together."

"I honestly never really considered self-care as important. On paper, I do a very good job of nurturing my mind, body, and spirit. My challenge is that I really need to push myself to keep at my routines — and when stress enters the picture, a lot falls apart. This exercise has been very beneficial for me in recognizing how little thought I have given to self-care. Moving forward, I will value it differently and will intentionally build self-checks into each day."

(continued)

(continued)

"I was asked to look for patterns in my responses. To take note if I was ***more active in some areas*** of self-care ***but ignored others*** which revealed: I seem to be heavily responding and active in Emotional self-care, Spiritual self-care, and Relationship self-care. This exercise revealed more attention is needed in Physical and Psychological self-care. I do see and find value in all these areas to promote a balanced and healthy internal self. That I am the only one to make my self-care the priority it needs to be."

"I completed the Self-Care Assessment. In the past five years, I prioritized self-care and this was reflected in the assessment. I learned self-care is a dynamic practice that requires continued reflection and flexibility enveloped in compassion for myself. I find printing this and posting it in strategic locations provides a reminder to prioritize myself."

"During this exercise it became obvious that self-care is something that is difficult for me as a caregiver. There are times that my world is so wrapped up in caregiving (making doctors' appointments, cooking, and cleaning) that I have an empty tank and am unable to give myself what I need. After this, I have a more direct approach to letting some of those things wait while I give myself what I need."

"What really stood out for me as I engaged in the task was an acknowledgement that I had begun writing feeling confident (maybe arrogant) that I had already developed a self-care program that was working for me, and I wasn't going to gain much in the process. However, as I reflected and wrote current practices in all the categories, I noticed that I could pay more attention to what I hold as important in my self-care routine. . . . In other words, I had to admit that maintaining consistency with the plan is something I need to refine and work on."

"In the past I have felt 'guilty' for taking time for myself and felt that it was frivolous. I see that focusing on self-care will assist me in completing all the things I want to do with my life."

"So, after a lifetime of trying not to take up space, I am now taking up space. I try to exercise and maintain my weight. I get massages and facials, and I tend to my health needs. I'm not perfect, but I'm a beginner after 65 years of neglect. I see a therapist and am taking this course. A huge part of my self-care is to go back and do things that are right for me and not just things that will make my parents love me. I never achieved that."

Creating a self-care plan

The last step to caring for yourself better is to develop a simple self-care plan that introduces some self-care into your life if you aren't already doing it or brings better balance to the current self-care you're already doing.

Choose a few self-care ideas that you want to incorporate into your life, particularly in the areas that need attention. You can improve things that you are not doing well enough (for example, sleep eight hours a night instead of six) as well as introduce new ideas (such as taking a walk three times a week for 30 minutes). Keep it simple so as to better set yourself up for success. Striving for balance in the overall plan is important.

Here are tips on how to think about a self-care plan to best set yourself up for success:

>> **Be aware of the challenges in getting started.** Your awareness of what you don't do well or enough of is already the first step for tipping the balance more positively but think about how to address any challenges.

>> **Establish a support system.** Enlisting others to help you with the challenges and to cheer you on is extremely important. For example, having a walking buddy will make your commitment to this self-care practice stronger as well as address your physical and social needs.

>> **Devise a method of keeping yourself accountable.** Keeping yourself accountable helps prevent slippage or excuses from creeping in and supports your commitment to self-care. Use a planner or ask someone to be your accountability partner.

>> **Be patient with yourself.** Don't try to do it all at once and overwhelm yourself. Think about how you would support a friend and then grant yourself that same kindness.

As you create your self-care plan, keep these tips in mind and be realistic on what you think you can achieve. Incorporate these new self-care ideas gradually into your daily life. And remember:

>> If it seems like a chore or produces more burden on getting other things accomplished or is producing stress, then it is not self-care.

>> If your self-care practices have become routine or mindless, then they are not self-care.

TIP

You need not find or introduce new self-care practices (although that can be good too). Instead, rediscover your current practices with a renewed sense of intention and presence.

Self-care is about loving yourself and treating yourself well because you deserve it. In this way, you show up in the best version of yourself for yourself and for others — not a tired, sad, or compromised version of yourself. And at end of life, you may often think of yourself as tired, sad, and compromised. That's okay. Because there will be moments when you are someplace or with others, then it will be easy to let who you are on the inside come out and really shine.

4

Social Preparation

Discover how good care requires social connection and community.

Create a support network of care for you, your loved ones, and your caregivers.

Explore the changing nature of relationships at the end of life.

Consider leaving a meaningful legacy to those you love.

Chapter **14**

Connecting to My Community

S ocial connection is a basic human need for our overall health and well-being. Just like shelter, food, and water, it is a necessity for survival. Having more of it helps us to grow and thrive.

As human beings, we have a need to be in community. This has personal benefits for our emotional and social well-being as well as immense benefits for our community and society at large. The ability to form social connections enables us to communicate and cooperate effectively, efficiently, and productively with others. Social connection is essential in life, and even more so, at the end of life when so much of our ability to function and be in this world depends upon the assistance and help of others. Our social community and social skills are critical to the care we will receive at end of life.

This chapter is about caring for each other as a community, showing that at end of life you cannot do it alone, and how good care depends upon our ability to connect and maintain social relationships with others.

Humans Are Social Creatures

Human beings are a social species. We are hard-wired for social connections because they basically have helped us to survive, reproduce, and thrive throughout our evolutionary history.

Many animals of all types are social, like the lions and ants shown in Figure 14-1, but apparently, compared to other animals, humans are intensely social. According to Dr. Joan Silk, a primatologist and anthropologist at Arizona State University, about two-thirds of mammal species live alone and not in groups. Individuals only meet up to mate; then the females go off and raise the children alone. The remaining one-third of mammals do live in social groups.

FIGURE 14-1:
Humans may be the most social animal.

A human infant cannot live on its own from the moment of birth. In fact, we need the help of others throughout our entire life. A person can't live on their own without interaction and help from other people — at least, not in a way without being negatively affected mentally and emotionally. Even in order to meet our own needs — even if the needs are as basic as just survival — we still require communication, interaction, and socialization with others to live happy and fulfilling lives.

Social connection is essential to our overall well-being. We need to interact with others, form bonds, and have deep, meaningful relationships. We are most comfortable when we're connected. We find great joy in sharing stories. We feel intensely close with others when we can share our experiences and deep feelings. And we find deep satisfaction in working together and achieving a goal. Research studies have shown that on average, people who have strong social connections are happier, healthier, and live longer than those who don't.

It is clear that the quality and quantity of an individual's social relationships are linked to mental health, yet research has also shown social connection influences health outcomes and increases the odds of survival by 50 percent. In other words, the influence of social relationships on mortality risk is comparable to other risk factors such as smoking or alcohol consumption. Therefore, a lack of social connection, or *social disconnection*, diminishes benefits and leads to poor health and other negative outcomes. Loneliness and social isolation are associated with a greater risk of cardiovascular disease, dementia, stroke, depression, and anxiety.

The advantages of social connection go beyond just individual well-being in that they have a positive impact on communities and society as a whole. Social connections allow us to communicate and collaborate with others. By working together, we are able to achieve more than we could individually. Human cooperation and collaboration address societal issues of public health, community safety, economic prosperity, and government. These are the foundations of a social, collaborative, and productive society. Therefore, social connections also have immense societal benefits as well.

We need each other.

LESSONS FROM THE COVID-19 PANDEMIC

While social connection had been declining for decades prior to the COVID-19 pandemic, the onset of the pandemic, with its lockdowns and stay-at-home orders, was a critical time during which the issue of connection came to the forefront of public consciousness, raising awareness about this critical and ongoing public health concern.

Many of us felt lonely or isolated in a way we had never experienced before. We postponed or canceled meaningful life moments and celebrations like birthdays, graduations, and marriages. Children's education shifted online — and they missed out on the many benefits of interacting with their friends. Many people lost jobs and homes. We were unable to visit our children, siblings, parents, or grandparents. Many lost loved

(continued)

(continued)

ones. We experienced feelings of anxiety, stress, fear, sadness, grief, anger, and pain through the loss of these moments, rituals, celebrations, and relationships.

Although the COVID-19 pandemic was a collective experience, it impacted certain populations differently. Frontline workers had a different experience than those who could work from home. Parents managing their own work and their children's online school had a different experience than single young people unable to interact in-person with friends. And those at greater risk of severe COVID-19, including older individuals, those living in nursing homes, and people with underlying health conditions, faced unique challenges.

Emerging data suggests that people with close and positive familial connections may have had a different experience than those without.

2023 Our Epidemic of Loneliness and Isolation/The U.S. Department of Health & Human Services

Creating a Community of Care

As people live longer, the challenge becomes how to support and care for an aging population. The issues of aging center on access to healthcare, social support, and appropriate living arrangements for older people. Addressing these issues is essential for creating an inclusive, supportive society for all age groups, requiring mutual respect and cooperation by everyone.

Needing each other

According to the United Nations (UN), intergenerational solidarity is essential for achieving sustainable development and addressing the challenges of an aging population. The UN defines *intergenerational solidarity* as follows:

"A relationship of sharing, mutual respect, and cooperation between generations, based on the recognition that the needs and interests of younger and older people are interdependent and that both have a contribution to make to the well-being of society."

This definition highlights the mutual dependence and mutual benefit that under-lies intergenerational solidarity, as well as the importance of recognizing and valuing the contributions of all age groups to society. It involves actions such as resource sharing, knowledge, and expertise between generations. The UN emphasizes the role of intergenerational solidarity in promoting social cohesion and building stronger, more inclusive communities.

Intergenerational solidarity relies on the social connections and shared responsibility between people of different generations. When these social connections are based on mutual respect, support, and cooperation, they can be an important source of learning, enrichment, and support for all age groups.

The bottom line is the old need the young, and the young need the old. We all need each other.

Allowing others to care

We need the help of others throughout our entire life, and we are completely taken care of at the beginning and end of life. From birth through to young adulthood, we grow from being completely dependent on others to being independent. Then at the end of life, we transition in reverse, moving from independent to dependent. It is our ending state meeting again our beginning state, creating the full cycle of life. Truly understanding and accepting this concept can ease the transition as you age, experience loss, and prepare for end of life.

Initially, you may try to continue to do as much as you can on your own. It is natural to want to retain control and autonomy over your decisions and actions. You ask for help only when absolutely necessary, even becoming frustrated and angry at yourself and others. You may get annoyed at family members and friends constantly asking if you need help. *Can I do this for you? Can I get that for you?* Communication between you and your loved ones may become awkward and strained. You don't want to ask for help, and others are cautious of offering help. Everyone is nervous and wary.

Eventually the time comes when certain tasks or activities that you once did with ease become increasingly difficult for you. Instead of constantly asking for help, you either cede the responsibility or you just give it up. This is hard. It is a hard change from the way you are used to operating in life.

At end of life, when you come to rely upon the help and care of other people for almost everything, the social connections you've established prior become important in your care — not only to continue to live well but to die well too.

REMEMBER

Giving and receiving care is all about love. We give care because we love another. I help you because I care about you. Therefore, when we receive care and help from others, it is an expression of love and care.

Receiving care from others while acknowledging their love and fostering the social connection is possible. In this way, we keep the bond of the relationship strong and nurture the love which drives the good care.

Feeling good about your care

Good care begins with kindness and gratitude.

Kindness fosters social connection. Intuitively, this makes sense, but this idea is also supported by research. Dr. Julianne Holt-Lunstad, a professor of psychology and neuroscience, and director of the Social Connection and Health Lab at Brigham Young University, has conducted extensive research into methods for promoting social connection. One such research project found that small acts of kindness performed for neighbors has the potential to reduce loneliness, social isolation, and social anxiety, and to promote relationships instead of conflict with neighbors.

In fact, in a separate research study, acts of kindness were shown to have *greater and distinct* benefits for social connection over just general social interaction. And another feature of acts of kindness, supported by research, is that it can be contagious. People who have received acts of kindness are more likely to be more generous themselves.

When you are kind to another, this small act generates positive, warm feelings, both in you as the giver and in the other person as the receiver. The recipient feels good for being seen and acknowledged. And you, the giver, feel good too, for being generous in words or action. It is a moment of connection between two people. A moment of kindness and happiness. Therefore, being kind does foster social connection and creates a more positive environment for all. There is only an upside to being kind.

Gratitude is also a prosocial intervention. Gratitude not only helps you find new relationships but also binds you closer to relationships you already have by reinforcing positive interactions. Jo-Ann Tsang, Ph.D., professor of psychology and neuroscience at Baylor University, researches gratitude in interpersonal relationships. She defines gratitude as a response that happens when someone else gives you something good. "Gratitude is social and interpersonal because you feel grateful for something someone has given to you."

For example, if someone else has helped you in some way, it generates a feeling of goodness and generosity — *gratitude* — within you to recognize the giver. It turns out that that expression of gratitude — *showing thanks* — to the giver is the key to social connection.

Gratitude is a prosocial give-and-take behavioral response. Evoking gratitude benefits both parties. You feel good because someone has given something to you or done something for you. You feel happy and generous. In turn, you offer an expression of gratitude (see Figure 14-2), which can be as simple as saying thanks, an acknowledgment and appreciation for the good act. That recognition makes the giver feel good and creates positive feelings within them. They are now more likely to be generous with their time, resources, and feelings moving forward. Therefore, gratitude maintains, benefits, and *strengthens* social relationships.

FIGURE 14-2: Gift-giving makes the giver and the receiver feel good.

REMEMBER

Acts of kindness and gratitude can be big and small. They do not have to be grand gestures. Even small acts can have big impacts.

TIP

Perhaps, you aren't comfortable with outward expressions of kindness or gratitude. Maybe your personality is not expressive or effusive; that's okay. Start small, very small. Others who know you well will recognize a small act of kindness or gratitude as a big gesture. Thank you.

Kindness and gratitude are about honoring each other and the relationships you have with others. These values are so important to embrace throughout your entire life, but more so at the end of life. You want to feel good about the care and help you are receiving from others.

I Don't Need Help! I Can Do It Myself!

I feel it important to acknowledge how difficult it may be for you to ask for help. This concept is a challenging one for many people to adjust to at end of life — especially for those who have not operated this way for most of their life prior.

Asking for help

One reason you may have difficulty asking for help is because we are conditioned by society to be strong and independent. We are not a community-oriented society, but a very individual-oriented society. We are taught to admire qualities like strength, endurance, resilience, and independence. "Do it on your own on your own terms." Or even, "Tough it out." But these concepts do not work well for us at the end of life when living well is about interdependency.

Even worse is if you perceive asking for help as a sign of weakness or failure in yourself. Would you get angry or yell at a baby because they can't feed themself? Infants are unable to feed themselves; they simply don't have the ability to do so. You may be angry at the mess a baby has made, but you aren't angry at the baby. Similarly, when you are at the end of life, old or sick, you may not be able to feed yourself. You will have lost the ability to do so. It is not a weakness or failure or inadequacy on your part, you simply cannot do it. It is part of the process of dying.

Another reason you may find it hard to ask for help is that you may see yourself as a giver, not a receiver. Many people describe themselves as givers and admit to being bad receivers of help themselves. They don't like to ask for help from others even when they really need it. Think about why this is so for you.

NEW

For whatever reason that asking for help is difficult for you, it's okay. It is difficult; it is challenging. But understand that asking for help is not a reflection of you as a person or an individual with needs. Asking for help is an opportunity for a moment of connection, a chance to create, maintain, or strengthen a social bond with the person you ask to help you.

End of life — dying — is hard enough. You don't have to do it alone.

Gifting a good feeling

When you help someone out, you know that good feeling you get because you did a good thing? That's part of the reason why you offer help to others — because *it makes you feel good inside*. The action makes you feel you are a good person and reinforces the positive image you have of yourself.

NEW

In my work as an end-of-life doula, I always tell my patients and clients to let others help them because *doing so gifts them a good feeling*. Give others an opportunity to feel good about themselves and the work that they're doing.

At end of life, when we're able to "do" so little, this is a small gift that you can give over and over again. It takes no physical effort and is free to give. Yet its value is immeasurable and limitless. It is boundless and rooted in care and love. So, give a gift and ask for help.

Choosing to be alone

At end of life, you can't be alone and care for yourself. As I emphasize throughout this chapter, you need others to help take care of you. However, I acknowledge that, outside of your care, you may want to be alone.

Maybe there are times when you would like to be alone to be quiet; to be with your thoughts; to not worry about how others are thinking, perceiving, and acting toward you. That's okay. Preparing for end of life is work. You're working hard. You, your mind, and your body are preparing to die. And you can still choose how to spend your time, energy, and resources while you're still living: alone or with company.

Very rarely, I have heard of someone asking to die alone. I respect that if that's your decision. You have the choice. If you want to do so, just decide to die alone for reasons that feel right for you.

REMEMBER

Out there are people who love and care about you, whether you realize it or not — maybe an old friend, a neighbor, your caseworker, a chosen family member, or a person in your community. You may be surprised at who shows up. Let them in.

Chapter **15**

Creating a Support Network

Having a good support network in place can make all the difference in how you face end of life. In your attitude, mood, and feelings about what's going on and what's happening to you. In the care you receive. In the connectedness and community you have with others. In knowing that you are not alone as you experience the final chapter of your life.

Support comes from a network of people — the web of community that you've built up over decades of living and all the social relationships in your life. Most everyone you know cares about you to some degree; therefore, let them support you to some degree as well. Each person plays a different role and offers a different level of care and support, giving what they're able and comfortable to do. Some become intimately involved in your care, while others may just cook some meals or run errands. All this support is needed and helpful.

Relying on just one or two people places too heavy of a burden on just a couple of people. You know that word — burden. We hear it a lot when people talk about being sick or old, and dying. Well, it can be a burden to a few, but less so if a network of people are offering support. So let everyone in and let them help.

In this chapter, I discuss why a support network is most useful at end of life, explain how to create one, and offer online resources and apps that are available to you and your network of care.

Caring Takes a Village

The phrase *caring takes a village* highlights the concept of community caregiving. It involves the participation and support of multiple people, rather than just one or two. It focuses on teamwork and shared responsibility — two crucial elements to the well-being of everyone involved — to bring about good care.

WARNING

Having just a couple of people responsible for caregiving places too much work, stress, and burden on too few. This is especially true when the extent of caregiving is extended or unknown. When this situation occurs, extra anxiety and uncertainty are added on top of all the other emotions of aging, illness, and loss. This is especially true for the caregivers, who may include friends or family for whom caregiving is not their full-time profession and who may not know how to handle the extra emotions and responsibilities of long-term caregiving. When this happens, the quality of care may be affected or reduced.

REMEMBER

Setting up and maintaining a strong support network for end of life is critically important.

TIP

I recommend doing this ahead of time instead of letting it form as needed. A common problem when something needs to get done is not knowing who to call for help. Having a support network not only establishes who is available and how they can help, but expands the resources available to you. You may be surprised to find out who is willing to be involved and the experience they bring. For example, a pickleball partner may have previously navigated the illness and death of a loved one and may become an emotional support person to you. Alternatively, it could be a neighbor from a faith group that offers home-cooked meal delivery to families in similar situations. You never know who are willing to help and what they can do unless you share what's going on and let them in.

Setting up a support network also allows you and your loved ones to prepare for and anticipate any challenges or emergencies that may arise. A time of crisis is not the time to be scrambling for what to do or thinking about decisions that need to be made.

As important, a support network also supports your caregivers, providing much needed respite for them. Sharing the responsibility and workload of care becomes essential when your needs become greater. Outside of the medical support provided by the doctors and nurses, all other support comes from your family, friends, or community.

A strong support network of care is a more compassionate and loving system for everyone involved. It does the following:

>> Offers emotional, social, spiritual, financial, and logistical support

>> Comes from a variety of sources, in which each person does what they can and are best able to offer

>> Fills in the gaps of care, beyond what any one person can do

>> Reduces caregiver burden on the primary caregivers

>> Allows for respite and self-care for the caregivers because they need to take care of themselves too

>> Is a collaborative effort; hence, it feels better for everyone to "be in it together"

>> Copes with difficulties, challenges, and changes better than one person alone

>> Reinforces the sense of community and social connections

>> Ensures the best care possible for the person in need

NEW

Good care is based on a reciprocal model of care. It is a community-based model of: I show up for you, and you show up for me. We care for each other, and we pay it forward.

Implementing the Ring Theory

A good support network is an understanding of who's involved and the roles everyone plays in your care. It is a collaborative system based on shared responsibility with the goal of providing the best care for you.

I offer one simple framework for thinking about your support network that works for identifying and organizing your people. Clinical psychologist Susan Silk and mediator Barry Goldman developed the *Ring Theory*, a framework for navigating the complex emotions and relationships surrounding a person in crisis or traumatic loss. It is designed to help individuals in your support network to provide the best possible support to you.

Identifying your circles of care

To understand the Ring Theory, begin by identifying the potential people in your support network. These steps can guide you:

1. **Draw several concentric circles, maybe four or five, as shown in Figure 15-1.**

2. **In the center ring, write the name of the person experiencing crisis, trauma, or loss.**

   In this case, this would be *you*, so you can write your name in the center.

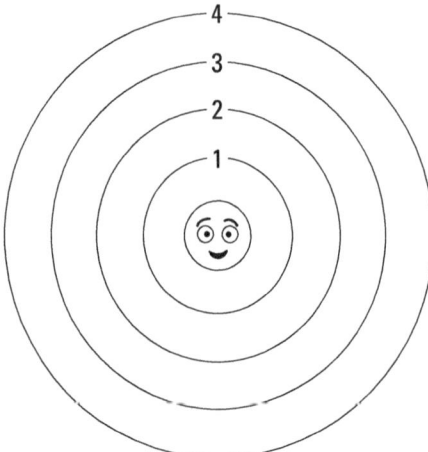

FIGURE 15-1: The Ring Theory exercise can help you identify who's in your support network.

3. **In Ring 1, write the names of your closest people.**

   These will be the ones who show up and are involved in your care. They're people you can call and depend upon to help. They also "get" you. The people in Ring 1 are usually only a small handful of people and may include your spouse, children, best friends, and parents. They may be your chosen family members and may not include biological family members. This is your *inner circle of care.*

4. **In Ring 2, write the names of the next closest people to you.**

   These are people close to you, but not the closest. They may be involved in your care but have smaller roles or responsibilities. They will show up if they can. They are people who you think could help, but are not the first people you think of. They can be your parents or extended family members. They can be good friends, or close friends who are busy or live afar. Close neighbors could be included in this ring. This is your *outer circle of care.*

5. **In Ring 3, write the names of people in your life who could lend a hand.**

   These may be people who you see regularly or are, in general, kind people. They could help with small tasks, such as running an errand or coming by to sit on short notice. They may be people you might have gotten to be better friends with if you had more time in your life. These can be distant relatives or estranged family members. They can be colleagues, neighbors, and acquaintances. They can be fellow churchgoers or people in your religious or spiritual community. They can be the people from a social activity you do or used to do, such as a book club or a running group. This is the *farthest circle of care*.

6. **Let Ring 4 contain everybody else.**

   You don't really have to identify these people as they won't be important in your care.

REMEMBER

As you go through this exercise, please be honest with yourself in evaluating the relationships with the people in your life. This is important in understanding what role each person can play and what they can give. Make no assumptions.

Dumping out

Look at your Ring Theory diagram from the preceding section. The person in the center ring — *you* — can say anything you want to anyone, anywhere. You can kvetch and complain and whine and moan and curse the heavens. You can say, "Life is unfair" and "Why me?" You can be angry or frustrated, and have a temper tantrum. This is the one payoff for being in the center ring. You get to *dump out* to anyone, anytime.

Everyone else can say those things too, but only to people in larger rings. This means people in the outer circles can complain only to people who are further outside of their own ring.

REMEMBER

Support people must remember that the crisis is about the person in the center circle. If you're a support person, don't speak or act like you know what the center circle person is going through. You simply can't and don't know. You showed up to support them in their sadness and distress in this time of crisis. Honor that. Reserve your emotions of sadness and distress about their situation. You don't want your reactions to be burdensome to the person in crisis. Their role is not to console us.

NEW

The result is that all complaining and negative emotions move outward, away from the person in crisis. Only support and comfort move inward toward the center, as shown in Figure 15-2. In this way, the person in crisis and their caregivers are best supported emotionally to handle the situation.

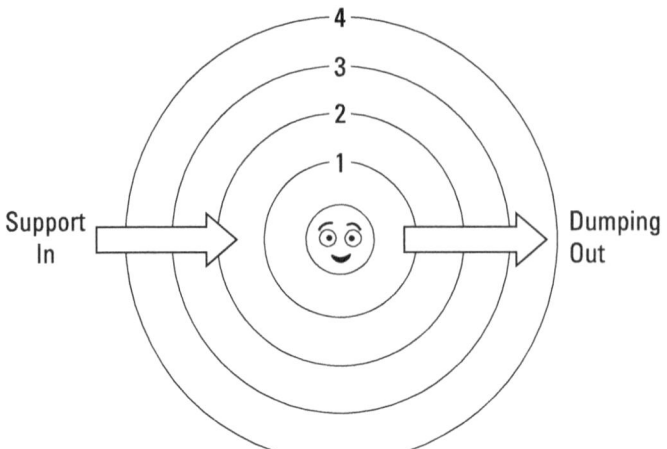

FIGURE 15-2:
Support comes into the person in crisis and dumping goes out.

Support in

When offering support, it can be useful to know what to say and to whom to say it when someone else is in crisis. When you are talking to the person in crisis (the center ring; refer to Figure 15-1) or a person in a ring smaller than yours, the goal is to help.

REMEMBER

Someone else is in trauma or loss. This is about them; this is their crisis. This is not about you. Of course, it may be difficult for you to see your loved one or friend sick or struggling. You may become overwhelmed and emotional, or feel unprepared and scared yourself to see them that way. This may trigger thoughts such as, "Oh my god! That could be me." This is a very normal response to seeing trauma. But remember, whatever you are feeling can't even come close to what the person in crisis is experiencing. Therefore, you must deal with your reaction and feelings, especially if they are upsetting, later at another time to someone who can support you. If you have showed up for the person in crisis — the person in the center circle — then you have showed up to support and offer comfort, love, and laughter.

NEW

As a support person, you may feel awkward or scared that you'll say the wrong thing. Ask yourself if what you are about to say is likely to provide comfort and support. If not, don't say it.

TIP

Here are a few examples of what to say to or what to do with someone in crisis:

>> "I'm sorry for what you are going through."

>> "I'm here for you."

>> "This must be really hard for you."

>> "Can I bring you your favorite ___ (food, stuffed animal, book)?"

>> Give a hug or hold their hand.

>> Recall a happy time or a funny moment together.

>> Just sit in silence and be with them.

Listening is often more helpful than talking. If you're showing up for the center circle person, you're showing up for a person *in need.* And you don't know what those needs are unless you listen.

Listening is the greatest gift you can give to a person who is in crisis.

Examples of what *not* to say to or do with someone in crisis include the following:

>> "You are going to be just fine."

>> "Don't talk like that! I don't want to hear you talking like that."

>> "This all happened for a reason."

>> "Be strong. You'll get through this."

>> "This is hard on me."

>> "I know how you feel."

>> "Here's what I would do if I were you."

>> Don't talk about how this is making you feel.

>> Don't offer a similar story about someone else.

>> Don't question or challenge decisions that have been made.

>> Don't lecture or give advice.

People who are suffering from trauma don't need advice. First, they are getting the advice they need from their doctors or other professionals in the field. Second, don't relate a story of something similar that happened to someone else. They do not need to know how your father, aunt, or friend handled a similar situation. Even though you think the story might be helpful, the circumstances are not the same. Explaining how someone else handled their battle with cancer is irrelevant and distracting. Besides, it removes the focus away from the person in crisis. This is their crisis; respect that.

REMEMBER

If you make a mistake and say a wrong thing, apologize. Say you are sorry immediately and sincerely. After the aggrieved acknowledges your apology, move on. Don't apologize again or make a big deal of it. You came to offer support, so make up for it now. Move on to something lighter, brighter, and happier.

Being the center of attention

As an end-of-life doula, I use Ring Theory all the time with my clients and their families to help them see themselves within this framework. It is a shift from how they may usually interact with others, but the results benefit everyone involved, emotionally and socially.

The hardest shift I've seen my clients make is putting themselves in the center circle (refer to Figure 15-1). Making themselves the focal point of everyone else is difficult. In response to a recalcitrant person, I say, "Com'on!!! You are dying! You deserve to be selfish and the focus of everyone else's attention. If there was ever a time in life to be so, the time is now."

NEW

Yes, this is absolutely true. End of life is not "business as usual." End of life is death; it is permanent. If only for this one time, please allow yourself to be the center of attention. Allow yourself to be taken care of. In fact, try to enjoy the luxury of the love, care, and attention that others want to give you.

Being the center circle is not only good for you, but it is good for the people in your circles of care. They want to take care of you. They want you to be as happy as possible. They want you to do the things that you want to do — to benefit yourself, not them. They want you to have as much joy in your life as possible until you die. They want all the things for you that you want for them in life, but this is their last chance to give it to you. This is where the people in your circles of care are coming from.

I've experienced that families who fully embraced care in this way coped better with death afterwards. They were able to express and give their love. They felt great peace of mind knowing that they gave you their best in caring for you. They experienced less regret and fewer what-ifs. The emotions of death are less complicated and more pure. For your family and loved ones left behind, all this leads to healthier coping and healing after death.

So be the center circle.

MARGARET'S STORY

Margaret was only in her 60s but had been battling ovarian cancer for 20 years. Now, she was dying from leukemia from the years of chemotherapy and radiation treatments.

Margaret was a petite, lovely woman, full of care and concern for others. She was a beloved community member and mother, adored by her two adult children. Margaret's daughter handled much of the care management and logistics while also working a full-time job. Margaret's son moved into her one-bedroom apartment so that he could care for her full-time.

While the three of them considered themselves close, Margaret had never really spoken much about dying with her two children. She clearly felt the disruption and burden that her illness was placing on her children's lives. When I asked her what she envisioned at death, Margaret replied, "I am a quiet woman. I thought I could just slip away while everyone else is going about their business."

"Really?" Did she think that she could be dying in the bedroom and everyone else would just be working — doing their own thing — while she lay dying?

Yes. Margaret thought this was possible.

We spoke much about the Ring Theory after this conversation. Margaret opened her heart, had discussions with her children, and envisioned a death worthy of who she was in life. In the end, Margaret was not ignored at death, but surrounded by those most important to her, cared for and loved.

Her son wrote to me, "I'm very grateful my mother was able to have things unfold as they did, just as she wanted ♥."

Adapted from https://www.latimes.com/opinion/story/la-timeless/ how-not-to-say-the-wrong-thing

Gathering Tools and Apps for Your Village

A good support network entails many people helping out, fulfilling tasks, and coming by to spend time and offer respite. Organizing and tracking all the people who are helping out can be a lot of work. And then there are all the people in your outer circles of care who would like to know how you are doing. Keeping up with all the social communication and coordination can become overwhelming. Having tools to help can be useful.

Many simple solutions are workable and inexpensive. A good old dry erase board or notebook are great tools in care management. A large calendar displayed in a central location is very effective for scheduling. And a group email or chat can manage communication needs.

If you're open to technology, many online tools and apps can help track or stream-line communication and care management. I offer examples of some useful apps available when I was writing this book. However, be aware that technology and apps change quickly. Some go away while new ones are launched. Be sure to research and see what's currently available and what would work best for your purposes and needs.

Communication and organization

Keeping everyone in your circles of care up-to-date can become a major chal-lenge. Everyone wants to know how you are, what they can do to help, and when they can see you. At times, it can feel great to have so many people concerned for your well-being; at other times, it can feel overwhelming to respond to so many people saying the same thing over and over again.

While group emails or chats can be great for disseminating information with a single "send" button, some apps aid in communication as well as provide other organizational tools.

Common features of these online apps include the following:

>> A calendar to organize appointments, visits, and reminders

>> An in-app messaging system to keep everyone updated about your health with announcements and important developments

>> A task request system for organizing help, both asking and receiving, and delegating tasks

>> Additional features like document storage, photo galleries, and a wellness journal

TIP

The need for coordinating your support network through an app is most useful near the end of life, when you have less energy, your condition is worse, and the demands are greater. Unfortunately, if you haven't set it up already by this time, it is too late to invest the amount of time and effort required for setup. If you're interested in using a support app, set it up early, so it's ready to go when you need it most.

Examples of apps in this category: CaringBridge, Lotsa Helping Hands, Caring Village, and Ianacare.

Medication management

Medication management apps assist you and your caregiving team with managing what may be an extensive array of pills that need to be taken at various times throughout the day. Taking the proper doses at the correct times ensures you are maintaining your health and well-being.

Common features of medication management apps include:

>> Dosage tracking

>> Refill alerts

>> Pill identification

>> Medication history

Users are also able to create a personalized medication schedule with schedule reminders. Some apps also offer sharing of information with healthcare providers and your support network to keep everyone up-to-date.

Examples of apps in this category: Medisafe, MyMeds Adhere, and Med Guide.

Resources and community

You can find a lot of information online for you and your caregivers, especially if you have questions or need tips, advice, and information on a specific issue, disease, or problem. Or if you need to find extra services or resources in your local area. Or if you are navigating a specific challenge and are not sure how to handle it, there are plenty of community forums to address your question. A ton of information is also available on the internet from professionals and nonprofit organizations.

Various online communities have formed around other people going through what you're going through, whether you're the person in need or the caregiver. Sometimes expressing your feelings or talking to a community that isn't too close to you is helpful. Or perhaps you would like to hear from people who truly are experiencing a similar situation. Nowadays, you can find online communities and forums for practically everything.

Examples of apps in this category: AARP, caregiving.com, Smart Patients, and Daily Caring.

Chapter **16**

Valuing and Healing Relationships

At every stage in life, people come and go. You meet new people. Depending on the location, time, interests, personalities, and needs of both parties, some of these casual introductions grow and develop into something more. You make new friends. Most of these friendships last only for a finite time or exist in certain contexts. A few may deepen and last a lifetime. Yet, every person you get to know is a social connection at a certain point in time. They become part of a social circle in your ongoing life. It is wonderful.

NEW

Yet it is the nature of life that circumstances change, people change, and thus, relationships change. This happens throughout your life. At the end of life, not only will the nature of your social relationships change, but they will eventually end due to your death. For you, thinking about this can be painful and filled with great sadness. However, in my experience, I have found this intense grief is often accompanied by a strong feeling of gratitude for having had those relationships. These two strong forces — grief and gratitude — complement each other.

In this chapter, I describe the changing nature of relationships at end of life, show how to appreciate the relationships we have, and offer guidance on how to heal from the pain that exists in our relationships or situations so that we can face death with peace of mind.

Understanding that Relationships Change

It is natural to want to keep the good times going when life is good. When life is easy and your relationships are good, you feel happy. But remember in Chapter 12, I talk about life being like a roller coaster. And it wouldn't be a roller coaster if it didn't have ups and downs, and twists and turns. You never know what lies ahead, what unexpected changes await on the path, and how you will react. This applies to life in general as well as to your social connections with others.

TIP

Pausing and evaluating the relationships in your life at different points is always a good practice. Taking time to identify who is in your life now, who you have lost, and who could potentially become more is helpful in understanding the changing nature of relationships. And especially at end of life, in doing so, it becomes crystal clear who is important to you and who you are important to.

Appreciating friends

The connections between people depend very much on circumstances. When the circumstances align, it can be easy to make friends, have friends, and be good friends. So, appreciate the ease of a good social life when it happens.

However, relationships change. You lose friends too. People move, you have less time, your interests change, the friendship is not as mutual or beneficial as it once was. For whatever reason, your social connections with people can and will change. This is natural and expected. Sometimes the loss in friendship is a mutual decision or a mutual drifting apart. Other times, a friendship ends because of a decision by one person, either you or the other person. Sometimes, you only realize a friendship has ended after you've been *ghosted* (cutting off contact with someone without telling them). This can be more painful and is more like a loss, leaving you with feelings of "what ifs" and "what could have been." Yet, for a time, there was a loveliness to the relationship — a mutual togetherness — that was good for both of you. Instead of focusing on the relationship that no longer is, appreciate what you had for the time that you had it.

Once circumstances change, it takes a concerted effort and desire by both parties to keep a relationship close. It must be a reciprocal effort. Thus, while you lose some friends and make new friends, value the people who choose to continue to be in your life. Having more than just a handful who stay on with you is rare. So, appreciate even more those who remain in your life.

As it is now clear, there is space for appreciation of all your past and current relationships, no matter their nature or how long they last.

Making new friends

You may be thinking, "Why bother making new friends when I am just going to die soon?!" This is true. It is perfectly valid to be thinking this. Most friendships take a long time to develop into something mutually beneficial and meaningful. With limited time left to live, you may be thinking that you don't have the time or care enough to bring new people into your life.

In my work as an end-of-life doula, I have observed that normal relationship building is accelerated at end of life. I've considered a couple reasons why this is. First, perhaps with limited time left to live, you are more honest with yourself and your feelings. You no longer have the time, energy, or concern to play games, pretend, or have an agenda. You just are. This is one of the reasons I'm drawn to work with people at end of life. There is such sincerity in the interactions with others; people are more authentic. I have found it possible to develop a deep relationship with others in a relatively short period of time, a level of trust and intimacy that would take years to reach in "normal" relationships. Second, you need help at end of life, and new people can help. They can benefit not only you but your family and caregivers too. You and your support network will need knowledge, support, and respite in living and caring for you as you approach the end of life. By welcoming new people into your life to help, you create and are more open to new social relationships.

I'm not saying that every new person that comes into your life needs to, should, or will even become something more, a friend possibly. Maybe it'll happen; maybe it won't. Even if you don't have the time, energy, or care to invest in a potential new relationship, all I ask is you keep your heart open. Just be open to letting others in and seeing what happens. It can be a gift to you and others.

Losing friends

As you age or are ill, you are likely to see immediate changes in your current relationships. Friends — even good friends — may not be able to cope with what's happening to you and no longer know how to interact with you. This is a common experience.

To understand this situation more deeply, imagine you have a friend who's your running buddy, and on those runs, the two of you speak about everything. You feel surprisingly close to your running friend because of what you feel is a deep sharing of your life. Then you become ill and have to stop running. The friend doesn't know how to interact with you in another way and outside of running. Or the friend doesn't have the time to exercise and also be friends with you in another context. So while you still want to be friends and are willing to try to be friends in another way, the friend cannot adjust. What you thought was an important relationship disappears.

Relationships end or change at end of life due to many complicated, subtle, and sometimes, not so obvious reasons. Perhaps, seeing you sick and frail triggers something in others about their own mortality. Or maybe, seeing you reminds them of how another good friend died. Or maybe, they just don't have the coping skills for losing you, so they pre-empt the goodbye.

NEW

For whatever reasons, the resultant emotions and reactions in others are about them. Not about you. You did not cause them to feel a certain way. They must own their own feelings as you must own your own feelings. The only person you can be responsible for is yourself. All you can do is keep your heart open and invite others in. Hopefully, they can keep their hearts open too.

Yet, accepting and adjusting to any resulting change or loss in your relationships can be difficult, often because they come about due to factors beyond your control. The loss of these friendships compounds the losses and grief you're already experiencing.

While the loss of friendships will fill you with great sadness, appreciate the gift of friendship that you had with that person while you had it. That friend contributed something to your life through stories, laughter, good times, and intimacy. It was wonderful. And so, while the friend can't accompany you on the next phase of life — the end of life (as depicted in Figure 16-1) — knowing and having had them in your life was a gift.

FIGURE 16-1:
Sometimes our friends can't accompany us on our end-of-life journey.

Healing Relationships

Not all relationships are healthy, nor do they all end well. Relationships are complex and often have deep-seated emotions associated with them. Carrying the pain of a relationship with you is not good for your emotional well-being.

How you go about healing from the pain of past and current relationships is a very personal process. For some, it can be an inner process of introspection and healing. For others, healing may involve the other party in mutual retrospective forgiveness. What brings healing, closure, or forgiveness to you is a very personal process given the nature of the relationship that caused the pain and the depth of the pain.

I cannot begin to know the burden you carry with the social pain from your relationships, but I have seen how it can weigh on you at end of life. It is heavy. Similarly to emotional baggage (which is discussed in Chapter 11), it is important to address your relationship baggage, and the hurt from past relationships which pains you, in order to have more peace of mind at death.

You can also choose to nurture and appreciate the healthy relationships you are in while releasing yourself from the toxic ones which you have and are unhealthy. In this way, you are living the kind of life now that allows you to arrive at the end of life with peace of mind.

In the nearby sidebar, I recount Mark's story through end of life. I so appreciated the closure Mark sought with his relationships before he died. It was beautiful that he wanted to acknowledge his friends — both past and present — and offer gratitude for the closeness they had. Unfortunately for Mark, it was a slow, arduous process. Most letters were easy to write, filled with gratitude, and well received; others were more difficult to write because of the associated guilt. Mark thought he had the time to make amends, but Death came for him sooner than he expected. Upon reflection, Mark taught me a valuable lesson: to cherish the people in my life and tie up the loose ends of my social relationships.

MARK'S STORY

Mark was 55 years old and diagnosed with amyotrophic lateral sclerosis (ALS; commonly known as Lou Gehrig's disease). By the time I met him, he was in a wheelchair, could no longer speak, and had severe communication challenges. He would type with one knuckle of a clawed and weakened hand. He was amazing!

One of the major issues for him was to create a sense of closure, in particular with regard to the relationships in his life. "Although the vast majority of friends have risen to the challenge created by my illness, a small number have drifted away, which makes me sad."

Mark wanted to tie up the interpersonal relationships of his life. There were old friends that he had lost touch with and relationships with girlfriends that ended badly. Most friends had risen to the challenge created by ALS, but some had drifted away. Mark wanted to connect to his past and current friends, and acknowledge the role the relationships had played in his life. "The goal would be to simply say thank you for being part of my life."

Unfortunately, time was too short for Mark at the pace he was able to work. He died one evening unexpectedly, leaving so much unsaid and undone.

In the next section, I offer one method that is a path to healing based on an ancient Hawaiian tradition of reconciliation.

The Ho'oponopono Prayer

"A tangled fishing line requires hours of tedious unraveling, probably a lost fish or two, and the potential loss of the entire fishing line or net. When tacking, a tangled rope can snap a boat's mast. And for a sea turtle, entanglement in the net means death."

—James A. Wall Jr. and Ronda Roberts Callister,
Ho'oponopono: Some Lessons from Hawaiian Mediation

Drawing from these observations, the Hawaiians use the term *entanglement* to describe interpersonal conflicts. The process for bringing resolution between parties, or *disentanglement*, is called ho'oponopono (pronounced HO-oh-Po-no-Po-no). Translated from Hawaiian, *ho'o* means "to make, to cause, or to bring about," and *pono* means "correct, right, in order." Therefore, *ho'oponopono* means "to make right." The Ho'oponopono prayer is about making things right between people.

Ho'oponopono is a simple, traditional Hawaiian method of reconciliation. It is a process of bringing harmony with the people in your life, yourself, and the world around you. It is a practice rooted in the understanding that harmony and balance are essential for your well-being, concepts that are emphasized throughout this book. By addressing and resolving conflicts or the pain you carry with others, you heal and are more positive with yourself and those around you.

Ho'oponopono works by guiding you through a process of introspection and healing. You use this mantra:

I'm sorry. Forgive me. Thank you. I love you.

In the mantra, you acknowledge and take responsibility for any thoughts, actions, or emotions that you may have contributed to conflict or disharmony. Then, ho'oponopono encourages you to take responsibility for your life and actions and to seek harmony through love and gratitude.

Ho'oponopono has a positive impact on relationships. By actively seeking harmony, you heal and strengthen your connection with others. The benefits of practicing ho'oponopono include emotional healing, reduced stress, improved relationships, greater inner peace, and a deeper sense of personal responsibility and self-awareness.

Next, I look at each of the components of ho'oponopono in a little more detail.

I'm sorry

When you say I'm sorry, you acknowledge your part in creating negative situations or feelings, both within yourself and in others.

When you say I'm sorry, you recognize that you are responsible for your own thoughts, beliefs, and actions that contributed to the pain, in yourself and others.

When you say I'm sorry, you realize that you are not being the best version of yourself.

Acknowledging all of this begins the healing process.

I'm sorry for _____.

Forgive me

When you seek forgiveness, it is for yourself, not for others. It is about forgiving yourself and allowing yourself to move forward.

When you seek forgiveness, it is about releasing the negative emotions you may be carrying of anger, guilt, or shame and saying you no longer want to carry the burden.

When you seek forgiveness of another person, it does not mean that they are right or excused for their behavior. You are releasing yourself from the power held over you by their actions, words, and thoughts.

Acknowledging all of this frees you — and the other person — from the entanglement of pain.

Please forgive me for _____.

SALVATORE'S STORY

Salvatore was a 93-year old Italian man, beloved by all. He was described as "an angel" by everyone who knew him because he was always helping people. Now, his house was full of family and friends, coming in and out, to pay their respects to Salvatore in his last days and say goodbye.

Maria, the hospice nurse, expected Salvatore to die that day, within hours. His vitals were so weak; he was showing all the signs and symptoms of imminent death.

Two days later, however, Salvatore was still alive, and the family was in distress with his condition. Maria asked the family repeatedly, *Has everything been taken care of? Is there something unresolved in Salvatore's life that is causing him to hold on?*

No, no, the family said, *We have all said goodbye. The priest has already come.* Then, an uncle said, *What about Pietro?* There had been a big fight and falling out between Salvatore and Pietro 40 years ago. Pietro had once been very close, but no one had thought of Pietro in decades. Maybe this was it.

Pietro was found alive in Sicily, but he was an old man himself. With technology, Pietro faced a dying Salvatore and said, in an old Sicilian dialect: *I forgive you old friend. We have been fools and wasted 40 years of our lives. Please forgive me.*

The call ended. Salvatore took one deep breath, exhaled, and died . . . . The power of forgiveness.

Maria went home that night, contacted all her siblings, and asked for mutual forgiveness for all their past troubles. From that point on, Maria has lived with a different view of life.

Thank you

When you say thank you, you are expressing gratitude and appreciation for all that you have in your life.

When you say thank you, you are treating yourself with kindness.

When you say thank you, you are sharing the happiness or wisdom of your being with others.

Acknowledging all of this begins the growth that comes from every experience.

Thank you for _____.

I love you

When you say I love you, it is an affirmation of the powerful healing force of love.

When you say I love you, it is an affirmation of self-love and accepting yourself just as you are, because to share your love with others, first you must love yourself.

When you say I love you, it is an acknowledgment of unconditional love for yourself, the others involved, and the situation as a whole.

Acknowledging all of this brings true healing, balance, and harmony in you and in relationships with others.

I love you.

Putting it all together

Ho'oponopono transforms negative emotions and thoughts into positive ones and paves the way for deeper understanding and a more meaningful connection with others. The practice encourages you to look inward, to address and heal your own inner conflicts first. What negative emotions and thoughts weigh on you with regard to the other person or situation?

NEW

By acknowledging and taking responsibility for any negative energies or actions you may have contributed, you begin to heal. Then, by introducing thoughts based on understanding, harmony, and love, you bring a more positive energy into your thinking about your relationships. Healing, that initially began from just within yourself, now radiates outwards.

REMEMBER

If you begin to practice ho'oponopono, remember this:

>> Ho'oponopono is simple and universal. Ho'oponopono can be practiced by people of all ages and backgrounds.

>> Ho'oponopono can be done anywhere and at any time. It is a personal practice.

>> The ho'oponopono mantra can be said aloud or silently, whatever resonates with you. Some prefer to chant it in a quiet, meditative space, while others might incorporate it into their daily activities, such as during a walk or while washing the dishes.

>> It is the repetition of the words, which is powerful. Repeating ho'oponopono helps to embed the meaning into your consciousness.

The ancient Ho'oponopono prayer concludes,

"So be well, and as you heal, I say to you: I am sorry for the memories of pain I share with you. I ask your forgiveness for joining my path to yours for healing, I thank you for being here in me, and I love you for being who you are."

Chapter **17**

Leaving a Legacy

L egacy is not a high falutin' idea meant just for wealthy people or celebrities or world leaders. Legacy sounds like a grand concept, but instead, it is a simple concept for everyone. You have a life story, so you have a legacy. Your life story is made up of the events of your life, the work you did, the people you knew and loved, the places you've been, the choices you made, the accomplishments you achieved, the challenges you encountered, and the profound lessons of life you've learned. All these components over the course of your lifetime make up a unique story of you. Legacy is defining the end of the story and what lives on afterwards.

Thinking about your legacy is honoring your life and the contributions you have made to others and the world. Everyone has a legacy. You may not know it. Or you may think your legacy is unimportant, miniscule, or irrelevant. Yet, everyone has a legacy. And you have an opportunity to discover, define, and determine it. You just have to decide if you want to do so or not.

At end of life, even just thinking about your legacy can make all the difference in feeling like your life meant something. This is a pretty powerful thought to have in your mind as you leave this world.

This chapter covers what is legacy, the meaning-making component of exploring legacy, and the different forms of expressions that legacy can take through a legacy project.

Defining Legacy

How you want to be remembered after death is the essence of *legacy*.

NEW

It is your life and your story. You get to determine how that story is remembered after your death. It is not about controlling when or where that story is told. It's about having a say in *what* is told. It is you saying to others, "This is what I want you to remember about me. This is what was important to me. This is who I am."

Legacy has two components: meaning-making and a legacy project. While exploring legacy often leads to the creation of a legacy project, these two elements are not necessarily connected. The meaning-making and the creation of the legacy project can be two stand-alone processes. A person can explore meaning and contemplate their legacy but not be interested in creating a legacy project. Or a person may not connect to the idea of exploring meaning but love the idea of creating a legacy project. Either is fine.

I talk more about each of the processes of meaning-making and creating a legacy project in the following sections.

Meaning-Making in Legacy

Exploring meaning in your life is very much a part of legacy. It naturally occurs as we age or edge closer to death in illness. We look back on our life and take stock. This review of your life, which I discuss in Chapter 12, helps you determine and clarify the most important qualities, aspects, accomplishments, beliefs, decisions, or times of your life. And having a fuller picture of yourself — the tapestry of your life — can help you see the impacts you've made and the meaning your life held.

Also in Chapter 12 in life review, I talk about the concept of editing your tapestry to create a slightly different version of yourself. That at every moment, you have a choice about who you want to be in the future: the same or different. Legacy takes it further: to think about and determine the last picture of yourself.

Honoring yourself

What do you want to say about yourself in that last picture of you? Having an opportunity to paint that last picture is a chance to determine what picture gets to hang up in the hallways of time. It is your say in how you will be remembered after your death.

Think of it like this: Imagine you are the president of the United States. Traditionally, each president has commissioned an official portrait as recognition and remembrance of their time in office. The portrait is not just a visual record of the president's appearance. Through the medium, dress, props, symbols, and background used, the portrait aims to capture the president's personality and style. It tells something about how the president wants to be *perceived and remembered* by the public. Figure 17-1 shows representations of two such portraits, with a space for you to consider yours.

FIGURE 17-1: Consider what you'd like your last portrait to say about you.

On the left, George Washington is a commanding figure. The portrait reinforces the image of Washington as a general and leader, the first president of the United States of America. In contrast, the portrait of John F. Kennedy in the middle tells a very different story of a man. The portrait depicts JFK as a president who is a thinker and is humble.

For you, imagine your portrait in the third frame on the right. What would you want it to say about you? Legacy is about that last picture of you — a way for you to honor yourself and the life you have lived. It's an opportunity to say something about *how you want to be perceived and remembered by your family and friends.*

What's my legacy?

What do you want your legacy to say about you? Your legacy is a very personal reflection of you; therefore, give some serious thought to its content.

TIP

Here are some things for you to consider:

>> **What do you want to say or express about yourself?** Legacy is a very personal expression of you, so consider which aspect of you is the part that

you want to live on. Like JFK's portrait, it could be about a personality trait or your character.

» **Is your legacy about who you were in life?** This could be about your work or the major role you took on in life, like in Washington's portrait. Or another example is, if you were a dancer your whole life, your legacy might be about your love of dance and career as a dancer.

» **Is your legacy about something that is important to you?** For many people, their family is their legacy; this is a very common subject. Or your legacy could reflect something else important to you that you want to share with others. For example, if you love nature and the environment, your legacy might be about the places you've been and the environmental impacts you've made in your lifetime.

» **Do you want your legacy to reflect a theme across your lifespan?** This could be something like working with children throughout your life or an important hobby.

» **Would you like your legacy to inspire future generations? What words of wisdom would you want to leave?** You may want to leave your thoughts on life, death, love, time, or other existential topics you've learned from contemplation and past experiences.

» **Do you want to express your thoughts and advice about important future events?** For example, parents often like to leave their thoughts and advice to their children for future milestone events. That way, the children can feel like they're with them in spirit.

REMEMBER

Your legacy can encompass one or more of the considerations presented here. Think carefully and thoughtfully about your legacy. How you want to be remembered is an important decision only you can make. Listen to your heart, and go with a message that feels right for you.

Creating a Legacy Project

A *legacy project* is a concrete physical object or process that is an outward expression of meaning of the deceased. Its purpose is to help the family and friends left behind to reconnect to the deceased after death.

The creation of a legacy project asks you to consider your life and your social relationships, especially those closest to you — your family and loved ones. This is where legacy extends beyond yourself to touch your community. This is when legacy intersects with the social aspects of preparing for end of life.

Painting your last portrait

Just thinking about your legacy and honoring the life you have lived can be incredibly meaningful all by itself. And that may be enough for you.

If you want to take it further, beyond the meaning-making, you can actually paint that last picture of you, for others to hang on their wall. Here I mean, metaphorically, for you to paint that last portrait. While you could actually have a painting done, instead the intention is for you to explore and create something to leave behind for others.

NEW

The idea here is to turn the thinking — the meaning-making — into a physical expression of the meaning — the legacy project.

The legacy project shifts the focus from the life you have lived to preserving a piece of your past. It can increase your sense of control at end of life because you are determining the lasting narrative of your story.

NEW

Creating a legacy project becomes an opportunity to decide on how you will be remembered by others. The legacy project allows you to express that meaning about yourself which becomes a lasting remembrance.

Reconnecting to me

After you are gone, that last picture of you is often what your loved ones hold onto in grief and remembrance. Therefore, the legacy project becomes a means by which others reconnect back to you.

TIP

You can begin a legacy project at any point in life, but it is best to begin well before death. Because legacy is all about you, it's good to do this while your health is still good. You may begin a legacy project on your own or with your family and friends. But it's good to enlist the help of others when your health begins to decline. It can be a beautiful time spent together; it feels incredibly meaningful for everyone. For your loved ones especially, it allows them to continue to connect to you in life and to be part of this important process of leaving something behind.

If you aren't interested in a legacy or don't have the cognitive capacity or energy to be involved, then your family or loved ones may decide to create one for you. That's okay. For your loved ones, creating a legacy project can be part of the grieving process and a healthy expression of loss and love.

A legacy project that is completed before death can be a wonderful addition to any memorial or after-death remembrance event. After all, that is the purpose of a legacy project — a means for those left behind to reconnect to you in a way that you would like to be remembered. And what better time for you to have a say in how people remember you than at a celebration of you!

A legacy project can also be completed post-death by your family and loved ones. The focus of the meaning-making process for them would be to explore meaning in their relationship to you. Understand that this legacy project wouldn't then necessarily reflect your life and what's most important to you. A legacy project done by a loved one after death may be more of an expression of what you meant to them, how they connect to you, and what they want to remember about you.

Considering Common Legacy Ideas

Legacy projects can take many different forms. Since the project is something "left behind" for your family and friends, it often results in a physical object or product. The ideas are endless.

I offer some thoughts for you to consider, and then following, present a few of the more common legacy projects.

>> Choose what resonates with you and what you are able to get done with the time, energy, and resources you have available.

>> Involve your family and friends. This is a process that creates love, joy, laughter, and tears.

REMEMBER

In the end, whatever you create to stand as your legacy will be a gift to the people that you love.

Letters and notes

This is the most common and simplest of legacy projects that you can do, and do on your own. It allows you to put down in your own words your thoughts, ideas, hopes, and dreams. And this is one of the main reasons to write to your loved ones at end of life: so you can be sure that they know exactly how you feel. Especially if you hadn't been able to express your feelings previously, for whatever reasons, this is a great way to make sure that they know exactly how you feel.

Writing individual letters to specific important persons in your life — your spouse or partner, best friends, parents — is best as they're each a unique individual. And in the case of writing letters to your children, who are also unique individuals, write a personal letter to each child. Don't write a group letter to all your children.

TIP

Be specific. In each letter you write, recall special memories together and describe specific things that you love about the person you are writing to. No detail is too small.

Especially for parents leaving behind young children, I've known some moms to write a series of notes to their children. *To be opened on your 16ᵗʰ birthday. To be opened upon graduation. To be opened upon getting married. To be opened at the birth of your first child.* It is a way for you to still share your thoughts, hopes, and advice for your child as they face a major life transition. And for your child, it is a way for them to feel your presence at an important moment in their life.

WARNING

Letters and notes to loved ones are usually written while preparing for end of life. One of the worse things that I've seen is that sometimes people wait too long to write their letters. They want to do it, they have so much to say, but they procrastinate. For some, doing this task brings the reality of mortality too close. Or it's just too emotionally difficult and sad to contemplate such a task — imagining life going on without you. Or, by the time you are able to face writing a letter, you no longer have the energy, ability, or cognition to do so. Try not to put it off. A letter becomes such a precious point of connection between you and your loved one.

If the task of writing letters is too taxing or challenging, you can:

>> Keep the letters short.

>> Get someone to help by writing the letter for you. You supply the thoughts and words; they put pen to paper.

>> Speak your words into a recording device and have it transcribed speech-to-text.

REMEMBER

Make sure you say what you want to say since these are lasting words. The length of the letter doesn't matter; the sentiment is what counts.

Legacy letters and notes are usually given to family and friends after death, either soon afterwards or at certain milestone events. Make sure that you designate someone to be in charge of this responsibility of distributing the letters. Or leave clear instructions about the letters, perhaps putting them with your important documents.

Legacy and memory books

Sometimes it is not so much about what you want to say to others, but what you want to share about yourself. This is when legacy books or memory books, focusing on you and your life, can be really wonderful legacy projects.

A *legacy book* is a keepsake book that preserves your history, memories, and stories. The content is written by you with photographs to accompany the text. Legacy books are created to document and celebrate you and are often shared with others.

Creating a physical keepsake of your stories in a memory book can be a lovely and natural outcome of doing a life review. I talk about life review in Chapter 12 and how meaningful a process this can be for you to reflect back on your life. So if you are doing a life review, consider creating a memory book or other legacy project afterwards.

Creating a legacy book is a bigger project and can be difficult to do on your own. Fortunately, many online services can simplify the process to make it easy for you. Online services can help with every step, from writing the stories (for example, with prompts and editing), and putting it all together (such as proofreading and layout), to printing and shipping the books.

There are also many options and features to make the process as user-friendly as possible. For instance, some services send you topic prompts to help with the writing. You may find prompts helpful so you don't feel lost about how to start and what to write about. And the prompts are often inspiring and cover topics that you may not have thought of yourself.

Another great feature is speech-to-text transcription. You record your stories by talking into a recording device. The audio file is then uploaded to the service where it is transcribed and edited to create a written story in your words. Some upscale services also include professional research into family history, genealogy, and other historical records to create a broader and richer picture.

REMEMBER

Keep in mind a legacy project like this takes time. Most online services recommend a year, so that the collection and telling of stories is a slow, thoughtful, and fun process that doesn't feel like drudgery.

If you are interested in creating a legacy book, do it while your health is good. You can begin this process on your own, but if your health declines rapidly, consider pulling in someone to help. Not only can a family member assist you, but doing it with someone else can also have its own reward in spending time together.

Dozens of available legacy book apps can help you in this endeavor. I give a few examples here, but by no means is this all that are available. Please do your research to find a service that offers options and produces a product that you like.

Examples of legacy book apps include Remento, Storyworth, My Stories Matter, Meminto, Circa Legacy, Legacy Books, and Anderson Archival.

Photo books

Photo books do essentially the same thing as legacy books and memory books, but tell more of your story in photographs rather than words. In a world obsessed with the use of phone cameras, almost every moment now is captured digitally. And old print photographs can be easily digitized by archival services. Thus, digital photography makes this an easy method to tell your story through images.

Creating a photo book is an especially attractive option for those people who are not as comfortable writing or speaking about themselves. Perhaps, it's not so much what you want to say, but what you want to express through imagery and pictures showing you, people, places, and things that you've done.

"A picture is worth a thousand words."
—adage attributed to Fred R. Barnard, *Printers' Ink Journal*

Similarly to legacy books and memory books, many online services are available to help you put this all together. These programs offer ease in uploading images, photo storage, designer templates, customizable options, and even printing and shipping photo books. Some upscale services even send a professional photographer to your home to capture you and your family in everyday moments, offering a more personalized and higher quality end product. Again, please do your research to find a service that is within your budget and produces a final product that you like.

Examples of photo book services are Mixbook, Shutterfly, VistaPrint, and The Photo Legacy.

Audio and video

The ease of recording digital audio and video nowadays makes this an attractive option. So many editing applications are available online, making this a relatively easy legacy project to do on your own or with a little assistance.

The purpose of creating an audio or video legacy project would be the same as discussed previously in the "Letters and notes" section. It allows you to put down in your own words your thoughts, ideas, hopes, and dreams so that your loved ones know exactly how you feel.

And since your words and image are captured by audio and video, your family and friends will actually hear and see you too. I have heard family members say after a death how precious it is to hear the voice of their loved one. Something that they will never hear again is now held everlasting in the legacy video.

A legacy project of this nature can be as simple or professional as you want it to be. It can be as simple as recording a file on your mobile phone. Or if you want help in creating a more expansive video legacy project, ask around to find someone with experience in video production in your community. There are also a lot of online services offering legacy videos. Some professional services offer skilled interviewers to create the conversation and keep it going. A production team comes to your home, sets up the environment, conducts the interview, and records it live. A compromise alternative is to do the interview live but remotely. In both situations, the focus is on a "live" experience, speaking to an actual person.

I give a few examples of online services, but this is not an exhaustive list. Please do your research to find a service that offers options and produces a product that you like. If you want to do a live interview, try to find a videographer in your local area or region.

Examples of audio and video services are Loving Legacy Video, Family Legacies Videos, Family Tree Video, and Ezra Productions.

Legacy and memory boxes

A *memory box*, also known as a *keepsake box*, is a place to store mementos or items from special moments, events, or occasions. In terms of legacy, a type of memory box that focuses on you and is given to others in anticipation of or after a death can be called a *legacy box*. In this situation, a legacy box is a specially curated collection of items that are meaningful to you and remind others of you.

Look around your bedroom or home now. Those "things" that you have held onto over time are meaningful and important to you. Why have you held onto them? What memories or stories do they hold for you? Passing on a keepsake of yours will preserve a bit of you and your history.

What's nice is that you get to select what goes inside the box. An item placed in a legacy box should be something very much associated with you or very meaningful to you. An item could recall a specific shared time or place or event. Examples of stuff that could go in a legacy box are a favorite piece of jewelry, photos, a bottle of perfume, notes and letters, souvenirs, memorabilia, and trinkets. Almost anything can go inside a legacy box as long as it can fit.

Creating and giving legacy boxes to the important people in your life can be a lovely project. It is an incredibly meaningful and heartfelt process to acknowledge your relationships with them and leave a piece of you behind for them. Whatever is given will be cherished.

Recipe collections and more

Legacy projects can also focus on a part of you, which could be a passion, endeavor, or hobby. Although it emphasizes only one particular aspect of you, in fact, it tells much about you as a whole person — why you did it, what you brought to it, and what you achieved by doing it. It says something about what you love about life, what is important to you, and the qualities in you that enabled you to do it. It can say a lot.

A common legacy theme for many people centers around food, meals, or eating. I have heard stories of Sunday family gatherings around the table with Nonna's famous spaghetti or of the traditions of annual Thanksgiving dinners with all the trimmings. Many of us hold close the memories of meals filled with good times, laughter, love, and full bellies.

So a legacy project can focus on bringing that passion, endeavor, or hobby to life. Whether it be meals together, cooking, climbing mountains, bird watching, mentoring kids, travel, photography, fashion, coaching soccer, or whatever, this activity brought you to life and gave you great joy. That is something to share about yourself and a pretty good way to be remembered.

SONDRA'S STORY

I once created a legacy project that was a collection of recipes and stories of meals spent together with the deceased. Over 25 people contributed stories and photographs to the legacy book. There were memories of delicious tiramisu, spicy Korean food, Thanksgiving dinners in the Poconos, hot apple turnovers on cold winter nights, annual reunion lunches, matzah balls and gelfite fish at Passover seders, hotel buffet breakfasts, sesame chicken from Tang's, hand-cut fries, the same soup and sandwich ordered at the same diner every single time, homemade stuffed bell peppers, and French silk dark chocolate pie topped with whipped cream.

Food had played a large part in the social life of my client Sondra. She had used meals as a way of bringing people together and connecting with them.

In one of the stories, a niece writes, "Almost every single time I met my aunt, her first question to me was 'Did you eat?' She asked this of everyone who stopped by to see her." The niece went on to explain that the question of "Did you eat?" was often meant as a way to ask whether you were okay in life. "Do you need anything?" "Can I do something for you?" It was Sondra's way of expressing that she cared about you.

This question was such a beautiful reflection of the great care that Sondra had for other people that it became the title of her legacy book: *Did You Eat?*

Crafts, quilts, and more

If you work with your hands or are a crafty person (and I don't mean sly!), consider making something to give to the important people in your life. Or give them something that you have already made. A crafted object is a wonderful legacy product that can embody you and spark memories.

I remember my grandmother spending so much time in her sewing room making quilts. These were not the kind of quilts that were pictures or told stories. My grandmother's quilts were made up of hundreds of hexagons, cut from colorful scrap cloth and sewn together. She spent countless hours cutting cloth, laying out the hexagons, finding the right color combinations, and sewing them together on the ancient foot-powered Singer sewing machine. My sisters and I each have several of the quilts my grandmother made. For me, one quilt holds all the memories of my grandmother in it — and that is all I need to keep my grandmother close to my heart.

NEW

My grandmother didn't make the quilts with the idea of creating a legacy, but they became her legacy. So, a legacy does not even have to be something created with the idea of being remembered.

Your legacy already exists. Just look around. Look at yourself and your home with a discerning eye. See what things or objects embody you and are meaningful or important to you. Then, just share that with others.

5

Spiritual Preparation

IN THIS PART . . .

Recognize the value of spirituality for hope, comfort, strength, and connection.

Lean into your spiritual practices and traditions for support.

Strive for compassionate care at end of life.

Chapter **18**

Embracing Spirituality at End of Life

Spirituality is an important factor that affects our overall health. People who are ill often evoke spirituality to find inner strength and develop a new way of thinking about their situation that allows them to transcend the difficulties and challenges of illness and cope emotionally.

It is the same at end of life when spirituality helps the dying cope with approaching death and make sense of what awaits them after death. People turn to a higher power to seek support, bargain for more time or a cure, or seek answers where science and medicine fail them. Our connection to this higher power — God or Mother Nature or the universe — is the basis of spirituality.

Learn to lean into your spirituality at end of life. If your spiritual beliefs and practices have been there for you throughout life, remember that you are living up until the last breath. Your spirituality can give you hope, comfort, strength, and connection.

In this chapter, we discover more about spirituality, the distinctions between spirituality and religion, and some of the common spiritual issues that can arise at end of life.

What Is Spirituality

Spirituality is a broad term for a big concept. In simple terms, spirituality is the connection to something bigger than yourself. Or in more complex terms, spirituality is the aspect of humanity through which individuals seek meaning, purpose, and transcendence, and connect to self, others, nature, the moment, and to the significant or sacred.

Spirituality is universal

Whenever I look up into the night sky twinkling with thousands of stars, I get a sense of awe — that there is more to this universe than my own being. I feel the existence of something bigger than myself, of which I am blessed to be a part of. It may be a very, very small part, but I am a part of something bigger, nonetheless.

Gazing at the night sky is a spiritual moment for me. Moments of awe are often spiritual moments for many people. During these moments, we may think about:

>> Our meaning and purpose in life

>> Our sense of belonging

>> Love

>> Hope, peace, and gratitude

These are universal ideas that we all seek as human beings. They're our spiritual needs.

When we connect to something bigger than ourselves, whether God or Mother Nature or the universe, we may ask about our own existence and our relationship to self, others, our community, and the greater world. Whether it be gazing at the night sky, standing on the edge of the Grand Canyon, or praying in church.

Spirituality is diverse

The concept of spirituality is found in all cultures and societies. Culture and spirituality, as concepts, are closely intertwined and greatly influence one another.

NEW

Culture is not synonymous with country or ethnicity. Rather culture describes communities of shared key beliefs, values, behaviors, routines, and institutions. For example, New York City is a "salad bowl" of different cultures with over 200 nationalities, or ingredients, represented. Each cultural heritage brings its own distinct flavor, while coexisting with the others. These "flavors" can be expressed through language, religion, faith, rituals, practices, and traditions.

One way culture is expressed is through one's spirituality or religion. Given the incredible diversity existing in society and the many cultures represented, the expressions of spirituality are just as diverse.

TIP

Therefore, we must be open to the unfamiliar and acknowledge different forms and expressions of spirituality. You may not recognize an action, an idea, or a wish as a spiritual expression or preference. What is sacred to you may not be seen or understood as sacred to someone else.

REMEMBER

If you are preparing for end of life, it is important to incorporate all forms of personal expression, including spirituality, into your process. This is what makes the journey of life — and death — meaningful, purposeful, and personal.

If you are caring for someone at end life — or in life in general — it is equally important to have cultural sensitivity in spiritual matters and its forms of expression.

Distinguishing Spirituality and Religion

While *spirituality* encompasses all that is unknown and possible related to existence and the divine, *religion* represents a specific set of beliefs concerning the cause, nature, and purpose of the universe and connecting to the divine or God. Therefore, religion and faith tend to fall under the larger umbrella of spirituality.

The broader context of spirituality encompasses both religious and secular ideologies, as depicted in Figure 18-1. The former includes things like interpersonal relationships, cultural interactions, or connection with nature.

For example, nature is a source of spirituality for many people. The divine is Mother Nature, and spending time in nature is one form of expression of that spiritual belief. This is a practice that does not fall within the purview of religion.

Note: For the purposes of this book, the word "spirituality" is used to encompass spirituality, religion, and faith. If a discussion refers specifically to religion, then the word "religion" or "religious" is used.

FIGURE 18-1:
Spirituality can
be felt and
expressed in
different ways by
different people.

Spirituality versus religion

Religion is one of the ways through which spirituality is expressed.

Yet, there are important distinctions between spirituality and religion:

SPIRITUALITY	RELIGION
Individual	Collective
Personal path	Structured path
Informal	Formal
Flexible	Rules
Broad/inclusive	Must be a believer

For many people, religion is the framework for a spiritual life. But it's possible to identify as **religious but not spiritual**. Some prefer the structured, communal path with specific doctrine, rituals, and practices, but do not feel internally connected to the divine. And it's possible to be **spiritual but not religious**. Many people identify in this way, preferring to do inner work and pursue a personal path of meaning and purpose. This can also include those who do not practice a religion and identify as agnostic or atheist.

Lastly, it is possible to be **both spiritual and religious**. You can pursue a life of deep spiritual meaning while also using the rituals and practices of a religious place of worship. In this case, when the two work together, it allows for a rich personal journey within the structure and support of a shared faith community.

Global religious landscape

The purpose of this brief summary section on the global religious landscape is to help you understand and recognize the diversity and concentrations of religions that exist in the world today.

In 2020, according to global demographic studies, more than three-quarters of the world's people identified with a specific religion (see Figure 18-2). The three major world religions are Christianity, Islam, and Hinduism. The share of all the other world's religions is only 6.5 percent and includes Buddhism, Baha'i, Daoism, Jain, Sikh, Judaism, and folk religions.

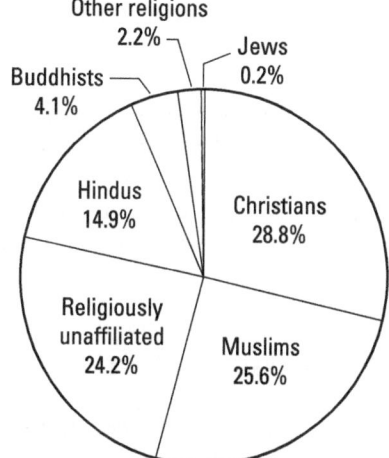

Almost a quarter of the world's people have no religious affiliation. This makes it the third largest group behind Christians and Muslims. It is interesting to note that this category is only one of two groups which are *growing* as a percentage of the world population (the other group being Islam). People in this group consistently say they are spiritual and have spiritual beliefs and practices, but are not religious.

TIP

An excellent, informative resource guide on the religious needs in palliative and end-of-life care can be found at Opening the Spiritual Gate, a website maintained by the Cheshire & Merseyside Palliative & End of Life Care Network. It lists 41 faiths, many of which would fall into the "other religions" category. Concise information for each faith is provided on its beliefs; key issues; eating, food, and drink; and death and dying.

Recognizing Spiritual Distress

The end of life is often a time when spiritual matters come to the fore. Recognizing what arises as spiritual issues is important so they can be addressed properly and with appropriate spiritual support. Symptoms of spiritual distress are easily mistaken as symptoms of illness or a changed mental state; medication is not the remedy for spiritual issues.

Spiritual distress and spiritual crisis occur when you are unable to find sources of meaning, hope, love, peace, comfort, strength, and connection in life. Or when conflict occurs between your beliefs and what is happening to you in life. This is common in illness and impending death, which often trigger spiritual distress in individuals. To make matters worse, the distress then impacts and worsens your mental and physical health.

This section covers some of the common spiritual issues that may arise at end of life. A complementary discussion on spiritual loss can be found in Chapter 9. More importantly, in the next chapter, I talk about how to stay connected with your spirituality and instead, use it as a means of support in illness and at end of life. Then you can be better prepared to address spiritual distress when it arises at end of life.

Feeling scared, needing comfort

People facing their own death are often drawn to spirituality as comfort. Spirituality helps the dying cope with their condition and make sense of what awaits after death. Especially if a person fears death or has death anxiety, spirituality can be a source of comfort and security.

I have seen this to be the case in many dying individuals. A patient of mine was in severe pain and grimacing, but as soon as I began reading from the Bible, she began to relax, nod in agreement, and forget about her pain. Another man dying from cancer grew uneasy whenever we spoke about end of life and what it might be like, but he wanted the information so he could prepare mentally and physically. After our conversations, we would close with meditation and chanting. Afterwards, he was calm and could move on in life with clarity and understanding.

For many people, nature is the source of spirituality. When they approach death and are mostly indoors and in bed, they can feel very disconnected to the restorative and rejuvenating qualities of nature. I have played nature sound tracks of birds singing, rain, and ocean waves. The dying close their eyes and transport themselves to the wilderness, forest, or beach. They transcend their current condition and feel connected to something greater than themselves.

One woman I cared for found spirituality in nature, and in particular, gardens and flowers. Unfortunately, she had limited mobility and relied on others to take her out. Whenever I visited, I would face her to the open window with fresh air on her face and place a vase of flowers on the sill. In this way, she could be comforted as we talked of difficult matters.

It is clear that spiritual individuals find comfort and solace with their circumstances when connected to their source of spirituality.

Even non-religious individuals, who are scared of death, often turn to spirituality or religion when faced with illness or a limited time left to live. Even when they do not believe, they will turn to anything else to find comfort. Spirituality is that powerful.

Experiencing existential distress

I have heard many people at the end of life say, "My life had no meaning" or "My life was insignificant." This sentiment is full of sorrow. It is so easy for a dying person to forget the significance of their life when they are doing nothing all day and everything is taken care of for them. It is my belief that people who feel insignificant at the end of their life are only looking at their current situation. Yes, I know that it is hard to feel that life has any meaning when you are bed bound, in pain, treated like a child, and wearing a diaper. It is hard to see the purpose in living. Yes, it may be hard — even impossible — to identify the current meaning of your life, but certainly, it is not the case that your entire life had no meaning. You have simply lost the connection to the meaning that your life once had.

"There is no reason to pity old people. Instead, young people should envy them. It is true that the old have no opportunities, no possibilities in the future. But they have more than that. Instead of possibilities in the future they have realities in the past — the potentialities they have actualized, the meanings they have fulfilled, the values they have realized — and nothing and nobody can ever remove these assets from the past."
—Vicktor Frankl, *Man's Search for Meaning* (Beacon Press)

More than likely, there were probably many times in your life when you felt significant in this world. Powerful, invincible, and at the top of your game. You raised a family or succeeded at your job. You cruised the road with the wind in your hair or traveled the world and spoke five languages. Or there were times when you loved or were loved deeply. In those times, you felt that you mattered to someone and someone mattered to you. It feels so unbelievably good and worthwhile to be alive when you are connected to someone in a mutual love.

Right now, you may feel none of these feelings — neither strong nor free nor loved. A person who is concerned over the lack of meaning or the worthlessness of their life is a person in existential distress.

Frankl, a Holocaust survivor, goes on to argue that even for those who are in the most miserable of conditions, the value of each and every person stays with them based on the meanings in life they created in the past rather than the usefulness of the person in the present. Unfortunately for us, society places value on a sense of usefulness to society. And it is so hard to constantly remind yourself that once your life did have meaning.

Losing faith

Grief, loss, and approaching death can cause you to question your faith. Feelings of anger with or abandonment by God are common and can be deeply painful and confusing. Whereas God was once a source of love and strength, you now feel betrayed by God and turn away. You doubt God's love for you.

People go through a lot of emotions with the diagnosis of a serious illness, the losses that occur with illness, and dying. We want answers for why this is happening and why this is happening to *me*. We often look for something or someone to blame. We may blame ourselves, thinking "if I had only done this" or "maybe it was because I did that." Or we might blame our faith or God for what is happening, which is completely normal and not unexpected.

If you blame God, you may try to distance yourself from God. You may be angry with God for having cancer. You may believe God caused this pain and suffering. You may believe that you don't deserve to die. If this is the case, how can you remain close to God? It would be natural for you — as it would be for any human being — to question your beliefs and even go so far as to lose faith.

MARILYN'S STORY

When I first met Marilyn, she was in a senior residence being taken care of 24 hours a day by home health aides. It was a small, dark, impersonal studio room with a hospital bed. Not an uncommon situation for many elderly people aging alone. She had limited mobility with assistance, but soon after I met her, Marilyn began lying in bed all the time.

Marilyn believed in God, but did not pray. She believed in heaven, but described herself as secular. There was no feeling or connection in the words she used to describe her relationship with God. Instead, Marilyn displayed reverence in the words she used to describe opera.

Opera was her religion. It was clear every time I witnessed Marilyn listen to opera — she had a transcendent experience. As the soprano's voice soared, so did Marilyn. I could tell that Marilyn was no longer in the room with me. Her body was with me, but her mind was free. She was communing with the divine in the arias of Puccini.

With her caregivers, I reintroduced opera into Marilyn's daily life. Marilyn awakened and began to appreciate being alive instead of just wanting to die all the time. She became more accepting of her condition and less angry and depressed. Eventually, I believe, through opera, Marilyn found her way back to her Christian God. And now, she had two sources of comfort, strength, hope, and peace.

Marilyn leaned much on God as she approached death, and she found much comfort in what awaited her in heaven. With opera playing softly to guide her, Marilyn died peacefully.

Making sense of death

Death is still, and perhaps the greatest, mystery of our existence. What happens to us after death is truly an unknown, and being faced with the unknown can cause death anxiety for some at end of life.

REMEMBER

Spirituality helps people make sense of what awaits them after death, and thereby, offers comfort and security to the dying in what awaits them in the beyond. This statement is especially true for all religions that have an afterlife belief and detail very specifically how to transcend from this physical world to the beyond. Afterlife beliefs greatly influence and impact the end-of-life experience by eliminating the uncertainty in what happens after death. What is unknown is now known for a person of faith.

There exists a confidence in knowing your destination and the continuation of your soul beyond death. That belief is what offers peace, comfort, and security as you move through illness and dying. That belief is what manifests in serenity and acceptance as you face death in the last breaths of life. I have witnessed it in others. There is power in the belief of what comes next to transcend the experience of dying.

Chapter **19**

Leaning into Spiritual Care

During hard times, what do you hold onto? Where do you go? Do you physically go somewhere? Or do you go somewhere in your mind? What do you think about? When the chips are down and life is all bad luck, what sustains you and keeps you going?

Answering these questions will clue you in to your inner resources — what grounds and supports you in life's difficulties and challenges. Identifying your inner resources helps you to understand more about what gives you hope, strength, comfort, and peace in life . . . and in facing death.

Spirituality is the source of these inner resources and plays a very large role in your overall emotional well-being. Staying connected to the spirituality, faith, or religion that grounds, centers, and strengthens you is essential if you are ill or dying. And actively working through any spiritual issues that arise at end of life is beneficial for more likely positive outcomes during the dying process and at death.

In this chapter, I talk about spirituality as support, how to lean into your spiritual practices and traditions to stay connected to your spirituality, and how spirituality helps create an end of life that is meaningful, purposeful, and sacred.

Finding Support in Spirituality

If your spiritual beliefs and practices have been an important part of your life and supported you during difficult times, then lean on your spirituality at end of life. Do not let the permanent nature of death and the complicated emotions of grief, sadness, and possibly anger dissuade you from turning to your spirituality even more. If your spirituality has been there for you in life, let it be there for you in death. It is no different.

At end of life, it is imperative that you:

>> Identify your spirituality and discuss your spiritual views with your family, healthcare team, caregivers, and other important people involved in your care.

>> Consider how much your spiritual views will influence the goals of care, medical decisions, and the dying process.

>> Share and clarify your spiritual views with others so that there are no assumptions about the degree to which spirituality will play into your end of life.

>> Involve others from your spiritual community to support you.

>> Incorporate spiritual practices and rituals into your illness journey or dying process.

REMEMBER

Spiritual preparation for end of life is just as important as physical, emotional, and social preparation. Tending to your spiritual needs keeps you connected to those deep inner resources within you of hope, strength, comfort, and peace — qualities you want at end of life. Therefore, don't ignore your spiritual needs. Stay connected to your spiritual beliefs and lean on others in your spiritual community. Spirituality plays an important role in your end of life and brings reverence and meaning into the experience.

Leaning into Others for Spiritual Support

In social preparation for end of life, I talk about how important it is for you to stay socially connected, build a support network, and ask for help. If you are a member of a spiritual or religious community, you already have a built-in community that is there for you and can provide support for your spiritual needs too. Don't hesitate to lean into others who can help at end of life.

Your spiritual leaders

The spiritual leaders of your community can work with you to explore your thoughts, worries, and doubts about end of life. They know well the experiences of illness, dying, and death and are usually readily available for support in these matters. Your spiritual leaders also know you well and can advise you from a spiritual perspective that is more relatable to your situation. As leaders, they can also enlist members of the community to help with practical matters as well as keep you connected to the community. Seek spiritual counseling from your spiritual or religious leaders.

TIP

If you're struggling with a loss of faith or any other spiritual issue and don't want to share this directly with your spiritual leader, you can reach out for spiritual advice and guidance elsewhere. You may feel more comfortable talking openly if you go outside of your immediate religious or spiritual circle. There's less risk of judgment when starting with someone new, but on the other hand, a new person doesn't know you well. Online spiritual counseling is also an alternative in seeking advice outside of your community.

Your spiritual community

You may be removed from your spiritual community, alone, without the support and practice of fellow practitioners to commune with, draw strength from, and reinforce your own beliefs. This can be one of the hardest parts of being removed from your home and cared for elsewhere, such as a hospital, nursing home, or even in a family member's home.

It becomes vital to stay connected to a spiritual community, not only to prevent spiritual distress, but for your physical, emotional, and social health.

TIP

Talk to members of your community, share with them what's going on for you, and ask for help with your spiritual needs. Spiritual care can take a lot of different forms. Consider doing the following:

>> Ask others to pray for you.

>> Engage with online worship services. It may not be with your own community, but it will allow you to stay connected with your faith.

>> Have spiritual texts read aloud to you.

>> Listen to spiritual music.

>> Ask for visits from members of your spiritual community.

REMEMBER

Spiritual and religious communities tend to be particularly kind, giving, and generous with their time and resources. Not only is it aligned with their beliefs, it's a sort of "pay it forward" system of support. They will be there for you in your time of need, and someone else will be there later for them. So don't hesitate; ask. Lean into your community.

Spiritual care counselors

If you are in a hospital or on hospice, then spiritual care counselors are often part of the healthcare team. They can help you explore and work through the spiritual issues that often arise as death nears. Ask staff if a spiritual care counselor is available for you.

Most spiritual care counselors tend to be more spiritual in nature than religious and are nondenominational. However, counselors are trained and knowledgeable on the spiritual issues of different religions and are available to address them with you. The spiritual care counselor can even work with your specified clergy or faith leader. The counselor can help arrange and set up rituals or ceremonies consistent with your spiritual beliefs or religion, if requested and as needed.

Caregivers

NEW

If you are caring for someone who is ill or dying, their current situation is not just a medical or physical one. Ask them how they are spiritually. A person's state of mind can be lifted and eased if they are supported spiritually.

TIP

Be open to considering spirituality as a form of support and look for small ways in which you can support their spiritual expression. Read religious texts aloud, find online worship services, or play spiritual music. Supporting another person in their spiritual needs is a kindness you can offer.

Leaning into Personal Spiritual Practices

What aspects of your spirituality or spiritual practices do you find most helpful to you personally? Prayer, meditation, or reading scripture? Or attending religious services, listening to music, or communing with nature?

Much of your time at end of life is spent alone in quiet time. Using this time for personal spiritual practice and deep inner work are ways to keep meaning in your life, stay connected to your spirituality, and make the time pass more purposefully.

Deep inner work

Most of us don't seem to have enough time to accomplish anything and everything we want or should do while living daily life. Yet, at end of life, there seems to be too much time.

Hence, this is the perfect time to focus on the deep inner work to prepare for end of life. Consider doing a life review (see Chapter 12); addressing past regrets, guilt, or shame (see Chapter 11); or healing past and current relationships (see Chapter 16). Or just take care of your own spiritual needs so you don't develop spiritual distress (see Chapter 18).

REMEMBER

Because so much time at end of life is spent in quiet time, it's important to find ways to keep yourself occupied with a sense of purpose and meaning.

Contemplation

When we are in times of need, we often find ourselves speaking to a higher power for guidance, wisdom, or solace. This is a way of connecting to our spirituality and the divine. And, the more we connect with the divine, the more we want to connect. Soon, you may find yourself connecting with the divine not only in times of need, but in good times or daily or whenever the spirit moves within you.

REMEMBER

Use the quiet moments at end of life to find the peace, hope, and strength you need to be in your situation.

TIP

Personal spiritual practices may be in the form of prayers, mantras, and meditation. If you need audio or visual aids, ask for help to set those up. Use whatever you need to stay connected to your spirituality.

Leaning into Spiritual Traditions

A person's spiritual beliefs also affect how they perceive death, the dying process, and the afterlife. Historically, when people died at home within their community, it was natural that spiritual traditions were part of the dying process and conducted with ease. In modern times, a great many people are dying away from home instead, in hospitals, nursing homes, or facilities. It's no surprise then that a conscious effort must be made to acknowledge and integrate spiritual practices and traditions into end-of-life care.

Rituals and ceremonies

Rituals and ceremonies are used to reinforce beliefs and act as sources of comfort and connection. As the end-of-life approaches, specific religious rituals and traditions may be conducted as part of the dying process and death. Incorporate the rituals from your religion, or have them conducted for you. These rituals and ceremonies offer strength and peace of mind by keeping you connected to your faith's beliefs in dying, death, and the afterlife. And they lend an air of the sacred and reverence to what's happening.

NEW

If you are spiritual and not religious, you may not have specific rituals already preestablished. If so, there is great benefit in designing your own rituals that speak to your spiritual expression. Ritual lends an air of seriousness and significance that carries weight in the intention and meaning of the act. I have found rituals — formal religious ones and informal, personally designed ones — to be profoundly moving and potentially transformative acts. You can brainstorm your own simple rituals, or ask your spiritual leaders and community members for help.

TIP

There are many online resources as well as books galore about rituals and ceremonies. For custom, secular rituals that you can design on your own, I like Be Ceremonial, an online website and app.

REMEMBER

Religions do have very specific rituals and ceremonies at end of life. They play a very significant role because they are tied to certain religious beliefs, both in preparation for death and after death.

Before-death rituals

Before death, many religions have rituals that prepare you for death. The purpose is to prepare your soul/spirit/essence to make the transition to the beyond. Rituals can be in the form of reading, praying, chanting, lighting candles, burning incense, meditating, or playing music. Families and friends visit and gather around the bed to pray, offer support, and be with you until death.

For example, in the Catholic church, *last rites* are the final blessings and prayers one receives before going to heaven and are administered to a person shortly before death. For a faithful Catholic, the rites offer forgiveness of sins and assure entrance into heaven.

In Buddhism, the state of mind at death is believed to influence the character of rebirth. For devout Buddhists, this means having a calm, clear mind in the period before death and at death. Therefore, monks and/or spiritual friends chant and read prayers continuously during dying, so these are the last things a Buddhist hears in their last moment of consciousness.

After-death rituals

After death, religions differ in the preparation of the body, including washing, dressing, and purifying. There are usually very specific guidelines and restrictions on when, where, and how these are done and by whom. Religions also vary when it comes to the final disposition of the body in funerals, burials, and cremation. You can find more discussion of these after-death arrangements in Chapter 7.

For example, in preparation for burial, Islam provides very specific guidance on the preparation and ritual washing of the body. It specifies the conditions for washing, who can perform the wash, and even the method of washing, including the water used and the order of the body parts to be washed.

Hindu after-death rituals are also very elaborate and specific. One of the simplest, but most important, rituals after death is to tie the big toes of the dead body together with thread. The belief is that this ritual prevents the soul of the deceased from reentering the body and therefore liberates it on its journey.

Ancestor worship

Ancestor worship is the practice of venerating deceased ancestors as still part of the family and whose spirits can intervene in the affairs of the living. Ancestor worship can be found worldwide and is common in many past and current religions *and* cultures.

Ancestor worship takes many different forms. Common practices include:

>> Altars to the deceased

>> Offerings of food, drink, flowers, or other goods

>> Gravesite maintenance

>> Lighting candles

>> Burning incense

REMEMBER

Everyone practices some form of ancestor worship. In some cultures and religions, ancestor worship is an integral practice of life with home altars, elaborate graveside rituals, and even holidays set aside to honor the tradition. In simpler forms, when you visit the graves of deceased loved ones and bring flowers, that is a form of ancestor worship. If you keep photos of deceased relatives, such as a spouse or your parents, on display and speak to them about what's going on in your life, as shown in Figure 19-1, that is a form of ancestor worship.

FIGURE 19-1:
One of the simplest forms of ancestor worship is talking with your deceased loved one.

NEW

And at end of life, if you find comfort in thinking that you will join your deceased loved ones, that is a belief in ancestor worship. It is common for dying persons to have visions of deceased people, either known or unknown, and be comforted by their presence. These experiences are not hallucinations or dreams.

REMEMBER

And if you are present when this occurs to a dying person, please respect their experience. If you are able, you can show support and even encourage their vision by validating it and showing curiosity. "Who did you see? Tell me more."

TIP

Another simple way to support ancestor worship is with the display of photographs of family and close loved ones, whether living or deceased. Every single person carries with them or displays photos of people they love. Underlying this practice is the profound idea and belief that you are part of a lineage of people and will not be forgotten.

We may not acknowledge all these practices as religious or cultural, or even consider them worship, but certainly, what we are doing is maintaining a connection with those we loved and acknowledging the influence and importance of those deceased in our lives. Lean into it.

Chapter **20**

Letting Go and Compassion

magine if, at the end of life, you could feel *equanimity.* In other words, you could look at yourself — see yourself dying — and feel calm and ready. You could look at your mental and physical house and see that it is all in order. You could look back at your life and appreciate it for all its ups and downs and twists and turns. You could look at the people surrounding you and know that you loved them and were loved in return. You could look at time and space and feel that your mind, body, and spirit are ready to let go.

Equanimity at death, and the related concepts of impermanence, compassion, and loving-kindness, are some of the main teachings of Buddhism. Yet, you don't have to be Buddhist or practice Buddhism to understand these concepts and apply them to your own life. These are universal ideals.

His Holiness the 14th Dalai Lama once said, "Do not try to use what you learn from Buddhism to be a Buddhist; use it to be a better whatever-you-already-are."

In this chapter, we discover the Buddhist concepts of compassion and self-compassion, what compassionate care looks like at end of life, and how to ease into death by letting go.

The Value of Compassion

Compassion is at the core of Buddhism. There are age-old and countless texts and teachings on this subject, including from the Buddha himself. In this section, I give a brief overview of the concept of compassion and how it applies at end of life.

Defining compassion

Compassion is the wish that others be free from suffering. You can understand, just based on this definition, how compassion is a desirable quality at end of life.

Practicing compassion is to recognize the suffering that exists in others and respond with a genuine desire to alleviate that suffering. When you see someone you love suffering, it breaks your heart. You want to do anything to alleviate that suffering. Therefore, knowing how to support others compassionately is crucial.

Cultivating compassion is taking the feeling of compassion, applying it to yourself, and extending it outward to include others. By cultivating compassion, it becomes possible to feel a sense of interconnectedness in the world. You develop a sense of commitment, responsibility, and respect toward others.

His Holiness the 14th Dalai Lama explains that when you can feel compassion for another person, regardless of whether they are a friend or an enemy, that is true compassion. The feeling of genuine compassion is much stronger, much wider; it is universal. It is the innate desire for all human beings to be happy and overcome suffering. Hence, the practice of cultivating compassion is not limited to Buddhist practitioners — it is seen as a universal quality that can be developed by anyone.

Compassion, empathy, and sympathy

In the family of care and concern, sympathy, empathy, and compassion are related. The three qualities are often mistakenly used interchangeably, but they are distinct from one another and evoke different emotional responses. Clearly understanding the differences of these three terms as they relate to a care situation is important.

When you are not feeling well, ill, or even dying, you will see many different reactions and receive many different responses from other people. Many times, you receive responses or actions that are insensitive, off-putting, and unsupportive. Or worse, they make you wish that you hadn't spoken to the other person in the first place.

In those situations, the other person usually isn't trying to be mean or insensitive. More often, they don't know what to say or do, and many times, it comes out all wrong. Or the other person does nothing, not acknowledging the pain or terrible situation you are in, and that response feels just as bad. While the intention to do good might exist in the other person, neither of their responses feel good to you, a person in need.

So how should one respond?

As an end-of-life doula, I teach about how to support the dying, the ultimate final passage of aging and illness. And certainly, at end of life, there is pain and suffering in one form or another. When I talk about how to support a dying person, supportive responses arise from either sympathy, empathy, or compassion. Therefore, it is important to clearly understand these three concepts and how, when offered, they are received by a person.

Imagine a person wearing and walking in shoes that hurt. You can think of "shoes that hurt" as a symbol for being in pain, ill, or dying. Sympathy, empathy, and compassion are expressed in different ways.

Offering sympathy, as shown in Figure 20-1, often does little good for a person in pain. While it is an acknowledgment that pain exists, it offers no comfort or relief. In fact, expressions of sympathy are often felt as pity. Because the pain is emphasized, sympathy is often perceived as noting the difference between my sick, poor state versus your whole, healthy state. Sympathy can feel a lot like an expression of superiority.

SYMPATHY

> I am sorry that your shoes hurt.

> A lot of good that does for me.

FIGURE 20-1: Sympathy is not a good supportive response and often feels like pity.

Many people believe that offering empathy (see Figure 20-2) is a good supportive response to someone in pain. Again, while it is an acknowledgment that your pain exists, it offers no comfort or relief. An empathic person may feel or experience the pain of another person, but they can't truly know or imagine another's pain. And unfortunately, an empathic person often responds with what provides comfort to them rather than what provides comfort to you. At end of life, the experience of dying for each individual is unique and it is their burden to carry until death.

EMPATHY

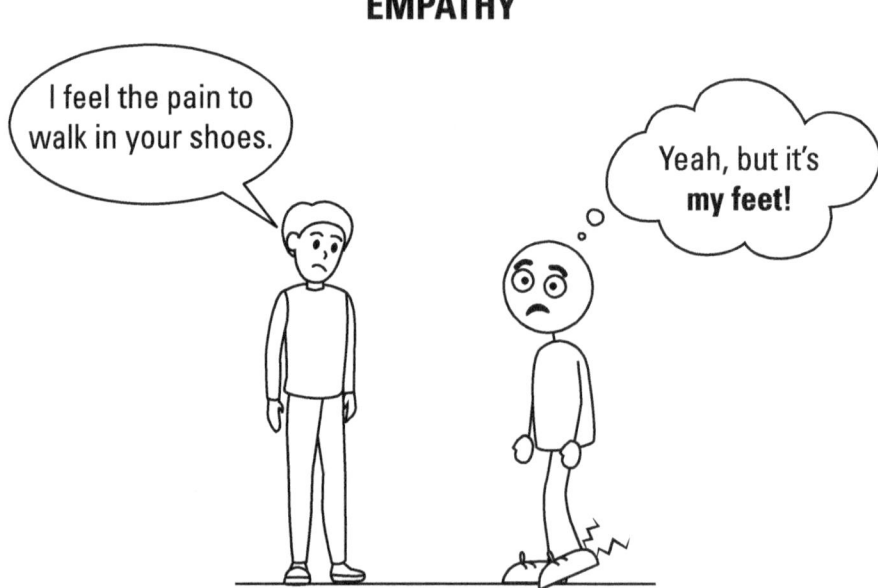

FIGURE 20-2: Empathy is not a good supportive response and does not honor the other person's experience.

Compassion is walking alongside the other person in their journey. I can offer a hand, as shown in Figure 20-3, and be someone to lean on. I can accompany and support you, all the while acknowledging that it is your journey. That is compassion.

REMEMBER

In summary, sympathy resides in our thoughts; we understand the pain. Empathy occupies our feelings; we feel the pain. Compassion goes beyond sympathy or empathy; it moves the heart to action. We provide support.

Compassionate care at end of life

If someone you love is dying, one of the hardest parts of it all is watching them die. And I don't mean watching them actively die in the last days, hours, and minutes of life. I mean watching them die in the weeks, months, and years prior to death. There is nothing you can do to stop the process of dying.

COMPASSION

FIGURE 20-3: Compassion is a supportive response which feels good to everyone.

The next best thing that you can do is to support with compassion.

>> **Honor the process.** It is the end of their life, not yours. It is their process, not yours. It may not be the way you would do things or the decisions you would make, but this is their process. They are doing the best they can under the circumstances. Give them the space, time, and support they need to move through the process at their own pace and level of comfort.

>> **Respect them as a capable person.** It may be hard to refrain from jumping right in and doing everything for them. But don't try to fix their problems for them, or tell them how you would handle it if it were you. If you must offer solutions — offer gently — but then respect the decision they make even if it is not the one you offered.

>> **Acknowledge their pain and suffering.** No one likes to see another suffer, but pain and suffering exist. Don't try to take it away, diminish it, or dismiss it.

>> **Let them talk and listen.** It's worth saying again: Let them talk and listen. Don't interrupt or try to silence them, even when they begin to speak of difficult subjects. Maybe you don't want to hear talk of dying, but if they need to talk about it, listen. Or maybe you don't understand what they're telling you. Regardless, let them talk and tell you what's on their mind, even if it sounds like nonsense to you. Give them space to be heard; just listen and be silent. You can work on your own feelings later.

>> **Trust that they know themselves best.** Trust in their decisions even if you disagree. This is not your end-of-life journey; it's theirs. Let them make the decision because they are the one to live by their decision and its consequences.

REMEMBER

There are already plenty of other "experts" involved, giving medical, legal, financial, and even care advice. Fill the gaps of emotional, social, spiritual, and physical care. When you keep the dying person you love as the focus and support them as a *whole* human being, that's offering compassionate care.

Self-compassion

"You can search the entire universe for someone who deserves your love and compassion more than you do yourself, and you will not find that person anywhere. . . . You more than anyone deserve your own love and compassion."

—Modern paraphrase of verse 157 of the *Dhammapada*, a collection of sayings of the Buddha

When we think of the ideas of care, kindness, generosity, or compassion, it's easy for us to think of these ideas in terms of others — those we love and especially those who are suffering. When we extend these qualities to others, we feel good about ourselves, thinking, "I am a good person to help others."

NEW

However, you cannot truly care for others with compassion if you are unable to extend the same courtesy to yourself. It is important to practice and cultivate self-compassion. Just as you want to alleviate the suffering of others, you must also recognize your own suffering and treat yourself with kindness and understanding.

As you prepare for end of life, treat yourself with compassion. This is hard work. As you work through emotional wounds and face your fears of dying, be kind to yourself. As you get your physical and mental house in order, be understanding of your limitations. As you heal your relationships with yourself and others, be forgiving of yourself. As you address unfinished business and lay to rest the shame, guilt, and regrets of the past, be gentle with yourself. And as you surround yourself with the people you love, be honest with yourself and them.

REMEMBER

Without self-judgment, you may find more equanimity in yourself, your circumstances, and your death. You will be more open to see things as they genuinely are. You may find yourself more at ease and accepting. With more equanimity, you will be able to let go.

Easing into Death

Ultimately, death is all about letting go. Letting go of life. Letting go of this existence to whatever might be next. Letting go of this reality to the unknown.

Say these words aloud. What do they mean to you? How do you feel when you say them? Say them often enough so that one day you feel the possibility of letting go.

Attachment versus non-attachment

Attachment is when we hold on or cling to other people, objects, ideas, or experiences.

Non-attachment is when we acknowledge, honor, and accept things as they are. It's a way of engaging with things with flexibility, not fixation. Our well-being doesn't depend on these things or on an outcome.

Clinging to anything or any idea is ultimately futile as everything changes. Clinging to life is futile as everything will die. If you cling to life or to the idea that you will not die, it will only lead to much suffering, for you and others around you.

Holding on versus letting go

It's human nature to hold on at end of life. However, how many times have you witnessed dying that seemed to go on too long? You wonder if the dying person is suffering, and because they are usually non responsive at this stage, it is impossible to ask. We don't know if they are suffering physically or mentally, and holding on for some reason.

There may be many reasons why you, or anyone, may hold on at end of life. Salvatore, whose story is discussed in Chapter 16, held on because of a broken relationship that was never healed. I have seen people hold on in the hopes of being visited by someone very important to them. When it happens, it is beautiful, but oftentimes, no one comes, and the person dies a protracted death. I have seen others hold onto life because of a fear of dying, and their dying process is not pretty.

WARNING

At end of life, if you are struggling to hold on, others can sense what's happening. There is stress, anxiety, or distress in the atmosphere. It does not feel calm or peaceful.

The struggle to hold on can manifest in upsetting physical symptoms, such as:

>> Pain

>> Restlessness and agitation

>> Flailing and violent movements

>> Shouting or calling out

>> Grimacing or frowning

>> Disorientation or confusion

>> Disturbing visions

>> Picking or pulling at yourself or things

>> Grabbing or grasping at real or imagined things

REMEMBER

And when you are suffering, your loved ones suffer. It pains them physically and mentally as well, to witness and not be able to do anything to alleviate your pain and suffering. Situations like this are very challenging emotionally and make it difficult for them to be present at death. In addition, watching you suffer can complicate their ability to cope and grieve after your death.

TIP

To avoid the distress of holding on, come prepared to face death. Develop a relationship with your own mortality and what it means before you lie on your death-bed. Do all the things in this book.

REMEMBER

By preparing yourself for end of life, you can relieve unnecessary suffering for yourself and your loved ones, ease into the process of dying, and let go in peace.

Giving permission

So here we are at the end of life. You know that death is near and are ready physically, emotionally, socially, and spiritually. You've done all the hard work of preparing for this moment. You've gotten all your affairs in order, you've taken care of unfinished business, and you've addressed past regrets, wounds, and relationships. You feel good about the life you've led and the person you are now. You are cared for with respect and surrounded by love. Congratulations for making it this far!

NEW

Oops, there is one last thing to do. It is a reciprocal action that you and your loved ones do for each other. You give permission to let go.

If you are the one dying, begin by reminding your family and friends of how much you love them. Tell them that you know that they will be sad for a very long time, but that they should hold the memory of you in their hearts with happiness and love. Let them know you're ready to die and you're okay. Ask them to not hold onto you and to let you go.

If you are a family member or a close friend, begin by telling your loved one who is dying how much you love them. Thank them for everything they've given you in life — friendship, love, wisdom, laughter, and memories — and anything else that is specific to your relationship. Tell them that you are going to be okay. Assure them that all of you who are left behind will take care of one another. Give your loved one permission to let go.

When should you have a conversation about letting go? You and your loved ones will know when the time is right. It may be an easy conversation to have, or it may be a hard thing to do. Of course, don't wait too long for the very last minute. The sooner permission is granted, the more ease there can be in the process of dying. So listen to your heart. You will get a sense of the appropriate time.

TIP

Even if your loved one is close to death and unresponsive, you can still talk to them. Tell them everything you need to say for yourself and give them the reassurances they need to let go. Hearing is believed to be the very last sense to go before death. So continue to talk to them as they may very well hear you.

Giving permission is something only you as a loved one can do. It is an act of great kindness to say, "You may go when you are ready. I will be okay."

6

The Part of Tens

Dispell common misconceptions about death, dying, aging, and illness.

Start life anew with integrating death into living.

Chapter **21**

Ten Myths About Death and Dying

D ue to society's taboo approach to death, a lot of myths and misconceptions have grown out of our ignorance, avoidance, and fear of death. Many of them are deeply entrenched in our thinking as to how to approach the end of life or what it is going to be like. Unfortunately, these misconceptions can lead to serious misunderstandings about end-of-life care, the dying process, and even pain and suffering.

If you're going to prepare for the end of life, you'll be thinking about death and dying a lot. This chapter offers you some straight talk about common myths.

Nobody Thinks About Death

Nobody is *talking* about death. And because we are not talking about it, we think no one is thinking about it. In fact, everyone thinks about death, but we are all too afraid to bring up the subject. We have created a culture of having no one to talk to about death and dying.

Recently, a person — let's call her Diana — told me this relevant story. (By the way, Diana is not in the end-of-life space, but when she found out I was an end-of-life doula, she related this story.) Diana was in a group with three other strangers. It came about that she mentioned that her father had recently died and she was now thinking about death a lot. One of the group members exclaimed, "Oh my gosh! I think about death all the time!" Another person said, "Yes, a close friend of mine just passed, and it's been on my mind a lot." And the last stranger agreed, "I too am obsessed with death." Wow! It was the beginning of what turned into an enriching, intimate connection between four individuals for a brief moment in time.

TIP

Be brave. Bring up the subject casually, but don't make it a big deal. It's amazing how quickly a connection can be made with others when talking about death.

Thinking About Death Will Make It Happen

Thinking about something happening is not the same as planning for something to happen.

The problem is that we use the tool of visualization all the time in achieving goals, working at our jobs, and playing sports. Visualization is an extremely effective tool by helping us to imagine, anticipate, feel, and prepare ahead of time. In most of life's situations, when we visualize something, it is our intent to actually do those plans, activities, or movements.

Not so in the case of death. You can still use visualization as a tool to imagine, anticipate, and feel what death is — as introspective personal work. And if it motivates you to then prepare for end of life, like doing the things in this book, great.

But in the case of death, you don't then actualize it. You go on with living life, more aware and appreciative, and ready.

Thinking About Death Just Makes Me Sad

Okay, I accept that the basic premise of death is sad. You will be dead and no longer living the big, beautiful, fun, crazy, happy life you have. But being sad is not a bad emotion, and it's okay if thinking about death makes you sad.

However, thinking about death can also evoke other positive feelings, such as gratitude, love, contentment, calm, hope, and compassion. Thinking about death can make you look at your own life and appreciate what you have, what you are doing, and who is in your life. My question to you is this: Are you allowing yourself to feel those positive emotions too?

REMEMBER

When you allow yourself to feel sadness and happiness, calm and anger, love and hate, you are acknowledging that life and death both exist. Life is full of opposites, and living both makes it rich.

Preparing for End of Life Is Only for Old or Sick People

You may think that people only think and prepare for end of life when they are old or sick. While the majority of people die from old age or illness, you can't wait until you are either old or sick to prepare for end of life. Under these circumstances, it is not the best time to be facing the difficult questions of mortality and making important decisions about legal, financial, and medical matters. Especially if you have a terminal illness, you will not be feeling well physically and might be having chemotherapy, taking strong medications, or undergoing surgery. In fact, you may feel pretty crappy a lot of the time. And under these conditions, how are you supposed to make important decisions?! Better to prepare for end of life ahead of time when you are calm, confident, and clear-headed.

Nowadays, more and more people are preparing early. So don't procrastinate! Help yourself and others by preparing for end of life now, so you can be prepared whenever death should happen.

Hospice Means Giving Up

Too many people wait to get on hospice until they are almost dead. Because of this, you may have the impression that hospice is only an option at the very, very end of life when it is certain that you will die . . . and soon.

The other factor contributing to this misconception is that one of the eligibility criteria for hospice is that you are no longer seeking curative treatments for your illness. More often than not, nothing more can be done. You have already spent years battling cancer with multiple rounds of chemotherapy, radiation, and off-label drugs. The cancer is no longer reacting to treatments. When you go on hospice, it is not that you are giving up but that nothing more can be done for the illness.

Or it may be the case that you decide you no longer want curative treatments anymore. The rigors and side effects of treatment are not offering a quality of life worth living for. You are tired.

REMEMBER

Regardless of your personal reasons and circumstances, understand that hospice is a support service for you and your caregivers, and it's essential if you want to stay at home. Hospice personnel come to your home and monitor your health, manage medications, and help with practical matters. Hospice offers home health aides as well as complementary therapies. Hospice also sends supplies to your home and provides durable medical equipment to make staying at home easier. Hospice provides support.

I've seen some people do really well on hospice and heard many people say they wished they had gone on hospice sooner. The extra support reduces anxiety, worry, and burden on everyone, allowing you and your loved ones to spend more quality time together in the time remaining.

Pain Is a Part of Dying

You do not have to die in pain. This is a common misconception that contributes to so much suffering at end of life.

There is an entire branch of medicine called *palliative care,* which is devoted to making sure that you are not suffering from your condition or symptoms. Pain management is a vital part of palliative and hospice care, and pain can be managed through a number of ways. Yet, too many people bear pain and suffer. The consequence of doing so challenges your mental and emotional states and effects a lower quality of life. It may even impact your desire to live. It is imperative that you speak up about your pain.

However, it is true that many pain medications produce drowsiness. You end up sleeping a lot more. This is one reason that you may resist pain medication.

REMEMBER

The balance between alertness versus suffering is not an easy one, but know that at the end of life, pain can be effectively managed. You do not have to die in pain, unless it is your choice.

Morphine Kills You

This misunderstanding of morphine is another reason that too many people die in unnecessary pain. Morphine does not cause death; the underlying illness causes death.

Morphine and other opioids are pain-relieving medications that are used when pain does not respond to lower-level pain medications. Morphine is not addictive when used for pain relief, prescribed by a doctor, and monitored by the healthcare team. Also, tolerance does not develop. Increased use of morphine may be required because the disease progression may cause increasing pain; therefore, there is an increased need for pain relief.

REMEMBER

Morphine does not hasten death. Yet, whether you take morphine or another pain-relieving medication, it is always your choice.

I Need a Lawyer to Complete My Advance Directives

While advance directives are legal documents, they do not have to be completed by or with a lawyer. This misconception prevents many people from completing these vital documents. To encourage flexibility and get more people to complete advance directives, most forms become legal when simply witnessed and signed by the witnesses. In some states, notarization may also be required. There are notaries in local businesses and institutions, such as hospitals, banks, post offices, and churches; you just have to ask to find one.

A document is not any more legal if an attorney completes it. The use of an attorney can still be beneficial for other reasons. Many free downloadable versions of advance directives are available online. Some are very user-friendly with simple language and colorful graphics. These are just as effective and legal as a black and white form full of legalese. In fact, the user-friendly forms may be more understandable and accessible to you, but that doesn't make them less "legal." It is more important that you use a form you are comfortable with and enables you to clearly express what you want. And get the necessary signatures to make it legal.

My Family Knows What I Want

Wow, I've heard these statements a lot: "My family knows what I want" and "My eldest child will make the decisions and know what to do for me." And then I go and talk to the spouse or eldest child, and it's not so clear what they would do.

Yes, your family member can and will make decisions for you because you asked. They do it out of love and/or a sense of obligation to you. But unless you have specifically discussed *in detail* what you want, they truly don't know. There is no benefit in letting your family member decide how you want to live until your death or how you want your life celebrated after death. This often just leaves them with an inheritance of conflict or doubt about the decisions they made. Besides, any close family member won't be in a good emotional place to make these decisions, and typically, will decide to either do what they would want or take the most conservative action.

TIP

If you can be clear on what you want and are able to tell them, this conversation does much for relieving anxiety, burden, and uncertainty from your loved one's state of mind. It is much easier — and peaceful — for them to carry out someone else's wishes.

Living Longer Gives Me More Time

Have you ever wished to live longer or forever? This thought has probably crossed your mind at some point in life, but did you ever stop to think about what you are wishing for?

When you wish for more time, *you don't get more time now*. Time does not stop, and you don't get more time when you are young, healthy, or on a high in life. *What you get is more time at the end of life*. What you get is more time when you are old, frail, and feeble. This is the extra time you get — is this what you are wishing for?

REMEMBER

Instead, live life now. Appreciate being young, appreciate being healthy, appreciate the high moment in life you are on. Make the most of it and then live on.

Chapter **22**

Ten Tips for Thinking More Positively and Getting Started

This book began with the concept: You are living until the moment you die. So, if you want to prepare for end of life . . . in order to die well, you have to know how to live well.

In this chapter, I want to focus on the final concept of living well and offer you some tips on how to think more positively and get started. This is knowing how to live well with an awareness of your own mortality, not just having a good time all the time and ignoring the possibility of death. In the latter situation, you may think that you are living well, but you're not if you are not prepared for the possibility of dying. Living well is living contentedly without a fear of dying and being ready to face your death with calm and peace.

So as you prepare for the end of life, start living well. You may find some of the following tips occur naturally as you begin preparing, or you can begin with a conscious effort.

Stopping to Smell the Roses

There are two possible ways you may be experiencing life: One, you are walking around with blinders on, just going through the motions. Don't just let life pass you by! Or two, you are so very busy, cramming in more and more things to do, accomplish, and achieve. Get off the hamster wheel!

If one of these two ways describes you, that's okay. I am not suggesting that you change your lifestyle completely by taking off the blinders or getting off the hamster wheel *forever* (although it is something worth considering). What I am suggesting is that occasionally, maybe once a day, you *pause*. Take a moment to check in with yourself and look around you. How are you? Where are you? What are you doing? What is going on around you?

REMEMBER

There is so much more to life to notice if you just pause for a moment and smell the roses.

Living in the Now

What this is not: This is *not* about living now as if there is no tomorrow. While the possibility exists that tomorrow may not come — you could die suddenly by an accident — this is not about using this possibility as a reason for doing extreme, crazy, fun, wild stuff with abandon.

What this is: This *is* about learning to live in the now — in the moment, such that wherever you are and whatever you're doing, you are fully present. You are fully engaged in whatever is going on. Whether it be participating on a zoom call, having a meal, taking a walk, or listening to a friend, you are not thinking about the past (in other words, the would'ves, could'ves, or should'ves) nor planning or worrying about the future (such as, what you're going to eat for dinner). You are present in the now.

Saying I'm Not Fine

Start talking about death, dying, illness, and aging. Our society needs to bring these topics — which we all encounter and experience — out from the shadows and into the light. We should talk about these subjects as if noticing the weather. It exists, and it happens; some days are bright and sunny, while other days are rainy and dismal.

If your mother is not doing well, share the news with others. If your pet just died, let others know how you're feeling. If a good friend just got bad news and you don't know what to do, talk with others and get support. Don't make it a big deal. Bring it up in your normal voice, not in hushed tones. And don't apologize for sharing an intimate piece of information. The other person is privileged to hear this news.

However, there is the possibility that you won't get the kind and understanding response that you hope for. Often, people say or do something insensitive or inappropriate, but usually, the reason is that they don't know what to say or do, and therefore do the wrong thing. Tell the other person that their response made you feel bad or it wasn't helpful. Give them a chance to apologize and then see what happens. Hopefully, it will lead to a real, sincere expression of support. But more importantly, what you are doing is showing others that it's okay to talk about it.

If this all sounds like a big step to take, you can start even smaller. When someone asks, "How you are?" don't say, "I'm fine." Say how you are really feeling.

Writing Down Your Thoughts

We all need outlets for expression. If you don't have a safe space to express yourself verbally with a friend or a therapist, begin by writing down your thoughts. And even if you do have a safe space, you may want to have a specific place and time to be with the subject of death, like in a journal.

In the beginning, writing down all your fears, worries, and concerns about death, dying, and anything else that weighs on your mind may feel more like a brain dump. Hopefully, you can get to a place where you begin to explore your thoughts on the many positive and celebratory ideas and concepts of death and dying. A person once said to me, "You are so courageous to work in a space of mystery." This perspective evokes curiosity, wonder, and the unknown. Maybe you can explore death from that vantage point.

Whatever comes up in your mind is between you and your journal, and by writing down your thoughts, you can see how your thinking evolves over time.

Talking to The Elderly

In most ancient, indigenous, and non-Western societal groups, the elderly are revered. Old age is honored and celebrated, and the elderly are still considered integral members of society. The elderly carry wisdom and perspectives on living a fulfilling life based on a life lived. The wisdom doesn't just come from a life well-lived, but more often, the wisdom comes from the struggles and challenges of a hard-lived life. It is wisdom gained from experience.

In many places around the world, for example in Asian countries such as India and Korea, the elderly are granted great respect and may even still be heads of households. It is common in Latin and African cultures for families to be multigenerational, with the elderly playing a key role in family decision-making and caring for the young children.

Begin a conversation with an older individual. What has changed since they were young? What do they enjoy more now that they are older? What is more difficult? What advice would they give to you about life? Listen and see where the conversation goes . . . .

Volunteering in Hospice

If you like the idea of talking to the elderly, this idea takes it one step further: Go volunteer in hospice. For me, it is not at all depressing or sad to volunteer and be with people as they approach the end of life.

What I see in the dying is strength, serenity, calm, peace, acceptance, and immense courage. Yes, the situation may also present difficult emotions, such as fear, pain, anguish, doubt, anger, and suffering, but I remind myself that these are real people and that they are struggling. We are all human beings and we all struggle. If a nugget of gold can be had on how to struggle, cope, and hopefully, find peace with death, it is a wisdom that can be used to face anything in life. And if my presence can offer some small comfort to a dying person in their time of passage, it is a benefit for both of us. There are many lessons about life and living that can be learned from the dying.

Dr. Elisabeth Kübler-Ross famously said, "Those who learned to know death, rather than to fear and fight it, become our teachers about life" (*On Children and Death*, 1985).

Relishing Simple Joys

Countless people at the end of life say that it is the simple things that matter most. *The simple things.* It's because simple things have the ability to give you great joy for very little effort.

Write down five simple things that you can do on your own that bring a smile to your face. They should be things that take only about 5 to 8 minutes to do or less. Not more. A simple joy has the ability to shift your mind to happiness. It tells you that the world — and you — are going to be okay. Examples could be standing with your eyes closed and the sun on your face feeling its warmth, or putting on headphones and immersing yourself in your favorite song.

REMEMBER

A simple joy takes only minutes but has the ability to shift your whole perspective. Learn to access and lean into these simple joys because you deserve to feel good.

Writing a Letter to Your Future Self

Often what gives peace at death is being a fulfilled person. You are content with who you are, the life you've lived, and where you are now at the end of life. To that end, how can you best explore who you might become?

Write a letter to your future self. This activity is about imagining who you are going to be sometime in the future. Five years is a reasonable time frame to envision, as it is both far enough away and close enough to seem real. In your letter, address prompts like the following:

>> Who do I want to be?

>> Where do I want to be?

>> What do I want to have done?

>> Who do I want to be with?

>> What advice would I give my future self?

>> What do I want to thank my future self for?

After you write your Dear Me letter, reflect on how to make your vision a reality. What changes do you need to make to move toward that future? How can you make room for change? What are the first steps you can make today? After you physically write the letter, put it in an envelope, and store it someplace safe to be opened in the future.

REMEMBER

While your vision of the future is likely to change, doing this activity occasionally keeps you on the right track to becoming the person you want to be.

Writing Letters of Gratitude

Gratitude is good for you. You know how good it feels to be acknowledged and thanked, especially when it comes unexpectedly. Gratitude enhances appreciation and fosters positive emotions. It contributes to a sense of well-being, happiness, and social connection.

Make a list of the people who have been influential in your life or have positively impacted you. Rather than a simple thank you note, write a letter describing how you feel about what they have done for you and why you are grateful to them. Be specific about how meaningful they've been in your life.

Send your letter, or better yet, deliver and read your letter to that person. Remember you cannot guarantee the response the letter receives. The benefit and reward for you is in the act of writing the letter of gratitude.

Spending the Inheritance

When you are dead, what lasts for your loved ones — and gives them solace in your absence — are memories. Not the jewelry, house, car, or bank account. What helps with their grief is to have memories to access and hold on to as they find a way to a new reality without you in their life.

So while you are alive, spend time together and create memories. Use your money to have experiences of adventure, learning, and fun. Be together in a new environment, exposing yourselves to new foods, new sights, and new people. Laugh, make mistakes, let go of everyday worries. Feel love, tell stories, and share precious moments. Be there to experience the gratitude and impact of creating new memories with those you love. Memories are what lasts.

Index

A

AARP, 36, 225

acceptance stage of grief, 153

acknowledging death, 119. *See also* death

ADs. *See* advance directives (ADs)

  advance care planning, 47

  advance directives (*see* advance
    directives (ADs))

  conversations, 48–49

  healthcare proxy, 50–54

  living will, 55–58

advance directives (ADs), 58–59, 67

  healthcare proxy, 50

    appointing your, 53–54

    changing your, 54

    choosing, 51–52

    fighting for, 51

    recognizing synonyms for, 54

    selection of, 50

    trusting of, 50–51

  with lawyer, 285

  living will, 55–56

    completing your, 57

    creating your, 57–58

    medical treatments, 56

  sharing your, 59–60

  up to date, 60

agent/attorney-in-fact, 45

aging population, 208

agonizing process, 89

AIDS epidemic of the 1980s, 30

alkaline hydrolysis, 101–102

Allow Natural Death (AND) medical
  order, 68–69

ancestor worship, 267–268

anger stage of grief, 153

anticipating grief, 152. *See also* grief

appetite, 137

Aquamation process, 101

attachment *vs.* non-attachment, 275

audio, legacy, 245–246

B

bargaining stage of grief, 153

Barnard, Fred R., 245

bereavement counselor, 80–81

birth, 8–9. *See also* death

body

  after death (*see* body after death)

  disposition form, 97–98

  disposition options, 98

    alkaline hydrolysis, 101–102

    cremation, 100–101

    green burial, 100

    natural organic reduction, 102

    organ and tissue donation, 99–100

    traditional burial, 100

  donation, 102–103

body after death, 96
  body disposition options, 98
    alkaline hydrolysis, 101–102
    body donation, 102–103
    cremation, 100–101
    green burial, 100
    natural organic reduction, 102
    organ and tissue donation, 99–100
    traditional burial, 100
  paperwork, 97–98
Buddhism, 269, 270
Button, Diane, 125

C

CAAP, 194
Callister, Ronda Roberts, 233
cardiopulmonary resuscitation (CPR)
    process, 67–68
caregivers, 264
CaringInfo, 53, 57
Celebration of Life gatherings, 84–85, 108
ceremonies, 266
certified death certificate, 97
cognition, 139–140
communication apps, 224–225
community, 205
  care, 208–211
  COVID-19 pandemic, 207–208
  good feeling, 212–213
  grief in, 156–157
  human beings, 206–207
  LGBTQ+, 30–31
  mourning in, 156–158
  online, 225

resources and, 225
  social animal, 206–207
  spiritual supporting with, 263–264
community-based model, 217
community-led death care, 105
compassion
  definition, 270
  end of life care, 272–274
  family of care and concern, 270–272
  self-compassion, 274
  supporting with, 273–274
confusion, 139
Connecticut Hospice, 71
constant process, 146
Conversation Project, 48
COVID-19 pandemic, 207–208
crafted object, 248
cremains, 100
cremation, 100–101
crematoriums, 101
culture
  and cultural heritage, 111
  experience death, 111–112

D

daily mortality vitamin, 122–123, 126
death, 11–13, 116–118, 281–282,
    284, 287–292
  ADs with lawyer, 285
  approach, 172
  attachment *vs.* non-attachment, 275
  birth and, 8–9
  body after (*see* body after death)
  certificate, 97

compassion
  definition, 270
  end of life care, 272–274
  family of care and concern, 270–272
  self-compassion, 274
  supporting with, 273–274
in doorstep, 163
embracing, 121–126
emotions, 222
end of life, 283
family member, 286
friends with, 118–121
future, 179
happening, 282
holding *vs.* release, 275–276
hospice, 283–284
illness and, 216
journey, 188
legacy (*see* legacy)
loved ones, 183, 276–277
morphine, 285
motivates, conscious awareness of, 123
peaceful, investing in, 163–164
personal, 23–25
  identification of, 25–27
  incorporate personal elements
    into, 28–31
post-death arrangements (*see* post-death
  arrangements)
pre-death planning
  celebration of life gatherings, 84–85
  sensing death, 85–90
  vigil plan, 90–93

remembering me after death
  funeral, 105
  gatherings after death,
    103–104
  home funeral, 105–108
  memorial, 108
  obituary, 109–110
  viewing, 104–105
  wake, 104
ripple effect of, 20
roses, moment and smell,
  288
scared of, 256–257
sensing, 85–86, 259
  MAiD, 87–89
  natural death, 86
  planned death, 87
  sudden death, 86
  VSED, 89–90
spirituality (*see* spirituality)
thinking, 282–283
uncertainty about, 16
deathcare space, 121
decision-making process, 64
De Fina, Anna, 183
denial stage of grief, 153
depression stage of grief, 153
devices, to stock information,
  39–40
digital
  file cabinet, 38–40
  information, 39, 40
dignity therapy, 178–180

distress symptoms
  spirituality
    death sense, 259
    existential distress, 257–258
    faith loss, 258
    scared of death, 256–257
doctors, 74–76
Do Not Attempt Resuscitation (DNAR) medical order, 68
Do Not Intubate (DNI) medical order, 68
Do Not Resuscitate (DNR) medical order, 67
durable power of attorney (DPOA), 44–46
dying. *See* death

E

embracing death, 121–126. *See also* death
emotional baggage, 162
  shedding, 164–165
    guilt, 166–168
    regrets, 165–166
    shame, 168–169
emotional self-care, 192
emotions, 154–155
empathy, 270–272
encompasses symptoms, 73
end-of-life, 172, 174, 178, 180, 181, 183, 272–274, 281–284, 286
  basics, 7–8
    birth and death, 8–9
    death, 11–13
    I will die, 9–11

care, 70, 152
  goals of, 62
  hospice, 70–72
  palliative care, 72–74
community, 205
  care, 208–211
  COVID-19 pandemic, 207–208
  good feeling, 212–213
  human beings, 206–207
  social animal, 206–207
compassion
  definition, 270
  end of life care, 272–274
  family of care and concern, 270–272
  self-compassion, 274
  supporting with, 273–274
doula, 78–79, 93, 109, 111, 121, 122, 145
healing relationships, 231–233
  Ho'oponopono prayer, 233–236
  Salvatore's story, 234–235
legacy (*see* legacy)
life review, 171
  benefits, 177
  definition, 171
  dignity therapy, 178–180
  experience of life, 288
  methods, 178
  pretty darn amazing, 172–173
  roller coaster, 175–176
  Stanford Letter Project, 181–182
  storytelling, 183–185
  tapestry, 173–174

network (*see* network)

planning for, 15, 42

  death, 16, 20–22

  healthy, 17

  wedding, 17–20

self-care (*see* self-care)

social relationships change, 227–231

spirituality (*see* spirituality)

End-of-Life Doula Professional Certificate
  program, 183, 199

energy, 136

equanimity, 269

Estate Planning For Dummies (Simon and
  Mashinski), 42

estate planning process, 41–42

  components of, 42–43

    general durable power of attorney, 44–45

    Last Will and Testament, 43

    revocable living trust, 43

  get help with, 46–47

  keep the documents up to date, 47

  will, trust, and DPOA, 45–46

executor, 43

existential distress, 257–258

experiencing grief, 152–154. *See also* grief

  in community, 156–157

  different for everyone, 155–156

  emotions, 154–155

  time, 158

expression, outlets for, 289

F

family

  care and concern, 270–272

  member, 286

fearing death, 124. *See also* death

file cabinet, 36, 38–40

financial

  durable power of attorney, 44–45

  information, 37–38

  instability, 21

"Forbidden Death," 117. *See also* death

forgetfulness, 138–139

14th Dalai Lama, 125, 126, 269

frailty, 86

Frankl, Vicktor, 257, 258

funeral services, 105

  Gaelic funerals, 112

  jazz funerals, 112

  living funerals, 84–85

G

Gaelic funerals, 112

general durable power of attorney, 44–45

global religious landscape, 255

goals of care, for end of life, 64–66

Goldman, Barry, 217

good care, 205, 210

good death, 124–126, 162. *See also* death

good feeling, 212–213

gratitude, 210–211

  letter writing, 292

green burial, 100

grief, 20–22, 149–150

  and mourning, 151

    anticipatory grief, 152

    experiencing grief, 152–158

    transformation of, 158–160

guilt, 166–168

H

HCP. *See* healthcare proxy (HCP)

healing relationships, 231–233
  Ho'oponopono prayer, 233–236
  Salvatore's story, 234–235

healthcare
  team, 74
    bereavement counselor, 80–81
    doctors, 74–76
    end-of-life doula, 78–79
    home health aide, 80
    nurse, 76–77
    social workers, 77
    spiritual care counselor, 79
    support staff, 82
    volunteers, 81
  workers, 121

healthcare proxy (HCP)
  appointing your, 53–54
  changing your, 54
  choosing, 51–52
  fighting for, 51
  recognizing synonyms for, 54
  selection of, 50
  trusting of, 50–51

health information, 38

Holt-Lunstad, Julianne, 210

home
  funeral service, 105–108
  health aide, 80

Ho'oponopono prayer, 233–236

hospice, 283–284
  bereavement counselor, 80–81
  chaplain, 79

doctors, 74–76

eligibility criteria for, 72

end-of-life doulas, 78–79, 93, 109, 111, 121, 122, 145

home health aide, 80

nurse, 76–77

origins of, 70–71

vs. palliative care, 73–74

social workers, 77

spiritual care counselor, 79

support staff, 82

volunteers in, 81–82, 290

human beings, 10, 190, 205–207, 252, 270, 290

human composting, 102

I

"identity searching," as young adults, 128

inheritance, 292

Institute for Healthcare Improvement, 48

intergenerational solidarity, 208–209

I will die, 9–11

J

jazz funerals, 112

Jonsson, Alexandra, 189

K

Kaiser Family Foundation survey on Aging and End-of-Life Medical Care, 65

keepsake box, 246

Kennedy, John F., 239

Kübler-Ross, Elisabeth, 154, 155, 290
  On Death and Dying, 152

Kübler-Ross Change Curve, 155

L

Last Act of Caring, 106
last rites, 111, 266
legacy, 237
  box, 246
  definition, 238
  ideas
    audio and video, 245–246
    collection of recipes, 247
    crafted object, 248
    letters and notes, 242–243
    memory books, 243–244
    memory boxes, 246
    photo books, 245
  meaning-making component, 238–240
  product, 178
  project, 240
    last portrait, 241
    reconnection, 241–242
legal paperwork, 35–36
  advance care planning, 47
    advance directives, 49–50, 58–60
    conversations, 48–49
    healthcare proxy, 50–54
    living will, 55–58
  estate planning process, 41–42
    components of, 42–45
    get help with, 46–47
    keep the documents up to date, 47
    will, trust, and DPOA, 45–46
  organization of files
    devices, to stock information, 39–40
    digital file cabinet, 38
    digital information, 39, 40

file cabinet, 36
    financial information, 37–38
    health information, 38
    important docs, 36
    personal information, 37
less recognized mourning behavior, 151
letters, legacy, 242–243
LGBTQ+ community, 30–31
life, 7–8
  birth and death, 8–9
  death, 11–13
  I will die, 9–11
  quality *vs.* quantity of, 63
  review, 171
    benefits, 177
    definition, 171
    dignity therapy, 178–180
    experience of life, 288
    methods, 178
    pretty darn amazing, 172–173
    roller coaster, 175–176
    Stanford Letter Project,
      181–182
    storytelling, 183–185
    tapestry, 173–174
listening-based professional, 180
living
  funerals, 84–85
  healthier, 123–124
  trust, 44
  will, 55–56
    completing your, 57
    creating your, 57–58
    medical treatments, 56

loss, 127
  major and minor, 128–129
  navigating dimensions of
    mental loss, 137–140
    physical loss, 132–137
    social loss, 141–142
    spiritual loss, 143–145
  sitting with, 148
love, self-care, 188

M

MAiD. *See* Medical Aid in Dying (MAiD)
Mashinski, Joseph
  Estate Planning For Dummies, 42
Medical Aid in Dying (MAiD),
    87–89
medical logistics, 61–62
  end-of-life care, 70
    hospice, 70–72
    palliative care, 72–74
  healthcare team, 74
    bereavement counselor,
      80–81
    doctors, 74–76
    end-of-life doula, 78–79
    home health aide, 80
    nurse, 76–77
    social workers, 77
    spiritual care counselor, 79
    support staff, 82
    volunteers, 81
  medical decisions, 62
    essential question, 62–64
    goals of care, 64–65
    goals with others, 65–66

medical orders, 66–67
  AND, 68–69
  change your mind, 70
  DNAR, 68
  DNI, 68
  DNR, 67
  out-of-hospital DNR, 68
  POLST, 69
medical treatments, 56
medication management apps, 225
memorial service, 108
memory
  books, 243–245
  boxes, 246
mental
  loss, 138
    cognition, 139–140
    confusion, 139
    forgetfulness, 138–139
    mood swings, 140
  self-care, 191–192
mobility, 135–136
mood swings, 140
morphine, 285
mortality awareness, 125
Mount, Balfour, 72
mourning, 151
  anticipatory grief, 152
  in community, 156–158
  different for everyone, 155–156
  emotions, 154–155
  experiencing grief, 152–154
  with time, 158
  transformation of, 158–160
multicultural blending, 30–31

N

National Alliance for Care at Home, 53, 57

National Cancer Institute, 122

National End-of-Life Doula Alliance (NEDA), 79

National Home Funeral Alliance, 105, 107

national registry records, 99

natural

  death, 86. *See also* death

  organic reduction, 102

navigating dimensions of loss

  mental loss, 138

    cognition, 139–140

    confusion, 139

    forgetfulness, 138–139

    mood swings, 140

  physical loss, 132

    appetite, 137

    energy, 136

    mobility, 135–136

    physical appearance, 134–135

    roles, 134

    working, 132–133

  social loss, 141–142

  spiritual loss, 143

    disconnection, 143–144

    hope, meaning, and purpose, 145

    uncertainty and doubt, 144–145

NEDA. *See* National End-of-Life Doula Alliance (NEDA)

network, 215–216

  Ring Theory, 217–223

  tools and apps for village, 223–224

    communication and organization, 224–225

    medication management apps, 225

    resources and community, 225

  village care, 216–217

non-attachment *vs.* attachment, 275

notes, legacy, 242–243

nurse, 76–77

O

obituary, 109–110. *See also* death

old age, 283, 290

On Death and Dying (Kübler-Ross), 152

OPTN. *See* Organ Procurement and Transplantation Network (OPTN)

organ and tissue donation, 99–100

organization

  of files

    devices, to stock information, 39–40

    digital file cabinet, 38

    digital information, 39, 40

    file cabinet, 36

    financial information, 37–38

    health information, 38

    important docs, 36

    personal information, 37

  tools, 224–225

Organ Procurement and Transplantation Network (OPTN), 99

out-of-hospital DNR medical order, 68

P

palliative care, 72–74, 121

paperwork, for after death, 97–98

peaceful death, investing in, 163–164

peace of mind, 36, 41, 46, 66, 78, 90, 96, 118, 161–165, 167, 222, 228, 232, 266

Pearlman, Laurie A., 194

personal/personalizing

death, 23–25

identification of, 25–27

incorporate personal elements into, 28–31

information, 37

post-death arrangements

cultural, 111–112

religious, 110–111

spiritual practices, 264

contemplation, 265

deep inner work, 265

photo books, 245

physical

loss, 132

appetite, 137

energy, 136

mobility, 135–136

physical appearance, 134–135

roles, 134

working, 132–133

self-care, 190–191

Physician Orders for Life-Sustaining Treatment (POLST) medical order, 69

planned death, 87. *See also* death

planning, for end-of-life, 15

death, 16, 20–22

healthy, 17

wedding, 17–20

POA agent, 45

portable medical orders, 69

post-death arrangements, 95. *See also* death

body after death, 96

body disposition options, 98–103

paperwork, 97–98

bother with planning, 96

personalizing

cultural, 111–112

religious, 110–111

remembering me after death

funeral, 105

gatherings after death, 103–104

home funeral, 105–108

memorial, 108

obituary, 109–110

viewing, 104–105

wake, 104

pre-death planning, 83–84

celebration of life gatherings, 84–85

sensing death, 85–86

MAiD, 87–89

natural death, 86

planned death, 87

sudden death, 86

VSED, 89–90

vigil plan
  benefits to, 90–91
  elements of, 91–93
  help for, 93
probate process, 43

R

regrets, 165–166
religion/religious, 193
  beliefs, 143
  into post-death arrangements, 110–111
  vs. spirituality, 253–254
remembering me after death. *See also* death
  funeral, 105
  gatherings after death, 103–104
  home funeral, 105–108
  memorial, 108
  obituary, 109–110
  viewing, 104–105
  wake, 104
resources, 225
resuscitation, 67
revocable living trust, 44
right of self-determination, 55
Ring Theory, 217
  center of attention, 222
  dumping out, 219–220
  steps, 218–219
  support in, 220–222
Ring Theory (Goldman), 217
ripple effect, of death, 20

rituals. *See also* death
  after-death, 267
  before-death, 266
roller coaster, life review, 175–176

S

Saakvitne, Karen W., 194
sadness, 150
Saunders, Dame Cicely, 71
Schiffrin, Deborah, 183
secondary losses of grief, 20–21
self-care, 187, 189–190
  assessments, 194–198
    evaluation, 198
    learning, 199–200
    planning, 201–202
  emotional self-care, 192
  future, 291
  love, 188
  mental self-care, 191–192
  physical self-care, 190–191
  social self-care, 192–193
  spiritual self-care, 193–194
Self-Care Assessment Tool, 199
self-compassion, 274
sensing death, 85–86. *See also* death
  MAiD, 87–89
  natural death, 86
  planned death, 87
  sudden death, 86
  VSED, 89–90
The Seven Tasks of Life Review, 183

shame, 168–169

shedding emotional baggage, 164–165

  guilt, 166–168

  regrets, 165–166

  shame, 168–169

sick people, 283

Silk, Joan, 206

Simon, Jordan S.

  Estate Planning For Dummies, 42

simple joys, 291

social

  animal, 206–207

  connection, 205–207, 209–210

  loss, 141–142

  self-care, 192–193

  workers, 77

social relationships change, 227–228

  friends

    appreciation, 228–229

    losing, 230–231

    making, 229

speech-to-text transcription, 244

spiritual/spirituality, 261

  care counselors, 79, 145, 264

  caregivers, 258–259

  concept

    diverse, 252–253

    universal ideas, 252

  distress symptoms

    death sense, 259

    existential distress, 257–258

    faith loss, 258

    scared of death, 256–257

global religious landscape, 255

loss, 143

  disconnection, 143–144

  hope, meaning, and purpose, 145

  uncertainty and doubt, 144–145

personal spiritual practices, 264

  contemplation, 265

  deep inner work, 265

vs. religion, 253–254

religious beliefs, 143, 145

self-care, 193–194

supporting with, 262

  caregivers, 264

  community, 263–264

  leaders, 263

  spiritual care counselors, 264

traditions, 265

  after-death rituals, 267

  ancestor worship, 267–268

  before-death rituals, 266

  rituals and ceremonies, 266

stages of grief, 152–153

Stanford Letter Project, 181–182

sterile effluent, 101

stuff, 41

sudden death, 86. *See also* death

support staff, 82

suppressed grief, 155. *See also* grief

sympathy, 270–272

symptom burden, 73

T

Takin' Care of Business, 161–169

tapestry, 173–174

terror management theory (TMT), 123

testament, 43

time, grief with, 158

tissue donation, 99–100

TMT. *See* terror management theory (TMT)

The Top Five Regrets of the Dying (Ware), 165

traditional burial, 100

trust, 44–46

Tsang, Jo-Ann, 210

typical mourning behaviors, 151

U

uncertainty and doubt, 144–145

unfinished business, 161–169

United Nations (UN), 208–209

V

Vail, Kenneth E. III, 122

"Valuable Documents at Your Fingertips," 36

video, legacy, 245–246

viewing, gather after death, 104–105

vigil plan

  benefits to, 90–91

  elements of, 91–93

  help for, 93

village care

  network, 216–217

  tools and apps for, 223–224

    communication and organization, 224–225

    medication management apps, 225

    resources and community, 225

Voluntary Stopping of Eating and Drinking (VSED), 89–90

volunteers, 81, 82

VSED. *See* Voluntary Stopping of Eating and Drinking (VSED)

W

wake, gather after death, 104

Wald, Florence, 71

Wall, James A., Jr., 233

Ware, Bronnie

  The Top Five Regrets of the Dying, 165

Washington, George, 239

water

  cremation, 101–102

  effluent, 101

wedding planning, for life, 17–20

WHPCA. *See* Worldwide Hospice Palliative Care Alliance (WHPCA)

will, 43, 46. *See also* living, will

Worldwide Hospice Palliative Care Alliance (WHPCA), 71

About the Author

Virginia Chang, Ph.D. is a leading end-of-life doula, known nationally and internationally for her knowledge, integrity, and positive empowerment of a person's dying experience. She believes in every person's innate ability to transcend death and has witnessed countless individuals meeting death just the way they want.

Virginia is a strong proponent of autonomy, choice, and control in a person's end-of-life process. Her aim is to increase public awareness and reach as wide an audience as possible. To that end, she speaks regularly at hospitals, hospices, medical schools, colleges and universities, senior groups, community centers, libraries, and with just about anyone who wants to know more.

She is regularly featured in the media for her work as an end-of-life doula, including news articles, interviews, podcasts, and radio. Most notably, articles on Virginia's work can be found in *CNN*, *AARP*, *PBS*, *Crain's NY Business,* and *The Gothamist*.

Her work as an end-of-life doula was also featured in the short documentary film *A Good Death* by filmmakers Jean Chapiro and Alison Boya Sun. The film offers a unique profile on how Virginia guides, supports, and accompanies clients and their loved ones in the transition from life to death. The documentary continues to be in demand for educational purposes through community and organization screenings.

As an end-of-life doula, Virginia supports the dying and their families and caregivers to approach end of life in a positive, meaningful, and affirming way. She supports clients one-on-one and helps to advocate for and realize their needs and wishes. She serves with compassion, humbleness, and respect. Virginia works as a doula privately and as a hospice and vigil volunteer.

As an educator, Virginia teaches at the University of Vermont and Rutgers University. She is an established mentor in the field, supporting others to realize their potential as end-of-life doulas. She was trained in 2018 by the International End-of-Life Doula Association (INELDA) and the University of Vermont. She received her INELDA certification in 2019.

As an author, *Preparing For End of Life For Dummies* is her first published work. Other books on living well by facing aging, illness, and death are in progress. She continues to write essays to spread the word on positive dying.

Virginia's greatest wish is that she would not be needed as an end-of-life doula — that we would all prepare and care for each other at end of life with love, honor, and respect.

She works, teaches, reads, and writes in New York City. To find out more about Virginia and her work, please visit her website at tillthelastdoula.com.

Dedication

To all those who have died — our ancestors — for their wisdom about life.

To all those who have not yet died — the rest of us — may we face the end of life with grace.

To my children — Kyra and Jason — for your unconditional love, thank you.

Author's Acknowledgments

The opportunity to write this *For Dummies* book came to me out of the blue near the end of 2024, after spending most of the year writing my first book on end of life. I didn't expect to undertake this task. So my first acknowledgments go to all those who believed in me — that I had more to say. I am grateful for your confidence and encouragement, supporting me every step of the way this past year. It turns out that I did have more to say and have immensely enjoyed writing *Preparing For End of Life For Dummies*.

Thank you to Jennifer Yee, senior editor, who was the first person I met at John Wiley & Sons. I told you that I would seriously consider writing the *For Dummies* book if it meant working with people like you. And it's true, all the people at Wiley have been incredible. Special thanks go to Nicole Sholly, development editor, who helped me find my "Dummies voice" and whose guidance and feedback throughout the process were invaluable. And gratitude to the rest of the Wiley team for their efforts in bringing this book to readers: Chrissy Guthrie, development editor; Christine Pingleton, copy editor; Murari Mukundan, managing editor; Kristie Pyles, senior managing editor; and the entire illustration team at Straive.

I offer my deepest gratitude to Kris Kington-Barker, technical reviewer for this book. I hold you in such high regard as an end-of-life doula, colleague, and friend. Thank you for all that you have contributed to the field, for being a role model of the work, and for your time and efforts in reviewing these pages.

Merci beaucoup to the Virginia Center for the Creative Arts, le Moulin à Nef, for providing a nourishing and supportive residency to work on and complete this book project. It was such a pleasure and privilege to have dedicated, focused time.

I could not have written this book without the support and friendship of my doula colleagues, in particular those who have mentored with me over the years. Your compassion, kindness, curiosity, and passion for the work continue to motivate and inspire me. It's wonderful to work in a field with nice people. I offer heartfelt gratitude to Emma Acker and Diane Button — two special individuals who have been with me since nearly the beginning — thank you for being on this journey with me.

Also, many thanks to Maria, Kelly, Gillian, Emma, Lynn, and Holly for your ideas and input.

My sincerest gratitude goes to all my clients and patients who I have served at end of life. Thank you for letting me into your lives; I am honored to have known you. Thank you for sharing your wisdom — even if you didn't know it as such — about living, loving, and life. You will be remembered in hearts and stories.

My gratitude to all whom I may yet serve at the end of life. You give inspiration and meaning to my own life.

Finally, thank you to my children, Kyra and Jason, for being the amazing, loving, supportive presences you are in my life. I have felt that anything is possible. Thank you for sharing this world with me.

Publisher's Acknowledgments

Senior Acquisitions Editor: Jennifer Yee

Project Manager/Development Editor:
Nicole Sholly

Development Editor: Christine Guthrie

Copy Editor: Christine Pingleton

Technical Editor: Kris Kington-Barker

Managing Editor: Murari Mukundan

Production Editor: Tamilmani Varadharaj

Cover Image: © Raimund Linke/Getty Images